Because Somebody Asked Me To

Guy Vanderhaeghe

This book is dedicated to the memory of Morris Wolfe,
editor, mentor, and man of letters.

Thistledown Press Ltd.
Unit 222, 220 20th Street W
Saskatoon, SK
S7M 0W9
www.thistledownpress.com

Library and Archives Canada Cataloguing in Publication

Title: Because somebody asked me to : observations on history, literature,
    and the passing scene / by Guy Vanderhaeghe.
Names: Vanderhaeghe, Guy, 1951- author.
Identifiers: Canadiana (print) 20240355350 | Canadiana (ebook) 20240355393
    | ISBN 9781771872584 (softcover) | ISBN 9781771872638 (EPUB)
Subjects: LCSH: Canadian literature—History and criticism. | LCGFT:
    Essays.
Classification: LCC PS8593.A5386 B43 2024 | DDC C814/.54—dc23

Cover and book design by Michel Vrana
Cover image by marekuliasz/iStockphoto
Printed and bound in Canada

Thistledown Press gratefully acknowledges the financial assistance of SK
Arts, The Canada Council for the Arts, and the Government of Canada for
its publishing program.

Contents

The Writer and Writing 1: Thinking by Dreams

Books and Writers 2

Recollections 2

The Writer and Writing 2: History and Literature

Author's Note

MY FIRST BOOK, A COLLECTION of short stories called *Man Descending*, appeared in 1982. In the forty years following, I went on to publish novels, short stories, and plays, and to write a television miniseries based on my novel *The Englishman's Boy*. Despite always and forever thinking of myself as a writer of fiction, I also wrote occasional nonfiction: book reviews, talks about literature, magazine articles, short vignettes of various descriptions.

Years ago, an early mentor of mine, Morris Wolfe, started Grubstreet Books, a press committed to publishing what Morris loved to write and to read—literary non-fiction. At that time, he asked me if I would consider letting him collect, edit, and publish some of my nonfiction, but I declined his offer. He attempted to change my mind but didn't succeed; finally, he let the matter drop.

Morris Wolfe was a rare breed that no longer exists, someone who took writing seriously enough to want to write about it, not for his academic colleagues, but "for the 'intelligent general reader,' a category that now seems quaint," as he put it in the early 2000s. This he did superbly in the *Globe and Mail* as well as in the pages of magazines such as *Saturday Night*, *Books in Canada*, and *Canadian Forum*, once important organs of literary opinion that are now nothing more than fusty memories of a long-ago, once-upon-a-time world.

The literary landscape of Canada is far different terrain today than when Morris Wolfe tried to eke out a living in literary journalism and part-time teaching. When I published my first book, more than a decade after Morris had abandoned university teaching in 1970, the newspapers of every Canadian city with a population of more than a hundred thousand still had a books section; even an unknown writer like me could expect twenty or more reviews of my work to pop up all across the country. Late in the 1990s and early 2000s, the *Globe and Mail* and the *National Post* were busy *expanding* their book coverage and recruiting reviewers. When I received invitations to write reviews from Martin Levin at the *Globe* and Noah Richler at the *Post*, I agreed. The pay was negligible, but I believed that a discussion about books was important for readers and, more importantly, for writers.

This country's print media now shows little if any interest in the literary culture of this country. What passes for reviewing is now shunted off to Amazon.ca and Goodreads, where inanity proliferates. As the always delightfully acerbic Cynthia Ozick remarks, "Amazon encourages naïve and unqualified readers who look for easy prose and uplifting endings to expose their insipidities to a mass audience."

Gathering together these pieces, it struck me that they bore some resemblance to a spotty, desultory archive of my development as a writer and offered a record of my recurring literary obsessions and foibles. I was also prompted to think that they might give a sense of how the Canadian literary scene has evolved over the past four decades. My generation of English-speaking Canadian writers was preoccupied with defining themselves in opposition to the daunting cultural hegemony of the United States; we were struggling to learn how to write the reality of our country. With the passage of time, that impulse has slowly withered. The old cultural nationalism of the 1970s and 1980s is now regarded with suspicion and distrust by many of a new generation of writers who see it either as just another expression of Canada's tainted colonial past or as an impediment to international success. Of course, the new is always fated to someday become archaic. We never step in the same literary river twice, for it's not the same river and we are never the same person.

"Influences" was my first non-fiction piece. It appeared in 1984 in the twenty-fifth anniversary edition of *Canadian Literature*. Among the most recent is "From Hero to Villain and Villain to Hero," which was intended to be presented as a lecture in March of 2020 but was never delivered because of the onset of the coronavirus pandemic.

I have let all of these pieces stand pretty much as they first appeared, although I must admit that my writerly obsessiveness led me to substitute a word here or there or slightly rejig a sentence. In one instance, I significantly expanded a talk. However, most changes were entirely minor and cosmetic. For instance, introductions and afterwords to books were often published without a title and now, for the sake of consistency, I have named them. I have done my best to keep the original intact and avoided changing opinions that I may once have espoused but no longer hold. In looking them over, I see where circumstances may have altered arguments. For example, in the article "Literature and the Teaching of History," published in 1987, I made the claim that most high school students would have difficulty grasping the sort of mass fear and anxiety created by a pandemic because this was something they had never experienced. I suggested that Daniel Defoe's *Journal of the Plague Year* could provide vivid, concrete examples of people's visceral reactions to a devasting epidemic, that fiction could help students understand what it meant to live through such fraught times. Experience has overtaken this example, but I left it as is.

All the nonfiction I have ever written was solicited, which doesn't mean that I ever took on a task that I wasn't at least mildly interested in. Readers will note that, for the most part, my book reviews were uniformly favourable. This is because I made it a policy never to write about a subject that didn't at least mildly intrigue me, or about a writer whose work I suspected was unlikely to afford me pleasure or to elicit my admiration. In some instances, aspects of a book I was eager to read disappointed me and, if that happened, I did not hesitate to say so.

Of course, the sort of nonfiction that appears in periodicals or is delivered in talks comes with constraints. Newspapers and magazines impose word counts, and lectures have time limits. Nevertheless, it's not a bad thing for fiction writers to experience the discipline of boundaries. It helps the writer test the necessity of every word. If an editor asked for fifteen hundred words from me, she never got one word more.

It may have been because I lacked confidence in these pieces that had been written to order, chiefly "because somebody asked me to," that I dodged Morris Wolfe's offer to publish them, thinking that writing produced at someone else's behest was less worthy than writing driven by internal necessity. I feel differently now.

Morris Wolfe died in November of 2021, and when I learned he was gone, I felt a great stab of regret for having turned down his request. Of all the "somebodies who asked me to," he was the last one I should ever have refused.

Books and Writers I

Influences

IT WAS ONLY AFTER I had published a book that I was forced to consider the question of influences on my writing. Until that point, I had merely written. But reviewers made me aware of the problem of influence, drawing as they did convincing parallels between my short stories and the work of writers I had never read. Interviewers, too, were keen to unearth literary debts. Which writers and books, they asked, had most influenced me?

It was a question I wanted to answer honestly but I was not sure I could. For one thing, I had the impression that I was really being asked which books and writers I admired most, the questioner being certain that the answer to both questions would be the same. That might be so, but isn't necessarily so. *Ulysses*, for instance, is one of those universally admired works which has influenced writers less than one would think. Proust's *In Search of Lost Time* is another.

What I was coming to suspect was that literary influences are more various and varied than I had imagined. In my case, the threads of these influences resolved themselves into a knot which stubbornly resisted all my efforts to untangle it. For instance, when asked to produce a list of those authors I particularly admired, I was inevitably struck by the heterogeneity of the list. I could not but help imagine these writers incongruously yoked in conversation at literary cocktail parties. Flannery O'Connor and Anthony Powell? Christopher Isherwood and Rudy Wiebe? Alice Munro and Evelyn Waugh?

I could not see how these converging vectors of probable influence had shaped my writing. Worse, I felt I was suppressing another, perhaps equally important list of names. Names such as Zane Grey, Walter Scott, John Buchan, and Robert Louis Stevenson came immediately to mind. Yet I was afraid of being thought facetious if I gave these writers a nod of acknowledgement.

It was only when I read Vladimir Nabokov's autobiography, *Speak, Memory,* that I seriously began to define and elaborate a dim suspicion I had been harbouring, which is that "bad" writing is as influential in the development of a writer as is "good" writing. A brief reference by Nabokov to an article he had read as a child in the *Boy's Own Paper* strengthened that suspicion because it helped carry me back, back beyond my first acquaintance with Zane Grey, Stevenson, Buchan, and Scott, back to my earliest reading, to my introduction to the *Boy's Own Annual.*

During Nabokov's Edwardian childhood, the *Boy's Own Paper* was one of those bellicose boys' magazines which tub-thumped for the British Empire and the "right little, tight little Island!" It may seem strange that such a paper found its way into the Nabokov home, but Vladimir Nabokov's father was a wealthy anglophile who insisted on English governesses, governesses who, in turn, insisted that their little Russian charges read and wrote English before they read and wrote Russian. Thus, the *Boy's Own Paper.*

All of this smacks a bit of Alice in Wonderland. There is surely something absurd in the notion of a young Russian aristocrat, citizen of a xenophobic empire, reading, in English, the rival claims to glory of another xenophobic empire. The only thing possibly more absurd is that almost exactly fifty years later, in 1957 or thereabouts, I was poring over the *Boy's Own Annual,* which was the bound copy of all the issues of the *Boy's Own Paper* published that year. My volume was Edwardian, comprised of issues that Nabokov might conceivably have read on dark St. Petersburg winter evenings, a tome that had lost its covers and was coming apart in my hands and which I, at the age of six or seven, took to be a reasonably accurate picture of the world outside my bailiwick. No one told me that the fabulous world described in its pages had expired on the battle-fields of World War I more than forty years before.

Or perhaps I refused *not* to believe what I was reading. In any case, I held on to that illusion for something like three years before it finally evaporated in the face of reality. During that time, I confined my reading essentially to two books (aside from the insipid things assigned in school), and those books were an old school text of my mother's, *A History of the World*, and the previously mentioned volume of the *Boy's Own Annual*. In the beginning, I found *A History of the World* the more intriguing because of its illustrations: photographs of antiquities such as Mycenaean daggers and Etruscan coins, reproductions of "historical" paintings which showed Egyptian charioteers dramatically dying, transfixed by Hittite arrows. The *Boy's Own Annual* supplanted the *History* in my affections only as my ability to read improved, and then it became the staple nourishment of my imagination. I never read, or had read to me, any of the children's classics such as *Winnie the Pooh*, *The Jungle Book*, or *The Wind in the Willows*. In retrospect, I can say it might have been a good thing if I had read other books, but at the time I certainly didn't feel the lack of them. My pre–World War I issue of the *Boy's Own Annual* kept me entranced. I needed no other books. I was like a fundamentalist with his Bible.

The *Boy's Own Annual* fell into my hands by way of an elderly lady who was cleaning out her attic. This lady was typically English—or at least what North American readers of Agatha Christie mysteries might imagine as typically English. A widow, she lived for her huge garden, her budgerigars, and a cocker spaniel named Rusty. She presented me with the tattered copy of *Boy's* with an assurance that it was "just the thing for a lively young fellow." Against all odds, it was.

The contents of the *Boy's Own*, as I remember it, divided fairly evenly into three broad categories: practical knowledge; historical yarns which even I recognized as historical; and "contemporary" tales which were, at the time I read them, already more than forty years old. The latter I insisted on thinking of as accurate reflections of life in the British Isles and Empire. With hindsight, I conclude that this misconception of mine probably continued to flourish because my parents didn't own a television. A TV set would have rubbed my nose in the grit of reality. But I also must have practised self-delusion on a grand scale, some part of my mind censoring all evidence that contradicted the *Boy's Own* picture of the world. Still, in my defence I can say that this was also the age of Tarzan movies.

Anyway, who wouldn't wish to keep alive such magnificent delusions? How well I recall the *Boy's Own* article on self-defence. Here was practical knowledge indeed, a step-by-step, blow-by-blow account of the proper use of one's walking stick in repulsing assailants. The reader was advised to strike threatening black-guards with *glancing* blows, because glancing blows foiled any attempt at seizing one's walking stick, wresting it from one's grasp, and turning it against one. (It being understood that blackguards were clearly not the kind of fellows to carry walking sticks of their own.) Recommended targets for such glancing blows were elbows, shins, and, of course, the crown of the head. As a bonus, several policeman's grips were described and illustrated. When applied, these grips promised to bring about the instant submission of the felons. Young readers were cautioned to use minimum force when practising such grips on their chums.

The article incited in me a powerful longing. I knew there were no interesting blackguards stalking the streets of Esterhazy, Saskatchewan, of the type depicted in *Boy's Own*. Nor did I own an ashplant. However, that didn't mean I oughtn't to study the article very closely, particularly since after careful consideration, I had made up my mind to go off to England at some future date to enjoy the abundance of blackguards, villains, and ruffians found there, all suitable for thrashing.

The rest of *Boy's Own* was, if possible, even better, stuffed to bursting with plucky youths. There were plucky youths of the past: a ferreter-out of the Gunpowder Plot, an alarm-raiser at the Great Fire of London, an aider and abettor of the escape of Bonnie Prince Charlie to France. Then there were the plucky youths whom I mistook for my contemporaries. My favourite among these was a lad who had stained his skin with berry juice, wrapped his head in a turban, and embarked on a steamer ferrying pilgrims to Mecca. His mission? To uncover Arab slavers dealing in British subjects. After making fogbound London streets safe for respectable strollers I thought I might lend this chap a hand tidying up the Red Sea. My future bloomed.

If it was Nabokov's perfunctory comment about the *Boy's Own Paper* that resurrected memories which had lain mute under the dead weight of all the books that had followed the *Boy's Own*, books deposited year by year, stratum upon stratum, it was something else in *Speak, Memory* that made me wonder whether my writing hadn't been flavoured by this early infatuation of mine with the *Annual*.

Reading Nabokov's autobiography, I was struck by a curious thing. I noted that although Nabokov makes frequent reference to the authors of the great European and Russian masterpieces, he devotes more space to a man called Captain Mayne Reid than he does to Blok, Pushkin, Tolstoy, Gogol, Kafka, Flaubert, Dostoevsky, or for that matter, any other writer.

Who was Captain Mayne Reid? Captain Mayne Reid (1818-1883), Nabokov informs us, was a writer of Wild West romances. At the turn of the century, translations of his work were enormously popular with Russian schoolchildren. Young Vladimir Nabokov was, however, because of the diligence of his governesses, fluent enough in English to have the privilege of reading them in the original language. His favourite, he tells us, was *The Headless Horseman*.

From what Nabokov has to say in *Speak, Memory*, it is possible to deduce that Mayne Reid completely captivated his young reader. Nabokov even admits to rereading *The Headless Horseman* as an adult, and he maintains that the book has its points. It is instructive to note what these points are.

First of all, Nabokov takes delight in the artificiality and intricacy of Captain Mayne Reid's plots. Second, several passages of prose are quoted with approval. There is the whiskey decanter behind a Texas barman which looks like "an iris sparkling behind his shoulder," and the barman himself is improbably graced with "an aureole surrounding his perfumed head." Now it is true that in all this Nabokovian applause there is also more than a trace of Nabokovian mockery. But two things also came to my mind: Nabokov's own prose, touched as it is with the fantastic and a tincture of the archaic, and his own taste for studied melodrama and gloriously coincidental plot obviously display some affinity with Mayne Reid's own work. One has only to think of how improbably the nymphet's mother was despatched in *Lolita* to leave the field free for Humbert Humbert.

On such slender, even feeble evidence it would be foolhardy to argue a connection between Reid and Nabokov, to see the romancer's taste, filtered and purified by Nabokov's genius, later making a bow in the shadows of Nabokov's novels. But I sensed that, if clearly unprovable, it was still possible. Nabokov himself is frank in admitting that many of the books he later read resonated for him with Reidian echoes. Dwelling on Louise Poindexter, a young lady equipped with a lorgnette in *The Headless Horseman*, Nabokov writes:

> That lorgnette I found afterward in the hands of
> Madame Bovary, and later Anna Karenin had it, and
> then it passed into the possession of Chekhov's Lady
> with the Lapdog and was lost by her on the pier at
> Yalta. When Louise held it, it was directed toward
> the speckled shadows under the mesquites, where the
> horseman of her choice was having an innocent conver-
> sation with the daughter of a wealthy *haciendado*, Doña
> Isidora Covarubio de los Llanos (whose "head of hair in
> luxuriance rivalled the tail of a wild steed").

In just this manner the turbaned heads of Moslem pilgrims that I had met in the *Boy's Own Annual* sprang into view when I read *Lord Jim,* and walking sticks in the hands of Henry James's characters were suddenly transformed from the innocent appur-tenances of dandies into menacing clubs.

There was something else too. I had come to wonder if I had not begun the process of learning to write long ago with the *Boy's Own Annual.* The one problem with the magazine was that it was a serial, and I possessed only a single volume. Some of the stories had no beginning. Worse, some had no end. Several of the more harrowing tales had appended to their last page a cruel joke: *To be continued.* My favourite character, the berry-stained boy, I had to say goodbye to as he lay manacled in the bottom of an Arab dhow, on the point of being pitched overboard to sharks. What, I asked myself in torments of anx-iety, had happened to him?

I like to think now that he would have remained forever frozen in that limbo of near death if I hadn't assumed the responsibility of rescuing him. Because at some point in my childhood I came to realize that what I was reading was fiction, a structure created by the imagination. Or as I saw it then: *the boy can be saved!* At about the age of seven or eight I set about saving him, manufacturing ploys and desperate acts of desperate courage that would deliver him from implacable fate. In other words, I began an apprenticeship. I was learning to write.

Perhaps all my subsequent fiction has been marked by this experience, this revelation. Certain reviewers have remarked on my "traditionalism." Others have gently chided me for my interest in plot and "story." Is the *Boy's Own Annual* the obscure root of these tendencies? Have the stratagems concocted to elude the wicked slavers become, in some sense, second nature?

I don't know. The only testimony I can offer is the confession that when I sit down to write, it is only with the greatest effort of will that I manage to force the turbaned heads down, out of sight below the bulwarks of the dhows, or manage to master the violent and intoxicating urge to conclude every chapter with a clear suggestion of imminent peril.

It is, I suppose, only a matter of time before the will weakens and the long serialization begun twenty-five years ago resumes under a slightly different guise. I find that once acquired, the taste is hard to lose.

Canadian Literature, Spring 1984

The Weird Wild West

EVERYONE HAS HAD THE EXPERIENCE of reading a book that elicits a detached, calculated admiration for its virtues. Then comes a book that "provokes a spiritual shudder. It is like a deep note that cannot be heard but is felt, it is like a claw in the gut." I offer this description from Annie Proulx's *Close Range* since it comes closest to my own response to her wildly rambunctious, nervy collection of stories.

As her subtitle announces, Proulx's gaze is unflinchingly focused on the landscape and people of Wyoming. Her subject is the contemporary West, a place where a man telephones his estranged wife while viewing a porn video; where an eco-terrorist kills cattle by feeding them plastic bags drenched in molasses; and where highway billboards, illustrated with a "blown-up photograph of kangaroos hopping through the sage brush," trumpet Down Under Wyoming, Western Fun the Western Way. Proulx's Wyoming sheepherders conduct gay affairs out on the range and sushi is served in restaurants catering to Japanese tourists. Fans of Zane Grey and Louis L'Amour be warned, there are no mythic riders of the purple sage to be found in *Close Range*.

As in most fiction about the West, the landscape figures in Proulx's book as a palpable and inescapable presence. Refreshingly, however, it is a landscape transmogrified by human perceptions. An old man, returning to the West after many years, thinks: "Nothing had changed, not a goddamn thing, the empty pale place and its roaring wind, the distant antelope as tiny as mice, landforms shaped true to the past." Yet for another visitor, Wyoming is nothing but a list of natural disasters, "the fiery column of the Cave Gulch flare-off in its vast junkyard field, refineries, disturbed land, uranium mines, coal mines, trona mines, pump jacks and drilling rigs, clear-cuts, tank farms, contaminated rivers, pipelines, methanol-processing plants, ruinous dams, the Amoco mess, railroads, all disguised by the deceptively empty landscape."

Reality and unreality, the visible versus the submerged, a thematic chord resonating throughout *Close Range*, is signalled by the epigraph to Proulx's collection, a quotation from a retired Wyoming rancher: "Reality's never been much use out here."

There is plenty of "unreality" in these stories. In "The Bunchgrass Edge of the World," a derelict John Deere tractor woos an unattractive, lovelorn girl, seductively urging her, "Come on, get up in the cab. Plenty a bounce left." Similarly, in "Pair a Spurs," a rancher whose shattered bones are held together by dozens of steel pins is attracted to successive owners of spurs crafted by a member of a millenarian sect called Final Daze. The steel in his body mysteriously thrums, yearning for the metal of jingling spurs.

What makes these bizarre stories so believable is that the fantastic is embedded in a rich matrix of fully realized detail: weeds named, tractor parts enumerated, the anatomy of a spur (drop shank, star rowel, etc.) lovingly delineated. For Proulx, the hallucinatory blooms out of the commonplace.

What impressed me even more than Proulx's talking tractor or siren spurs is her gift for plumbing the minds of male characters. One of the most chilling moments in the book is a rape filtered through the consciousness of a young bull rider. His contempt for women, his sense of inadequacy is finally capped by one cold concluding sentence: "The girl had too much mustard and she'd find it out if she came his way again."

Scrope, in "Pair a Spurs," is an utterly convincing portrait of the husband set self-pityingly adrift when his wife walks out on him. Then there is ranch-raised Mero, who winds up "sixty years later as an octogenarian vegetarian pumping an Exercycle in the living room of a colonial house in Woolfoot, Massachusetts," a brilliant study of a proud old gamecock. Nor do the memorable male characters end with these; Proulx provides a roll call of at least a dozen more.

Only one of these stories, "A Lonely Coast," is told from a woman's point of view, and it is every bit as affecting and ruthlessly unsentimental as the others. This is Proulx's deft sketch of three women's desperate lives. "Nothing was too bold, nothing not worth the risk, they'd be sieving the men at the bar and cutting out the best three head, maybe climb on some guy's lap in the cab of his truck. If Josanna was still around at two in the a.m. she looked like what she was, a woman coming into middle age, lipstick gnawed off, plain face and thickening flesh, yawning, departing into the fresh night alone and sorry."

Despite the careless violence, the hardness that characterizes existence for Proulx's protagonists, it would be wrong to leave the impression that *Close Range* is nothing but a bleak recitation of the vagaries of trailer trash. It is also an uproariously funny book, laced with the black humour that is the last resort of people who know better than to expect much from life. For example, the women of "A Lonely Coast" scour the personals in the newspaper, offering wry commentaries on the prospects advertising in the back pages. "How about this one: 'Six-three, two hundred pounds, thirty-seven, blue eyes, plays drums and loves Christian music.' Can't you just hear it? 'The Old Rugged Cross' on bongos?"

The two most celebrated stories in *Close Range* are "The Half-Skinned Steer," chosen by John Updike for *Best American Short*

Stories of the Century, and "Brokeback Mountain," included in *The O. Henry Prize Stories 1998*. They open and close this collection, stunning bookends.

"The Half-Skinned Steer" is based on an old Icelandic folk-tale and, like most folk literature, it touches on humankind's darkest nightmares. Mero Corn and his brother, Rollo, live on a Wyoming ranch with their Everclear-swilling father and his girlfriend. The girlfriend tells the three men the story of a steer butchered by a rancher. The skinning is interrupted and when the rancher returns to finish the job, the steer has mysteriously disappeared. Then he "sees something moving stiff and slow, stumbling along. It looks raw and it's got something bunchy and wet hanging over its hindquarters." The rancher sees "the raw meat of the head and the shoulder muscles and the empty mouth without no tongue open wide and its red eyes glaring at him, pure teetotal hate." In that moment, he realizes that the animal was not dead, but only stunned when he began the skinning and that the baleful red eyes are announcing his doom.

Shortly after this, Mero, badly shaken by the story, flees Wyoming. Sixty years later, he returns for his brother's funeral. The piece concludes ominously with the old man "running now on the unmarked road through great darkness." What he meets with is the gory beast that precipitated his flight from home, patiently awaiting his return.

In "Brokeback Mountain," two young men, Ennis Del Mar and Jack Twist, commence a homosexual love affair during an idyllic summer. Nevertheless, they marry unhappily, have children and, for twenty years, meet for brief assignations. The two are the hapless prisoners of an iron code of "manliness" they dare not defy. In Ennis's words, "nothing could be done about it, and if you can't fix it you've got to stand it." "Brokeback Mountain" is Proulx's quietest, saddest, and most tragic story.

Finishing this collection, I was left feeling exhilarated by the range and power of Proulx's stories. In her introduction to *Close Range*, she makes two surprising comments. First, that she finds short fiction difficult. Every short story writer should have her problems. Second, Proulx states she was "fortunate in having a publisher who allowed me this side trip." *Close Range* is no side trip. It's a joyride down an interstate, pedal to the metal, a great book of stories by a writer driving flat out for some destination most of us can't even imagine.

Review of *Close Range: The Wyoming Stories,* by Annie Proulx
(Scribner, 1999)
Globe and Mail, May 1, 1999

A Magician of the Austere

THE TITLE OF RICHARD FORD'S collection of three long short stories, *Women with Men,* is a neat reversal and sly allusion to Hemingway's celebrated *Men Without Women,* a writer to whom Ford is often compared, sharing as they do a style remarkable for its simplicity, control, and ruthless austerity. In the 1930s, Cyril Connolly gave a name to this style, the New Vernacular, and pointed out that it succeeds only when ruled by the most meticulous attention to the whole of the structure of a work of art, "that discipline in the conception and execution of a book, that planning which gives simply-written things the power to endure, the constant pruning without which the imagination like a tea-rose reverts to the wilderness." Of this subtle art Richard Ford is a master. One may be first struck by the clarity and the exactness of his prose, but the apparent transparency is deceiving. The tip of the iceberg rises in plain view, but what lurks beneath it, a submerged mass of desire and longing, only bursts upon the reader at the moment of the magician's choosing.

This is the case in his two Paris stories, "The Womanizer" and "Occidentals." In the first, "The Womanizer," Martin Austin, a paper salesman to foreign textbook publishers, is troubled by "the uneasy, unanchored sensation he'd had lately of not knowing exactly how to make the next twenty-five years of life as eventful and important as the previous twenty-five." During a business trip to Paris he grows infatuated with Josephine Belliard; on his return to Chicago, his wife decides to leave him, providing him with an excuse to throw up his job and hightail it back to Paris to pursue Josephine.

Of course, this plot sketch neglects everything which makes the story so rich and mysterious. Like Chekhov's, the best of Ford's stories are unanalyzable, the result of a miraculous alchemy of language, image, and psychological insight. A Ford story is never a straightforward advance to a predictable resolution, but rather a circuitous journey marked by retractions, qualifications, and contradictions. Austin may steadfastly profess love for his wife; nevertheless, when she leaves him, he experiences a thrill of release. Obsessed with Josephine, he still can acknowledge that he finds her opaque and not even particularly sexually attractive. Typically, their first kiss is both momentous and unsatisfactory, making him feel "delusionary and foolish and pathetic—the kind of man he would make fun of if he heard himself described."

Yet despite his characters' hesitations and equivocations Ford's precise language, his gift for startling images and scenes, propel "The Womanizer" onward with a dreamlike intensity, pushing the reader into the midst of dark epiphanies which feel both surprising *and* inevitable. As "The Womanizer" nears its end, Austin is babysitting Josephine's small son, Leo, and the child attempts to smash Austin's gift to him, a delicate lacquered egg. The scene is feral, the child detestable, ugly. But then, Ford deftly reverses our sympathies. While waiting for Josephine in a park, Austin carelessly loses sight of the little boy. Leo is discovered huddled naked under bushes, left there by a child molester. Ford writes, "He was very white and very quiet. His hair was still neatly combed. Though when he saw Austin, and that it was Austin and not someone else coming, bent at the waist, furious, breathing stertorously, stumbling, crashing arms-out through the rough branches and trunks and roots of that small place, he gave a shrill, hopeless cry, as though he could see what was next, and who it would be, and it terrified him. And his cry was what he could do to let the world know that he feared his fate."

In the child's wordless cry each preceding moment of the story, held until then in liquid suspension, crystallizes terrifyingly.

"The Occidentals" is equally masterful. Charley Matthews and his lover, Helen, have come to Paris at the invitation of Charley's French publisher. However, Monsieur Blumberg inexplicably calls off their meeting to go on holiday, leaving the couple adrift in the City of Light.

At first, the story seems to drift also, like a guileless travelogue of Paris, or a catalogue of unconnected incidents and scenes. There are glimpses of the cemetery across from Charley and Helen's hotel, of a Christmas tree in an apartment window. The two make love, visit the Eiffel Tower, go to dinner, go shopping. Helen buys a garish tea towel stamped with the words The Glory of God Is to Keep Things Hidden. She claims it's a joke, she'll give it to someone who lies to her husband. The phrase is as enigmatic as Charley's desire not to feel he is the centre of things—despite it being hard to see how Charley could ever imagine he is.

As these apparently casual events multiply, so does the sense that something is not quite right here. Early in the story we are informed in an offhand manner that Helen "had cancer of the something a year before and was still officially in recovery." She strikes Charley as jet-lagged but as the story progresses her symptoms grow more ominous. One night he is startled to discover her body is covered with bruises "which looked like big gloomy expressionist paintings or else thunderclouds."

And so, losing himself in a foreign city, brought face to face with the possible seriousness of Helen's illness, Charley gets his wish. To his relief, he finds himself fading out of the centre of things. But the relief is short-lived when he arrives back at the hotel to learn that his lover has committed suicide. Just as in "The Womanizer," countless apparently insignificant and random details coalesce as the story concludes. The glimpses of the cemetery, Helen's desire to be "translated" like Charley, the bizarre tea towel with its inscrutable message, all echo in the words of her suicide note. "I think a good life is supposed to be to die knowing nothing. Or maybe it's to die knowing nobody. Anyway, I've almost succeeded at both of them."

The shortest of these stories, "Jealous," covers more familiar Ford territory: Montana, and a boy damaged by his parents' disintegrating marriage. "Jealous" works in the same oblique, elusive fashion as the other two stories, but it has a bonus, another one of Ford's incomparable portraits of the adolescent male. Lawrence is as arresting a figure as the narrator of Ford's magnificent novel *Wildlife*, or Paul, the hormonal time-bomb in *Independence Day*. Lawrence is worth the price of the book alone.

I have long been an admirer of Richard Ford (even before he wrote a blurb for one of my novels). For his sake, if not my own, I hope I can be credited with disinterestedness when I say *Women with Men* is a wonderful accomplishment. As a writer of fiction, I am reminded by this collection that the sinews of art are discipline and discretion. As a reader, this collection simply delights me. The long story allows Ford to put all his strengths on display. These are lit with the poetic illuminations which characterize the best short fiction, glimmers of what Nadine Gordimer has called "the flash of fireflies." There is an added dividend: they also feel as if they have the weight and amplitude of a novel. Fans of either form have plenty to admire in *Women with Men*.

Review of *Women with Men: Three Stories,* by Richard Ford
(Alfred A. Knopf, 1997)
Globe and Mail, June 29, 1997

Everyman in Autumn

IN RICHARD FORD'S *The Lay of the Land*, Frank Bascombe returns for another bravura performance. First met in *The Sportswriter* and subsequently reprised in Ford's *Independence Day*, Frank brings us news of his present state and that of the Shaky State of the Union. Comparisons may be invidious, but like John Updike's Rabbit Angstrom before a fatal heart attack on a basketball court laid him to rest, Frank Bascombe is now surely the character of record for the white, middle-class, suburban American male. A fact acknowledged by Ford in a sly, throwaway reference to "those primary caregivers" who measure "the Angstroms gone off your molars bit by bit."

The action of *The Lay of the Land* circles an iconic American celebration, as it did in *Independence Day*. The novel commences seven days before Thanksgiving, in the millennial year 2000, as chads are earnestly being scrutinized in Florida, and the citizenry of the United States is arrayed into two hostile, rancorous political camps.

One morning, Frank Bascombe, owner of a successful realty business on the Jersey Shore, opens his local newspaper and reads an article about the murder of a nursing instructor in Texas by a disgruntled male student. Before executing her, Don-Houston Clevinger offers a cliché posed as a question to Ms. McCurdy. "Are you ready to meet your maker?" he inquires. Whereupon she mildly answers, "Yes. Yes, I think I am," and is immediately dispatched by a Glock 9-mm pistol.

Ms. McCurdy's confident assertion strikes home with Frank because he is, at that moment, contemplating his own extinction. Recently diagnosed with prostate cancer at the age of fifty-five, Frank is well aware that the outcome may not be good and, more than anything else, he longs to quit life with the calm dignity Ms. McCurdy displayed. As Frank remarks, "I needed to get right, to get where Ms. McCurdy was at her ending song ..."

More things than prostate cancer are not right with Frank. His second wife, Sally, has recently vacated the premises after learning her first husband, Wally, a Vietnam vet who walked out on her decades before to go permanently missing from domestic action, and whom she had to have declared legally dead before she could remarry, has miraculously reappeared. After much soul-searching, Sally decides to reunite with Wally because she claims it is far more important to be with someone who needs you than someone who loves you.

As the United States prepares for Thanksgiving Day, complications multiply for Frank. He attends the funeral of an old buddy, gets involved in an embarrassing barroom brawl, stumbles on a bombing at a local hospital, tries to bear with the neighbours from hell, attends the implosion of a derelict hotel with an elderly friend who was once in the running for likely father-in-law, and is threatened with the resignation of his realty associate, a top-earning Tibetan Buddhist who has adopted the "American" name Mike Mahoney. What's more, he is confronted by an alarming proposal from his first wife, Anne, who has reversed her long-held view of him and is now suggesting it might be a good idea if they resumed, in every sense of the word, their former relations.

Then there is the forbidding prospect of what Bascombe calls Turkey Day, the dreaded family conclave of forced conviviality with the two children of his first marriage, Clarissa and Paul, and their significant others. His adored Clarissa, an irresolute lesbian, has recently acquired an unctuous new boyfriend. (Her father much prefers the old girlfriend.) Even more troubling is the impending encounter with his son, Paul, a Hallmark greeting-card writer in Kansas City. Much of *Independence Day* dealt with Frank and Paul's rocky father-son relationship, and the adolescent Paul depicted there would prompt most parents to offer up a prayer of gratitude for their own teenagers, however difficult and wayward they might be. Paul, it turns out, has not improved with age despite the best efforts of his current partner, Jill, to mitigate his toxicity.

As this partial description of incidents farcical and sad may indicate, *The Lay of the Land* qualifies as a bona fide page-turner, a book that keeps the reader up late at night eager to find out what happened to whom and how. But for me, the chief delight of the novel is its narrator's winning, pitch-perfect voice. In his stories, Ford strips the chassis clean, reducing wind resistance, paring his vehicle down to the bare essentials. In contrast, *The Lay of the Land* provides a ride in a high-end automobile, replete with deluxe appointments, driven by an assured chauffeur who glides you smoothly through the New Jersey landscape calling your attention to interesting views, passing on pertinent anthropological information about the inhabitants while playing the perfect raconteur.

Frank is adrift in what he has christened the Permanent Period, a phase he entered years earlier and that "portended an end to perpetual becoming, to thinking that life schemed wonderful changes for me, even if it didn't." Frank's struggle to accept what he is convinced is the unalterable condition of his life, his particular "lay of the land," is the heart of the novel.

Thankfully, what makes his journey so entrancing is that the usual whine and self-pity that corrode so many similar accounts of middle age are absent. Frank Bascombe is a decent, well-meaning, fallible, often hilariously funny fellow. An old-fashioned, nearly defunct term might best describe him. He is what my mother used to call "a real charmer."

Although a charmer, Frank Bascombe is not a Sensitive Male. As he tootles the highways and byways of New Jersey, the Kinkos, the Benjamin Moore "test farms," the Tight Butts Make Me Nuts! signs flowing by, he passes enough un-PC remarks concerning every race, religion, sexual preference, gender, and every other subdivision of the human family to have most of New Jersey up in arms. Why heaven forfend, he even has unkind things to say about the Dalai Lama. Of course, the first duty of the satirist is to provide offence to all those who want to believe things are exactly as they would wish them to be.

Needless to say, things come to a head with wives, children, difficult neighbours, etc. on Thanksgiving. More ominously, Frank also comes face to face with death, but in a fashion he never anticipated. In the aftermath of that most American of holidays, with the bird cooling on the festive table, Frank has renounced the Permanent Period to embrace the Next Level. All things are not settled, but some are. Life goes on, and Frank is damn glad it does.

As I finished this wonderful book, I thought of two favours I would ask of Richard Ford. The first is that Frank Bascombe pen that letter to the president of the United States he has long considered writing. I think the president needs to hear from him. My second request is that Richard Ford spare Frank the premature death Updike handed Rabbit and that he keep him knocking around for a long, long time. I, for one, look forward to whatever Mr. Bascombe might have to say in future.[*]

Review of *The Lay of the Land*, by Richard Ford (Alfred A. Knopf, 2006)
Globe and Mail, October 28, 2006

---

[*] Frank Bascombe has continued to ruminate on American society in the books *Let Me Be Frank with You* (HarperCollins, 2014) and *Be Mine* (HarperCollins, 2023).

Troubled Wit and Moralist

I WAS AN UNDERGRADUATE at the University of Saskatchewan when *St. Urbain's Horseman* was published in 1971. The temper of the times and my age predisposed me to welcome its black, mordant humour. Being young, I naturally assumed myself untainted by the hypocrisy, pretence, and stupidity Mordecai Richler so savagely pilloried, and I revelled in this exuberant novel without too many anxious second thoughts.

Rereading it, I am aware of what a different book it seems years later. For one thing, I can recognize now that a bona fide rural *goy*, genus *Saskatchewan*, who had never had a Jewish friend or set foot in Montreal, might be at a disadvantage in fully appreciating *St. Urbain's Horseman*. At the time, though, such thoughts never crossed my mind because I was too busy enjoying the book. All I knew was that this was the funniest Canadian fiction I had ever read, funnier even than several "serious" Canadian novels which had come my way. Passages fondly remembered still strike me as fresh and hilarious: the byzantine politics of show biz (and by extension, life itself) exposed during the Hampstead Heath softball game; Jake's feverish, slapstick attempts to dispose of his unflushable stool deposited in the Ormsby-Fletchers' toilet during the course of their classy dinner party; the plot summaries of Doug's socially conscious and stickily earnest radio plays.

Oddly enough, what I don't recall having noticed during the first reading was what a brooding, obsessed, and *serious* book *St. Urbain's Horseman* is, every bit as brooding, obsessed, and serious as Jake Hersh, a man who is constantly reminding himself, "Not all candidates pass." Much of Jake's character, his doubts and longings, is revealed in his questioning himself whether another troubled wit and moralist, Samuel Johnson (Reb Shmul to Jake), would have invited him to sit at his table. More than anything else, Jake Hersh wants to be judged worthy.

The observation that the impulse behind most satire and comedy is a moral one comes as news to no one. First cousin to this notion is V. S. Pritchett's remark that "Comedy can only be written by serious minds ..." *Certain* comedy at least, the kind that dares to undermine and subvert a reader's complacency. The sad truth is that most comic novels seek only to ingratiate. The targets of their satire are chiefly sitting ducks on very small ponds— military men above the rank of sergeant, television evangelists, university professors—anyone safely assumed to be ridiculous.

Although I am impressed by *St. Urbain's Horseman*'s carefully paced and crafted narrative, its epigrammatic prose, its characters who seethe and fulminate so magnificently and humanly, what impresses me most is the challenging, uncompromising quality of its comedy. Uneasy laughter is its natural accompaniment. The provoking of such laughter is not forgiven in some circles. Good writers, however, make lousy team players, forever letting down the side. Mordecai Richler, the mischievous Canadian, puts lines into the mouths of his characters such as "Canada's no joke. We're the world's leading producer of uranium. Walter Pidgeon was born in this country." (So was Saul Bellow, I heard a newscaster announce with pride when Bellow won the Nobel Prize for Literature.) As well as offending nationalists, Richler has been clucked at by some Jews for giving the world Duddy Kravitz and boring, sententious rabbis.

Admittedly, it is never pleasant to have it pointed out to you that apes may lurk in the midst of your angels. Woodstock still shone bright in the hippie heaven when I poked my nose into *St. Urbain's Horseman*. A smug twenty-one-year-old, I blithely snickered my way through a novel which appeared to be an entertaining indictment of the corruptions of the enemy, the middle-aged. Now I am no longer prompted to do that when Uncle Abe seizes the floor.

> This kid says when they have a rock concert, thousands
> of them from miles around, there's no rough stuff. I
> answered him, listen here, shmock, if I go to an affair
> at the synagogue, or a Mozart concert, we don't pour
> out of the halls with clubs, splitting heads. Why should
> you be amazed that your concerts don't end in a riot?
> What's so special? … Their bodies are beautiful, he tells
> me. When they swim nude, the sun shines out of their
> asses. Listen here, you little prick, you think I was born
> fat and bald, with a heart condition. Wasn't I young
> once, and aren't you going to grow old too? Aren't we all
> made of flesh?

Jake, like Uncle Abe, is given to contemplating the betrayals of the flesh, the ills and mishaps it is prey to. Gloomily he checks himself for signs of rot, anticipates cancer, air crashes, the ruin of his domestic happiness by the "injustice-collectors. The concentration camp survivors. The emaciated millions of India. The starvelings of Africa." Greater even than these pressing anxieties is his indignation with a world in which evidence of justice, human or divine, is largely absent and obscenities like Joseph Mengele walk free. "If God weren't dead," he thinks, "it would be necessary to kill him."

Between himself and this threatening world Jake interposes the Horseman. His transformation of childhood memories of his cousin Joey into St. Urbain's Horseman, a contemporary Golem, is as much an act of necessity as the original Golem's creation by a sixteenth-century rabbi to protect the Prague ghetto from pogroms. For Jake, the Horseman serves as a sheet anchor, an assurance that evil will be punished, that the compromise of principle is not a dirty inevitability. Corroded by contempt for the life he leads and the work he does, Jake adopts the Horseman as a moral editor, even an artistic conscience. Once again, he asks to be judged by the most impeccable magistrate. But with telling irony, Richler plants the seeds of doubt about the moral credentials of the Horseman. Although no final judgment of his character is offered, rumours of blackmail, card sharping, drug dealing, smuggling, wife and child desertion swirl about Joey. Even the *noms de guerre* (the Golem, the Horseman) bestowed upon him by his "acolyte" Jake are double-edged in their implications. While the Golem is the defender of the Jews, he is also a body without a soul. And the name of the Horseman sits ambiguously on a Jewish hero, recalling Isaac Babel's assertion that "When a Jew gets on a horse he stops being a Jew ..." What does he then become, a Cossack? After his wife's claim that Joey was a ringleader in an unprovoked attack on a peaceful Arab village, one has to wonder.

All of Richler's characters are, to a greater or lesser degree, invested with a marvellous ambiguity, something unusual in comic fiction where portraiture tends towards the simplistic and Manichaean. No one is clearly good or clearly evil in *St. Urbain's Horseman*, perhaps because the skeptical intelligence which makes Richler such a formidable counterpuncher when faced with dogmatism of any kind also prompts him to be leery of separating his characters into fictional sheep and fictional goats. Or it simply may be that for a book in which dilemmas of moral choice take centre stage, the dilemmas make sense only when they are the dilemmas of fully realized people and not caricatures. Here

Richler flirts with kicking the props out from under his comedy. How much of our common humanity can we recognize in a character like Harry Stein and still keep laughing? It is testimony to Richler's skill and tact as a writer that he pulls off this hazardous balancing act, coaxing from us a wiser, more rueful laughter than would have been possible if the Horseman's moral status had been unequivocal, or Uncle Abe had been definitely fingered as Joey's betrayer, or Jake's essential decency had not shown cracks, or the grotesque Harry Stein hadn't been allowed a few moments when his lunatic resentments didn't seem understandable and nearly sane. All this uncertainty, untidiness, ambiguity, and absurdity charge the novel with a nervous sense of life.

Absurdity is present even when Jake's worst premonition comes to pass. As he always feared, his happiness is put in jeopardy by an "injustice collector." Not, however, by one of the pathetic starvelings which haunt his conscience but by the sociopathic Harry Stein, who bristles with grievance because he doesn't have King Farouk's share of girls and other good things. Led astray by Harry, Jake has to endure a humiliating trial, facing shameful and embarrassing sexual charges. No sooner does the trial conclude than he has to undergo another trial, news of the death of Joey in an air crash. Flipping through the pages of the Horseman's journal, reflecting upon his cousin's death, Jake suddenly hears the old question with which Joey once confronted the timid, cautious Jews of St. Urbain Street: "What are you going to do?"

What Jake does is weep. In the tears he sheds for his dead father, his mother, Nancy, Harry, and Joey, his need for the Horseman dissolves, and a new question, unthinkable until now, presents itself. "What if the Horseman was a distorting mirror and we each took the self-justifying image we required of him?"

St. Urbain's Horseman begins with a nightmare and ends with one. There are echoes in this of James Joyce's famous statement that "History ... is a nightmare from which I am trying to awake."

Jake, too, wishes to awake from the nightmare of History summed up in the ominous refrain repeated throughout the novel.

"Mengele cannot have been there all the time."
"In my opinion, always. Night and day."

Richler's comedy is played out with this horror hovering in the background. As the sinister presence of Mengele grows in strength, the laughter grows more troubled and uncomfortable because the evasions, compromises, and duplicities that excite derision seem so trivial in comparison with those that gave birth to Mengele. Yet we know they share a common father.

A challenge is being issued. When Jake awakes from his final nightmare, he does so with new words on his lips, words that signal an acceptance of personal responsibility. "I've come" replaces "he's come." Joey no longer stands in for Jake against the ever-present evil (Mengele in all his guises). Jake has become his own Horseman.

What sort of Horseman awakes from the nightmare? It is pure speculation, but I would hazard a guess that he is not the sort of Horseman who searches for Mengele in Paraguayan jungles when he can be found closer to home. He is likely to be a less obviously heroic figure than Joey, a more ordinary man whose ordinary testament of faith is enunciated in the novel. "What Jake stood for would not fire the countryside: decency, tolerance, honor. With E. M. Forster, he wearily offered two cheers for democracy. After George Orwell, he was for a closer look at anybody's panacea."

Is this finally the point to which our reluctant laughter brings us, to a recognition that decency, tolerance, honour, and hard-headed skepticism are the best we have to offer in opposition to the dominion of Mengele? Perhaps. There are no absolute certainties in this splendid, skeptical book. The novel closes with Jake at last fallen into a deep sleep after having crossed out "died

July 20, 1967, in an air crash" in the Horseman's journal and written over it "presumed dead." One last ambiguity: Is Jake retreat-
ing, backsliding into the old fantasy? Or is it, as I prefer to think,
that the Horseman cannot definitely be pronounced dead as long
as there is hope for his reincarnation in a new, chastened figure,
that of Jake, an ordinary decent man.

Afterword to *St. Urbain's Horseman,* by Mordecai Richler
(McClelland & Stewart, New Canadian Library, 1989)

A Walk around the
Leacock Monument

THIS ESSAY should begin with an explanation. I came to read
Stephen Leacock late, beyond the bounds of a university, and
thus without benefit of supervision. Therefore, whatever I write
cannot be attributed to bad teaching. Nor can I pretend to be
familiar with more than nine or ten of his books. As you may
already suspect, this is an apology for what follows.

The first book of Leacock's that I read was *Sunshine Sketches
of a Little Town*, easily the best of the ones I know. This, I hope,
entitles me to call it his masterpiece. What I discovered in its
pages was that strange and exotic place, Mariposa, a town like no
other I have encountered in Canadian fiction. Since I have lived
all my life in the West, I am driven to wonder if in commenting
on the strangeness of Mariposa I might not be raising the spectre
of regionalism which so often haunts discussion of our literature,
sowing confusion and dismay. Yet I am convinced that what travels
under the name of regionalism is really only the result of looking
at the same thing, Canada, from different angles. And I would
like to suggest that we might learn something by taking a walk
around the monument which Stephen Leacock has become and
taking a look at him from a slightly different angle. In suggesting
this, I am not attempting to diminish that monument. No one

who wants to understand our literature or our nation can disregard or dismiss Leacock. His prominent position in Canadian letters could be assured on any number of grounds. His virtues as a stylist alone would cause him to be remembered. Few Canadians have written such elegant, lucid prose. But Leacock is a great deal more than a stylist. He is one of the great interpreters of this country.

And I might add that it was through Leacock that I came to understand a grandfather who had always succeeded in bewildering me. In turn, what I knew of my grandfather made Leacock seem more familiar and less peculiar than he might otherwise have been to someone who had spent his entire life on the prairies. Growing up in a small town in Saskatchewan, I was fortunate enough to have the benefit of the company of both my grandfathers. Each was an immigrant. One came from Belgium, the other from Ontario. It is the grandfather who seemed most foreign to me—the one who came from Ontario—that Leacock has helped me to understand.

What I perceived as my Ontario grandfather's foreignness, his bizarreness, was a result of context. In a town which was almost entirely populated by men and women of Eastern and Central European stock, he belonged to a tiny minority group. He had a British name. He was a Protestant. And he was animated and ruled by all the vices and virtues of old Ontario. Amid those representatives of the wretched and huddled masses of Europe, he was the only bona fide refugee from Mariposa.

What made him so odd, even in the eyes of his children and grandchildren, was that he lived by a set of assumptions that were very different from those of his neighbours. In a society which has often been loosely described as "progressive," where politics were inclined to be liberal or radical, and most people had little notion of, or interest in, ancestors and antecedents, my grandfather was one of the few people who was a loyal Tory and proud of a family tree he could trace back to what he felt were distant horizons.

My grandfather clung to his politics because they distinguished him from his fellow citizens. His politics were the tip of an iceberg of submerged values. They were a way of standing fast to his race, his religion, and everything he had been taught as a child. Everyone else in my hometown seemed to regard the vote as a way of asserting self-interest or expressing gratitude. Most Eastern Europeans supported Liberals because they were grateful for Clifford Sifton's immigration policies, while the more fiery and radical were partisans of the CCF or Social Credit. These people were not burdened by family notions of political tradition or loyalty. After all, given where most of them had come from, they had not been in the habit of voting. They were the kind of citizens Leacock describes as "people whose aim is to be broadminded and judicious and who vote Liberal or Conservative according to their judgment of the questions of the day. If their judgment of these questions tells them there is something in it for them in voting Liberal, then they do so."

Nevertheless, after reading *Sunshine Sketches*, I came away with the distinct impression that the body politic of Mariposa was leavened by voters of sterner principles, those who were, to quote Leacock, "Liberals or Conservatives all their lives and are called dyed-in-the-wool Grits or old-time Tories and things of that sort."

What differentiated my grandfather from so many of his fellow townsmen was that he followed this fine old Ontario tradition of being born with one's politics decided. Any change in allegiance dictated by a consideration of self-interest would have been an apostasy too horrible to be contemplated. His motivation was not really political, but tribal.

My other grandfather, my Belgian grandfather, approached voting with an alacrity that stupefied my British grandfather. My Belgian grandfather had been, in rapid succession, a CCFer, a Social Crediter, a Liberal, and even once a Conservative. When he had run through all the parties he went back to the beginning and started all over again. That is not to say that he did not demonstrate a passionate commitment to whatever party temporarily harboured him, but then it would adopt some misguided policy such as an increase in the tax on pipe tobacco and he would be forced to withdraw his support.

My British grandfather had no difficulties in this respect. He knew he was a Conservative because he had been born a Conservative. He liked things to be settled this way. In his mind, it was a noble arrangement which had served well his father, his father's father, his father's father's father, and so on, back into the mists of time that presumably shrouded that Neolithic Conservative from whose loins they had all proceeded. Nor was he blind to the defects in this system. He recognized and felt them. Particularly when he didn't agree with the party's policies, or hated the man nominated to carry the colours in his riding, or thought the party leader was an imbecile. But putting those things aside, my grandfather was always proud to be a Conservative.

As far as I could see he got nothing from this loyalty except a sense of who he was. He was like Leacock, who wrote, "I belong to the Conservative party, but as yet I have failed entirely in Canadian politics, never having received a contract to build a bridge, or make a wharf, nor to construct even the smallest section of the Transcontinental Railway." At one point in his life such political success appeared to be within my grandfather's grasp. After a Conservative electoral triumph, my grandfather had hopes of obtaining a clerkship in the local Liquor Board store, but the party, swayed by higher considerations, gave the job to a more influential member's cousin. Thirty years after the fact, my grandfather was still grumbling about the injustice of it all. What the poor innocent did not see was that the party knew he was a Mariposan Conservative and, like Judge Pepperleigh, he was no more capable of switching party allegiances than a leopard is of changing its spots. So why would anyone be dumb enough to buy support that did not need to be bought?

When election time rolled around my grandfather would breathlessly report that the Lawyer Mackenzie and the Doctor Mackenzie had told him they were voting Conservative, as if this news assured a Conservative sweep of the town. What he could not seem to comprehend was that he and my grandmother, the Mackenzies and their wives, the British element as it were, only accounted for six votes. What about all those Liberal Hungarians, Czechs, and Ukrainians? The truth was that my grandfather could not see them. Not really. Or if he did, he assumed they could be appealed to and touched in the ways he was and, of course, they could not. They had been shaped by different circumstances.

All of this is, of course, merely a long preamble to the point that what one is capable of seeing depends a good deal on the angle of one's vision. Perhaps reflecting on my grandfather's unique perspective helped me explain something about Leacock that had always puzzled me. I had wondered why it was that a man who had lived as many years as Leacock had in Montreal never, to my knowledge, introduced a French-Canadian into his fiction. And why were there plenty of Anglican rectors and English peers but no Catholics or Jews? Montreal could certainly boast significant numbers of these last two communities.

By remarking on this I do not wish to make a criticism of Leacock but to raise a point. I am not saying that we *ought* to find in Leacock's books French-Canadians, Catholics, or Jews, only that we do not. After all, a writer defines his fictional universe as much by what he excludes as by what he includes. It is not an original remark to say that writers who are contemporaries and who share a common citizenship produce very different work. Henry James is one kind of American writer and Mark Twain another. Writing at roughly the same time, these writers produced their finest work when their talents and imagination discovered what, for want of a better word, I will call their subjects. Their masterpieces proclaim to the world a part of what it meant to be American then and, by extension, a part of what it means to be American now.

The same, I think, can be said of Leacock.

What was his subject? Mariposa. And what is Mariposa? I do not think it is what the back cover of the New Canadian Library edition of *Sunshine Sketches of a Little Town* proclaims it to be when it announces that "although Mariposa can be identified as Orillia, Ontario, it is also true that it represents any small town anywhere in Canada." An orthodox opinion, I suspect.

But I don't believe it for a minute. To claim that Leacock's Mariposa *is* the Canadian small town, a generic village that can be plopped down anywhere in the country to do duty like a Hollywood set, is to misrepresent what the rest of English-speaking Canada is and to diminish what Leacock achieved in his portrait. What Leacock drew with such love and conviction is not necessarily common to us all. Leacock's small town is not Alice Munro's small town, nor Margaret Laurence's small town, nor Sinclair Ross's small town. Nor should we expect it to be. To ignore differences is to diminish Mariposa in all its glorious particularity. As Czeslaw Milosz has written in *The Witness of Poetry*, "we apprehend the human condition with pity and terror not in the abstract but always in relation to a given place and time, in one particular province, one particular country."

Mariposa is a small town of a particular time, place, and people. It is important not to forget that this is a picture of a lost world, an Edwardian town basking in a bright sunshine of confidence, peace, and stability; a town that has no inkling that it will soon send its sons to perish in the bloody mud of Flanders. We also ought not to forget that it is an Ontario town and a British town.

In some sense Mariposa is also the closest thing to a utopia that the small-c conservative who denies the notion of human perfectibility will permit himself to dream. Here is the organic society so much applauded, a society whose members are bound to one another by common values, traditions, a longing for stability, and a belief in a deity. For a writer of Leacock's convictions and temperament this was a subject he both loved and understood. In no other of his works does his gentle humour illuminate human idiosyncrasy with a steadier light or does the pathos he evokes seem so much a natural outcome of our common human journey.

Of course, perhaps this Mariposa he created was never more than a dream. But Leacock's dream tells me something about my country as Twain's and James's dreams tell me something about America. In *Sunshine Sketches* I am allowed to glimpse what people of a certain time and place wanted life to be. And such dreams, projected by the force of desire, have consequences far into the future.

Yet how can I, an admitted foreigner to Mariposa, offer these speculations, separated from it as I am by time, region, and perhaps even sympathy? I could offer the suggestion that the love and skill with which Leacock writes lead me to perceive these things. But I have recourse to something else. After all, I knew my grandfather. One test of the dream is to imagine him in Mariposa. I have no difficulty in doing so.

I have no doubt that my grandfather would have been completely at home in Jeff Thorpe's barber shop, as he would have been at his ease promenading the deck of the Mariposa Belle. And how gladly he would have raised his voice in a Mariposa church or a glass in Smith's hostelry. Best of all, I see him as a Knight of Pythias. His Eastern European neighbours were not given to joining fraternal organizations. And what pleasure he would have taken in fighting a *real* election, the kind they fought in Missinaba County.

It is in this fictional landscape that my grandfather appears at home to me, rather than the one he inhabited for most of his life.

Perhaps this is some kind of testament to the strange reciprocity which exists between Life and Art. If it is, it suggests another way of looking at *Sunshine Sketches*, not as the embodiment of some kind of vague "Canadianism," but as a distinct and local expression. Perhaps even, to press a point, as a regional and ethnic work. Looked at in this way, *Sunshine Sketches* can lay claim to being not only a fine, funny, sad book, but also a book which possesses the power to reveal one Canadian to another, even across the daunting gulfs of space and time.

"Leacock and Understanding Canada," in *Stephen Leacock: A Reappraisal*, edited by David Staines (University of Ottawa Press, 1986)

Fight All You Want but No Sex

MANY LAPSED BELIEVERS have a nostalgia for a lost faith, along with the conviction that they had perfectly good reasons for losing it. A description which fits me as a former hockey fan. I now find a televised NHL game as entertaining as the broadcast of a bladder repair operation on The Learning Channel. I still continue to play hockey with towering ineptitude both winter and summer but have discovered it is much more amusing to disappoint myself with my own on-ice antics than watch millionaire professionals disappoint me with theirs.

The American sportswriters Klein and Reif offer a compelling justification for hockey apostasy. Their complaints in *The Death of Hockey* are familiar enough: the NHL's refusal to enforce the rules; its preference for size over skill; the rampant expansion of the league; the flight of teams from traditional hockey centres to the Sun Belt; a bloated season of eighty-two games, too many to be meaningful, and far too many to develop healthy club rivalries; etc., etc.

What is refreshing about Klein and Reif is that they skewer NHL hypocrisy with the inspired lunacy of the Marx Brothers. Having heard so often that "fighting is part of the game," they decided to treat it that way in the pages of *The Village Voice*, running a column devoted to hockey donnybrooks. League officials were not happy. "Why do you print that garbage?" one of them demanded angrily. Klein and Reif describe this "as an example of the profound cognitive dissonance between what the NHL allows and doesn't like to see mentioned."

The NHL's response to mayhem on skates has been to institute thirty-eight rule changes in thirty-seven years, many of which could have been drafted by Woody Allen. Gentlemen, combatants will be thrown out of the game unless helmets with visors are removed before battle commences! Gentlemen, no punch-ups with tape on your hands! And perhaps the wackiest of all: if jersey and upper-body gear are stripped off, the bare-chested fighter will be tossed. This is a commandment chiselled in response to wily Rob Ray who tied his sweater to his gear so that when an opposing gladiator pulled his sweater over Ray's head, "Razor" would be free to flail away unencumbered. A ploy which caused telecaster John Davidson to hilariously shriek, "*It's not manly!*"

Well, yes. But at least Klein and Reif are clear-sighted about the solution. They confess to *liking* hockey brawls, but also recognize that they hurt the game, leading many people to equate these highjinks with roller derby and the World Wrestling Federation. Their solution? Something simple. Do what every other legitimate pro sport has done, outlaw fighting.

This is their style in exposing all the absurdities of the NHL: report them deadpan, mischievously puncture them, and preach common sense. The result is a lively, entertaining, vitriolic dissection of the game by two writers whose passion for hockey and whose desire to see it fixed is incandescent.

While the tenor of *The Death of Hockey* is Dadaistic and likely to raise the ire of Don Cherry's disciples, Bill Boyd's *Hockey Towns* is reverentially nostalgic, which should appeal to even quondam fans. In 1996, 1997, and 1998, Boyd criss-crossed Canada, visiting a host of towns like Viking, Drummondville, Trail, Brandon, and Timmins, locales that have produced bumper crops of hockey greats.

Boyd announces he is not interested in hockey as metaphor or sociology; his approach is simply to interview fans, players, ex-players, coaches, scouts, and owners. This technique can grow repetitious and plodding since most hockey people say much the same things. Old-timers condemn current hockey for the incessant clutching and grabbing, the hitting from behind. Former players declare their love for the game, acclaim hockey people the greatest people on earth, maintain they would gladly have played for nothing. Such heartfelt professions are touching in light of the naked greed which has sullied the game. On the other hand, it is disconcerting to hear players who were once bought and sold like cattle fondly recall their days of indentured servitude.

Out of these frequent reiterations, and others, a crude sociology of hockey does unwittingly emerge. Despite the relative health of Junior A hockey, the impression is left that the sport in many small towns may be failing. How else to explain the decision of the owner of the Truro Bearcats, winner of the Allan Cup, once one of hockey's most coveted prizes, to fold his team at the end of a triumphal season? When Boyd encounters nearly empty rinks, he is reassured that attendance will pick up after Christmas. But did it? Even stranger is the behaviour of hardcore fans like Andy Gurba who leaves a tied game with the enigmatic comment, "I'm tired."

A book like *Hockey Towns* stands or falls on the strength of its anecdotes, and this has some fine ones, my favourite involving the inimitable Eddie Shore. Andy McCallum, who served under Shore in Syracuse, remembers Shore summoning his players and their wives to the rink at Christmas. They gathered in a state of high anticipation, believing their legendarily parsimonious leader was about to spring for a Yuletide celebration. Instead, Shore read the riot act to the assembly, decreeing sex before games verboten. Surely a milestone in management-player relations.

For anyone who happens to live in one of the places Boyd stopped, this book will be a treasure trove of local hockey lore. For anyone like myself, who grew up in a small town where the game was a passion, it will also have considerable charm. I was carried back to a time when rink rats squabbled for the privilege of scraping the ice between periods at the senior hockey team's games, a time when entire lines were composed of brothers and a one-armed defenceman acquitted himself with distinction in the league. *Sic transit gloria mundi.*

Review of *Hockey Towns: Stories of Small Town Hockey in Canada,* *by* Bill Boyd (Doubleday Canada, 1998) and *The Death of Hockey,* *by* Jeff A. Klein and Karl-Eric Reif (Macmillan Canada, 1998) *National Post*, December 15, 1998

Elemental Truths

IN THIS SPLENDIDLY DETAILED, authoritative biography, Myriam Anissimov traces the two great influences on the life and writing of Primo Levi: a passion for chemistry, and the duty he felt to testify to what he and millions of others had suffered at the hands of the Fascists and Nazis.

The love of chemistry came at an early age. The son of bourgeois Jewish parents, Levi was born in Turin, Italy, in 1919. Even as a boy, he was disgusted by Fascist propaganda masquerading as education. This led him to embrace the study of chemistry, a discipline where the mindless, blowsy notions of "spirit" and "blood," so beloved by Fascist and Nazi ideologues, had difficulty worming their way into the curriculum. Through various loopholes in the Italian racial laws aimed at Jews, Levi succeeded in graduating with a doctorate from the Chemical Institute and in securing precarious employment until he joined a group of Italian partisans in 1943. That same year he was betrayed, arrested, and deported to a Nazi death camp.

Approximately a third of Anissimov's biography is devoted to Primo Levi's time in Buna-Monowitz, an Auschwitz satellite camp. She draws heavily on Levi's brilliant series of memoirs that relate this nightmare, supplemented by interviews conducted with former inmates and published records. That the frail intellectual survived the ordeal is little less than miraculous. His intelligence and tenacity of spirit were largely responsible, but luck also played a role. Lorenzo Perrone, an Italian civilian worker at the camp, befriended him, and ran great risks smuggling him food. Levi's degree in chemistry also helped win him a place in the I. G. Farben plant at Buna-Monowitz, where German war materiel was produced with slave labour.

After liberation by Soviet troops, and a long, chaotic repatriation, Levi was finally returned to his parents' apartment on the Corso Re Umberto in Turin. There he would spend the rest of his days, marrying, raising two children, and writing whenever he could steal time from a demanding job as a chemist at the SIVA paint factory.

Levi, however, was never to be freed from his ghastly memories of Auschwitz. In *The Periodic Table*, he wrote, "It seemed to me that I would be purified if I told its story, and I felt like Coleridge's Ancient Mariner, who waylays on the street the wedding guests going to the feast, inflicting on them the story of his misfortune." Out of this obsession was born his first book, *If This Is a Man*. It was during the writing of this account of Auschwitz that Levi's training as a chemist and the demands of his subject came together to forge the distinctive prose style which was to become his signature. Perhaps provocatively, Levi always claimed his prose was modelled on "the weekly report commonly used in factories." Of course, this remark was not intended to be taken literally; books such as *The Truce* and *The Periodic Table* are works of art, not bureaucratic memos. What Levi sought to convey by his style was his attitude to his testimony. If he was to be a witness, he believed it his duty to be a scrupulously honest one, reporting only what he had seen, and offering his evidence in language of utter clarity, stripped of all rhetorical flourishes. This seeming "coolness" in describing the horrors of Auschwitz lent his writings about the Holocaust an eerie power, subtly shifting the burden of judgment from author to reader. More importantly, Levi's approach prompted other questions in his readers' minds, such as: How would I behave in such a situation? What delusions, what compromises would I be capable of? Charles Conreau, a Frenchman who met Levi in Auschwitz, called him a "marvellous weigher of souls." He was certainly that, but he also asks us, his readers, to take on the job of weighing our own souls.

For those familiar with any of Levi's memoirs, the last half of Anissimov's biography offers a prospect of more unfamiliar territory. For instance, I was surprised to learn that his beginnings as a writer were inauspicious. His first work, *If This Is a Man*, sank with scarcely a ripple after its appearance in Italy in 1947, and the indifference with which it was met drove Levi to abandon writing for the next fourteen years. Only the book's reissue in 1958, and its subsequent publication in Britain and the United States, encouraged him to resume writing.

For a man of such prodigious gifts, his was an uphill battle for recognition. While Anissimov makes it clear that Levi had his champions from the beginning (among them Italo Calvino), she also suggests that many in the Italian literary establishment were inclined to view him as a mere curiosity, a chemist who happened to write.

Although a modest, unassuming man with little taste for controversy, Levi was not reluctant to voice unfashionable opinions. A champion of lucidity, he was distrustful of most "experimental" writing, a position which earned him a reputation for philistinism among the avant-garde. Similarly, when Marxism was all the rage in Italian intellectual circles, Levi managed to raise the ire of the Left. His temerity in publishing *The Wrench*, a work of fiction about a worker, caused a furor among journalists, trade unionists, and students. The extreme left-wing newspaper *Lotta Continua* (which had once stated there was nothing to choose between a factory and a concentration camp) attacked the bourgeois Levi for daring to write a book in which a proletarian was the hero. There was also outrage among trade union leaders because one of Italy's leading intellectuals had missed an opportunity to show his working-class protagonist actively engaged in the political struggle.

Even his works about the death camps raised hackles in some quarters. Jean Améry, a philosopher who had been in Auschwitz with Levi, accused him of being a "forgiver." According to Anissimov, Levi did not share "the idea that the German people were collectively responsible for the Holocaust." In answering Améry's accusation in the pages of the *The Drowned and the Saved*, Levi wrote, "I consider this neither insult nor praise but imprecision. I am not inclined to forgive, I never forgave our enemies of that time … because I know no human act that can erase a crime." It was Levi's contention that *personal* responsibility for criminal acts was the paramount consideration.

Over the years, Levi's reputation as a writer steadily grew, and reached its zenith with the publication of his masterpiece, *The Periodic Table*, which earned him great international success. This meditation on Mendeleev's chemical table, a meditation which expanded to touch on science and its relationship to human existence, provided Levi the opportunity to retire from the SIVA paint company where he had worked for thirty years. For the first time, he eagerly contemplated life as a full-time writer.

But there were to be no safe harbours, no fairy-tale endings for Primo Levi. Strains and disillusionments which had been building for years came to a head and culminated in his suicide on April 11, 1987. When friends and family learned of his death, a debate immediately ensued about whether or not he had taken his own life. The evidence offered by Anissimov suggests he most certainly did.

What perplexed those who knew him was that Levi had several times argued persuasively in his books against suicide. They also pointed to the fact he had spoken cheerfully to the concierge only moments before flinging himself to his death down the stairwell of his apartment building.

The mystery of suicide, the reasons which lead anyone to such a decision, are almost always a tangle, but Anissimov goes some way in explaining why Levi killed himself. He was finding it difficult to write. A strong sense of filial duty left him practically the prisoner of a senile, tyrannical mother who lived in the Levi family's apartment. It appears he also had a history of depression.

But there were also larger, disturbing issues that preoccupied him. He despaired of the publicity and occasional credence given to revisionist historians and Holocaust deniers. For years, he had visited schools to talk to the young about the destruction of European Jewry at the hands of Nazis and Fascists, but he found the new generation's ahistoricism, and general lack of interest in what he had to say, distressing. A fervent anti-Fascist, he was troubled by the resurgence of the old political enemy in Italy. An incident at a basketball game where Italian spectators stood and chanted the name of the notorious death camp, Mauthausen, at the visiting Israeli team further deepened his despair, leaving him with the sense that all his efforts to combat Fascism and anti-Semitism had been worthless and futile.

Levi always considered himself a man of the Enlightenment, a man who held that reason and a rigorous pursuit of the truth were sufficient to prevent another descent into bloody barbarism. As Anissimov suggests in the subtitle of her biography, Levi's tragedy was the tragedy of an optimist.

This is a sad and sombre book. But despite what I suspect must be a less than elegant translation from the French, it nevertheless achieves a moving eloquence thanks to the eloquent figure of Levi himself. Unlike so many of the subjects of literary biographies, the man emerges as the equal of his art—not only the author of many admirable books, but the author of an admirable life.

Reading Anissimov's book nudged me to mentally "weigh the soul" of Levi against those sordid types he pitted himself against all his life. When Levi is placed in the balance with the ludicrous Russian anti-Semite Vladimir Zhirinovsky, or Canada's own self-aggrandizing buffoon in a hard hat, Ernst Zundel, can there be any doubt which way the scale will tip?

Review of *Primo Levi: Tragedy of an Optimist*, by Myriam Anissimov, translated by Steve Cox (Aurum, 1998)
National Post, April 17, 1999

Strangerhood

READERS CHANGE but books with life in them survive readers' changes. When Margaret Laurence's *The Tomorrow-Tamer* was first published, the newly independent, emerging nations of Africa were much in the news and much on the conscience of the West, and it was assumed that the stories in this collection offered sociological and political insights into post-colonial Ghana.*

Now, in a different climate, assumptions have reversed. Concerns about "cultural appropriation" and "authentic voice" foster doubts about whether a white, middle-class liberal, a mere sojourner in Africa, could possibly render the continent and its inhabitants accurately. Regardless of where one stands on these controversies, an awareness of the arguments will subtly shape and colour one's response to *The Tomorrow-Tamer* and influence what one seeks and finds between its covers.

Of course, it has to be recognized that Laurence herself raised these issues now so hotly debated. Discussing her African novel *This Side Jordan* in her essay "Gadgetry or Growing: Form and

---

* The title story, "The Tomorrow-Tamer," was first published in 1961 in the literary journal *Prism International*. The book of the same title was published in 1963.

Voice in the Novel," she volunteered remarks which apply equally to *The Tomorrow-Tamer*.

> I actually wonder how I ever had the nerve to attempt
> to go into the mind of an African man, and I suppose
> if I'd really known how difficult was the job I was
> attempting, I would never have tried it. I am not at all
> sorry I tried it, and in fact I believe from various com-
> ments made by African reviewers that at least some
> parts of the African chapters have a certain authenticity.
> But not, perhaps, as much as I once believed.

In a typically honest and direct manner, Laurence was admitting how difficult it was for the outsider, the "stranger," to accomplish what she had tried to do, and admitting how lim-ited she felt her success had been. While stopping short of a disavowal of the African books and what they contained, she suggested that their real importance lay in the lessons she had learned writing them.

> I had decided I could never get deeply enough inside
> the minds of African people—or, at least, I'd gone as
> far as I personally could as a non-African—and had a
> very strong desire to go back and write about people
> from my own background, people whose idiom I knew
> and whose concepts were familiar to me.

Yet *The Tomorrow-Tamer* deserves better than this. It is more than a literary signpost setting Laurence's feet firmly on the road home to Manawaka, and more than a piece of reporting, a flawed record of Africa and Africans at a decisive moment in their history. No, these stories have lasted because they are profound and moving meditations upon the words *change* and *stranger*, and because they are a living testament to Laurence's gift for embodying in the flesh of her characters such poignant abstractions.

The word *stranger* obviously awakened in Laurence strong feelings. A passage from Exodus, "Thou shalt not oppress a stranger, for ye know the heart of a stranger, seeing ye were strangers in the land of Egypt," is quoted in "The Rain Child"—a verse which years later she returned to for the title of her collection of essays, *Heart of a Stranger*, in which she reflected:

> … for a writer of fiction, part of the heart remains that of a stranger, for what we are trying to do is to understand those others who are our fictional characters, somehow to gain entrance to their minds and feelings, to respect them for themselves as human individuals, and to portray them as truly as we can. The whole process of fiction is a mysterious one, and a writer, however experienced, remains in some ways a perpetual amateur, or perhaps a perpetual traveller, an explorer of those inner territories, those strange lands of the heart and the spirit.

The whole cast of "The Rain Child" is a cast of strangers. There are the obvious ones, foreigners such as Hilda Povey, futilely trying to coax an English rosebush to bloom in an inhospitable environment, while her compatriot, Violet Nedden, doubly exiled because she recognizes that in Africa she is an alien teaching an "alien speech," finds herself dreading retirement in a Britain which has, in the years of her exile, become nothing more to her than an "island of grey rain." Then there are the "outcast children": Yindo the garden boy, a Dagomba from the northern desert, forced to speak a hesitant pidgin because no one understands his language. Ayesha, the former child prostitute, returned from Lagos because someone there recognized her speech as Twi. Finally,

Ruth Quansah, raised and educated in Britain, an English girl with a black skin, ignorant of the language and customs of her homeland, rejected by her African classmates and, eventually, by her English friend, David Mackie, who has taken up the task of "showing Africa to her as she wanted to be shown it—from the outside." Ruth's father, Dr. Quansah, knows his daughter's pain because he is suffering it too. As he confesses to Violet Nedden, "I still find most Europeans here as difficult to deal with as I ever did. And yet—I seem to have lost touch with my own people, too."

This isolation, this losing touch, this failure to connect, for Laurence crystallizes the essence of the stranger. Knowing the frustration of her own struggle to fully enter the minds of her own characters, to fully *connect* with them, and through them to establish a connection with her readers, gave Laurence insight and sympathy with all forms of alienation. She knew, as every writer does, how hard-won and desperately fragile ties of any kind are.

In *The Tomorrow-Tamer* change is seen as a threat to such precarious ties. Any alteration in the equation of connection necessarily produces an alteration in the result, and the result most often is an individual adrift in a cold and comfortless universe. This is most likely to be the plight of the more vulnerable African, but it is a fate which can befall Europeans too. The European narrator of "The Drummer of All the World," who at the age of six knew Twi better than he did English, who was suckled by an African nurse, who learned all the proverbs and parables of Ghana, and, when his missionary mother fell sick, who prayed to the Ghanaian gods, returns after an education in England to find a country transformed by the rush to independence. "The old Africa was dying, and I felt suddenly rootless, a stranger in the only land I could call home," he laments.

Political change is a destroyer and an orphan-maker, but an even greater danger is religious change. Among Canadian writers in the last half of the twentieth century, Laurence was an anomaly—she took religion seriously, and nowhere in her fiction is this seriousness more evident than it is in *The Tomorrow-Tamer*, a god-driven and god-haunted book. Will Kittredge, trying to explain to his friend Danso why the missionary Brother Lemon does not want to live in the middle of an African shantytown, says that the people there are a threat to Brother Lemon and everything he is. But, as Danso points out, that only makes it even. In the African world of shades and omnipresent gods, a loss of faith means not only a rending of the most fundamental and meaningful connections with the deities but also a separation from the community of believers. Or, as Ludwig Wittgenstein put it, "If you have no ties to either mankind or to God, then you *are* an alien."

The link between change, strangerhood, and loss of faith is nowhere more clearly drawn than in the title story of the collection. There, the arrival of strangers (European engineers and administrators, urban African workers) to construct a bridge near a small, secluded village has dire results. At each step in the construction the villagers are certain that the gods will exact a terrible punishment for the sacrileges committed. When their holy grove is destroyed by earth-moving equipment they are left utterly bereft and bewildered.

> So the grove was lost, and although the pleas were made
> to gods and grandsires, the village felt lost, too, depleted
> and vulnerable. But the retribution did not come. Owura
> did not rise. Nothing happened. Nothing at all.

In their bewilderment, there are always those who will seek new allegiances, new meanings, new spiritual links. Kofi, a young villager chosen to work on the bridge, attempts to interpret the modern steel miracle in the light of what he has been taught by the fetish priests and the elders. In a discussion with the other villagers, Kofi declares that there is something in the bridge, something as strong as the old god Owura. He goes further and decides that

> the other bridgemen might go, might desert, might falter, but he would not falter. He would tend the bridge as long as he lived. He would be its priest.

Having taken this leap into apostasy, he ventures an even more daring one. Standing high on the exposed steel of the bridge, he is granted another vision. When he sees for the first time the new road that connects his village to the outside world, the desire to be the priest of the bridge withers inside him. A more secular wish replaces it, a wish to leave the village, rejoin the bridgemen, and continue the work of building bridges. Suddenly, he is filled with a sense of his own power.

> Exultant, he wanted to shout aloud his own name and his praises. There was nothing he could not do. Slowly, deliberately, he pulled himself up until he was standing there on the steel, high above the forest and the river. He was above even the bridge itself. And above him, there was only the sky.

It is as if Kofi, in a matter of months, has compressed a journey which took Europe centuries to complete. In the moment of self-exultation, he becomes, psychologically, a quintessential European, a quintessential Westerner. Significantly, the moment of self-exultation is also the moment of his death, a death interpreted by the other villagers in the light of the old religion. The bridge sacrifices its priest to appease the river god.

In the imaginations of characters such as Kofi, or Adamo in "The Voices of Adamo," in their struggle to make sense of a perplexing, ever-changing world, we can find analogies with their creator's own struggle to write truthfully and honestly. In their attempts to understand a foreign civilization they mirror Laurence's own attempts to enter the mind of the fictional "other." The Kofis, the Dansos, the Adamos, the Tettehs, are doubtless driven to do this by necessity, but upon reflection we may conclude that so are we.

Change makes strangers of us all. *The Tomorrow-Tamer* is, after all, ironically titled. There is no taming tomorrow. Over two thousand years ago Heraclitus stated, "Everything flows and nothing stays." More than most writers, Laurence felt this truth in her very bones, and it was the image of the Heraclitean river that she turned to for the beginning of *The Diviners*, the last of her novels.

> The river flowed both ways. The current moved from
> north to south, but the wind usually came from the
> south, rippling the bronze-green water in the oppos-
> ite direction. This apparently impossible contradiction,
> made apparent and possible, still fascinated Morag, even
> after the years of river-watching.

Margaret Laurence knew that life is like the river, fluctuation and contradiction. But she wished to remind us that the exigencies of a world in flux do not exempt us from a simple human duty, the duty to imagine and re-imagine, to strive with compassion to plumb the hearts of our fellow strangers. This, more than anything else, is what *The Tomorrow-Tamer* is about.

Afterword to *The Tomorrow-Tamer*, by Margaret Laurence (McClelland & Stewart, New Canadian Library, 1993)

Recollections 1

A Sense of Place

THE PRAIRIE LANDSCAPE is often described in terms of broad brushstrokes, one of earth, one of sky. This, of course, is a stereotype. No matter. Whenever I am away from home, what I yearn for most is the second part of that cliché. As a preschooler briefly exiled to British Columbia, I complained that there was nothing to see; all those mountains got in the way of a view. Even now, any big city's sterile thicket of skyscrapers can induce a mild claustrophobia in me.

It was my grandmother who tilted my eyes upward when I was a child. Born and raised on the prairies, she was a student of weather. For her the sky was the slate where tomorrow was written in a code of clouds and sundogs, sunrises and sunsets. She loved thunderstorms, and whenever one threatened, she would hurry me out to her veranda to breathlessly await it. There we had ringside seats on the rivers of dazzling electricity forking the sky. I learned that if you quickly shut your eyes tight at a lightning flash, it would burn beneath your lids for several eerie instants while you drew in the scent of rusty porch screens and dust. The claps of thunder you felt as much as heard.

My sharpest early memories are of prairie skies. The first is staged on a bitterly frigid night. I am four years old, maybe five, sitting bundled up in a cardboard box on a sleigh towed by my father. Above me, pink and green lights seethe and shimmer, my introduction to the aurora borealis. As if they happened yesterday, I recall evening summer drives with my parents. The excuse was that we were "checking on the crops," but since we always seemed to be heading west, we must really have been "checking on the sunsets." After these fiery affairs concluded and twilight fell, a green field of wheat would turn a dusky emerald, glowing as if it had captured a residue of the day's coruscating sunshine and was slowly releasing its radiance into the gathering darkness.

Even when I was a teenager, a night sky was capable of shaking me out of adolescent self-absorption, which is saying a lot. If I left the car at the local drive-in to head for the concession stand, the sight of millions of stars winking and wheeling in a coal black sky was capable of halting me in my tracks. The romantic agonies of those star-crossed lovers Frankie Avalon and Annette Funicello could not hold a candle to that.

Saskatchewan licence plates proclaim that the province is the Land of Living Skies. For once, sloganeers and boosters got it right. Like all living things, prairie skies are infinitely changeable and fickle, by turns dangerous and benign, sometimes breeders of hail, tornadoes, blizzards, thunderstorms, and drought, but also creators of a unique, heart-stopping and wholly ineffable beauty.

Time, October 11, 2004

Luck You Need,
When You Need It

FOR A WRITER from Saskatchewan like me, the invitation to give this year's Margaret Laurence lecture is a great honour since Laurence was a literary godmother for so many of us with roots in the West. In the toddler-years of my writing life, when I was lurching about, snatching at anything and everything that might keep me from falling flat on my face, she was an indispensable example as to what might be done if I turned my attention to what lay right under my nose—if I only chose to look hard enough at what surrounded me, and did my best to treat the material with the respect it deserved. After forty years of writing, what was true for me then remains true for me now; to reread Margaret Laurence always helps to restore a little of my perennially shaky balance and sense of purpose.

Unlike many of the writers who have delivered this lecture in the past, I never met Margaret Laurence. But she did touch me in a way I have never forgotten, a steadying touch that came at a moment when I was desperately in need of it. My first book, a collection of short stories called *Man Descending*, had just received the 1982 Governor General's Award for English-language fiction. It happened that that year another collection of short stories had been shortlisted for the award, Alice Munro's *The Moons of Jupiter*, and her book had been inexplicably passed over by the jury in favour of mine. My chagrin at this oversight was even more acute than that of those who were strenuously expressing their outrage over this travesty of justice. What made my discomfort even worse was that Alice Munro had very generously given my book a blurb. So, sweating clean through my pants with trepidation, I wrote her a letter that reiterated what everybody else was saying: that a book of short stories by a clumsy neophyte writer had no business getting the nod over the work of perhaps the finest practitioner of short fiction *anywhere*. Alice made a typically kind attempt to solace my distress with a gentle reply. But I was not easily solaced.

I would be lying if I didn't admit that some part of me was *happy* that I had received this recognition. I knew it would make some difference to a writer who was just starting his career. At that time, the G.G. was pretty much the only prize in town and it carried an undeniable cachet. On the other hand, the well of my pleasure was poisoned because I knew that I hadn't *deserved* what I had gotten, and I couldn't stop feeling like a fraud and a cheat. Self-doubt and embarrassment were making it impossible for me to get on with the next book, or even to believe I had any business attempting to write another.

Then, out of the blue, I received a letter from a stranger. The stranger was Margaret Laurence. Before beginning to write this lecture, I requested that the University of Calgary Special Collections send me a copy of her note so that I could check the accuracy of my recollection about what she had said. More or less, my memory hadn't failed me. I won't quote any of the complimentary things she had to say about my work—even though I know that there is nothing that writers like better than to hear one of their colleagues lavishly and unjustifiably praised. I'll merely mention some of her advice to a young writer. Such as: "You are just beginning now, and some … people will give you a whole bunch of bullshit about how marvellous you are," coupled with a warning not to let anyone "cannibalize you" because "in all the ways that matter, you do not need them." She concluded her letter with this: "I hope you will not think this is presumptuous of me. You do have the gift, and so I am concerned about you and wish to give you—from an old professional—my deepest blessing."

A blessing from the old professional, Margaret Laurence, couched in language that had a quasi-biblical ring to it, the elder's laying on of hands, my initiation into what she always referred to as the "tribe." Her gesture moved me greatly and still does, the thought that someone of her stature, someone whose path had never crossed mine, could be large-hearted and generous enough to take the trouble to express concern over a young man's future as a writer. It wasn't that Margaret Laurence waved some magic wand that dispelled all my discomfiture, self-doubt, and anxiety. But what she did do was to remind me that nothing mattered besides getting on with the work and doing it as well as I could manage. Everything else, whether praise or criticism, was in the long run nothing but mere noise, clamour, distraction. Remember, she was whispering into my ear, *You have only made a start, beware of the pitfalls into which it is so easy for a writer to blindly topple.*

I wrote Margaret Laurence an incoherent letter of appreciation but I never got the chance to thank her face to face. Less than four years after the date on the note she had sent me she was dead. So as you might guess, her memory is particularly dear to me, and to have been asked to present a lecture in her name presents me with the chance to pay her, in gratitude, a small act of homage.

In trying to whittle down this evening's topic, the Writing Life, to something manageable, I had to give myself the same advice that I give my creative writing students: don't try to calculate what might interest others, decide on what interests you and do it. I knew I couldn't make pronouncements about what the writer's life *ought* to be, or how writers *ought* to work because I still haven't figured any of that out for myself and probably never will. Reflecting on the four decades I have spent writing fiction, the only thing that intrigues me, given the long perspective available to me now, is how I came to choose the writing life or, perhaps more truthfully, how I stumbled into it. In walking into the thicket of this mystery, I found myself doing very much the same things I do when constructing a fictional narrative, muddling through a host of details, trying to find a path that meanders from A to Z, that gives a through line that will lend a series of haphazard encounters, unforeseen circumstances, and detours the illusion of sense and inevitability. Having performed that exercise, only one thing strikes me: how improbable it is that I ever became a writer.

Of course, in taking myself by the hand for a stroll down memory lane I have edited out the many blind alleys that I blundered into or wilfully chose. Escaping these missteps and stupidities has largely been a question of dumb luck, so what I offer you tonight is a picaresque composed of unlikely coincidences and happy accidents that improbably delivered me to where I find myself today. Happy accidents such as receiving Margaret Laurence's letter, a lifeline tossed to me just at the moment when I felt myself sinking. Sooner or later I may have bobbed back to the surface without her kindly intervention, but who can say?

Neither the family nor the place I was born into would seem likely to have produced a writer. My parents were not "bookish" people. Somewhere in *Wolf Willow*, Wallace Stegner remarks that for many of the earliest settlers of the West the pioneer experience had a corrosive effect, slowly eroding whatever sophistication or cultural accomplishments that might have been part of the baggage they brought with them to the frontier. That appears to have been the case in my mother's family. In 1891, my great-grandmother, Louise Chappell, was the eighty-eighth person to be granted a teaching certificate by the government of the North-West Territories. She must have been an adventurous woman to have set out on her own from Ontario for a part of the country that only six years before had been convulsed by Louis Riel's North-West Resistance. There, in the tiny settlement of Spy Hill, Saskatchewan, she eventually married Joe Davis, one of the school trustees who had hired her to take charge of a one-room school. Their marriage produced eight children, who preserved a memory of a mother of genteel Victorian refinement, an amateur naturalist, photographer, painter, pianist, and proud owner of a considerable library of English classics, which after her death, her family consigned to a granary, where they were pulped by rain and trampled to pieces by sheep, all except for her copies of William Pitt's *Orations on the French War* and Jane Austen's *Mansfield Park*, which somehow survived and came into my possession some forty years ago.

The cultural patina of my great-grandmother's offspring fell far short of hers. Rural schools and the endless drudgery of life on a hardscrabble farm took their toll, contributing to the steady chipping away of the refinements she had put such store in. And in their turn, her grandchildren, raised in the drought- and Depression-stricken Saskatchewan of the 1930s, gave up on school even earlier than their parents had. Most of my uncles were working on farms by the time they turned thirteen or fourteen or were clambering into boxcars to roam Canada in a fruitless hunt for work until the Second World War snatched them out of the breadlines.

My father's side of the family put even less stock in schooling. My grandfather Vanderhaeghe, an immigrant from backward and impoverished West Flanders, thought of his children mostly as a source of cheap labour to keep afloat the farm he rented from a local merchant. Book-learning and lollygagging about in classrooms were obstacles to that. Threats from the local school board and harassment by truant officers over his kids' spotty attendance record had no effect on him. His children certainly paid a price for my grandfather's hostility to education. My father is incapable of writing anything, not even a cheque. He has never read a word I've written.

Yet despite the circumstances in which my parents had been raised, when I was a small child my mother made a point of reading to me from a store of five or six Thornton W. Burgess animal stories she had got her hands on. Where these books describing the adventures of Peter Rabbit, Jimmy Skunk, Paddy the Beaver et al. came from I have no idea. The nearest bookstore would have been in Regina, 225 kilometres away. And my parents never ventured that far afield because they didn't own a vehicle until I turned seven or eight. So someone must have loaned or given these books to my mother, or perhaps she ordered them from the Eaton's catalogue. At any rate, they were the only children's literature I was ever exposed to; I have no memory of any Dr. Seuss, L. Frank Baum, Beatrix Potter, J. M. Barrie, Lewis Carroll, or A. A. Milne, none of the classics. Burgess was it, but he was enough. I had had my first sweet kiss from narrative and I fell in love with it.

My other exposure to the delights of story came by way of my mother's family, the Allens. They were all great talkers, acidly funny, and savage raconteurs with outlandish nicknames like Black Jack, Willis the Waltz King, Gordo, and Bàcsi. Of them all, Uncle Bàcsi was the most flamboyant and voluble. My hometown, Esterhazy, as the name suggests, was largely settled by Hungarians, and it was the Hungarians who christened my uncle Ralph as Bàcsi, which, I have been told, can be translated as either uncle or elder brother and is a traditional title of respect. In my uncle's case the implication was different. It had been sardonically applied to him back in the days when he was a thirteen-year-old auctioneer's assistant strutting about at farm sales, a fedora rakishly tilted down over one eye, a cigar clamped in his mouth as he fast-talked prospective bidders, a pint-sized wheeler-dealer.

Whenever my mother's family got together it was a no-holds-barred verbal brawl. Her brothers and sisters riffed off one another's anecdotes or served up set pieces that had been worked and reworked over the years until they had all the crispness and polish of a good stand-up comedian's monologue. They had no shortage of material. All my uncles, with the exception of the youngest, Willis the Waltz King, had racketed about Canada during the Depression years, and then they had racketed about North Africa, Italy, and the Low Countries during the Second World War. Their war stories were like Vonnegut's or Heller's, with the gruesome bits more or less expunged. I'm sure they had seen their share of horrors—one of them had been badly wounded in Italy—but they portrayed life in the army as an absurd comedy involving the sabotaging of stupid noncoms and officers; frequent scrapes with the military police; sprees in Glasgow and Belfast, their favourite destinations when they went AWOL; or their risqué adventures cruising the streets of Cairo, Naples, and Brussels. These stories had carefully crafted beginnings, middles, and ends and were always sharply focused on character: the mild, naïve Anglican chaplain who could always be prevailed upon to provide a sterling character reference at a court martial; the punctilious, pedantic drill sergeant who put them through their paces with the .22 single-shot rifles mounted on artillery gun carriages the Canadian army in Britain used for training because they had no real artillery; the Fascist crone who every night lay in wait on her balcony with a chamber pot to empty on their heads when they staggered back to bivouac after a night out on the town; the half-crazed army psychiatrist who saw shell-shock cases everywhere.

I suppose that like one of Konrad Lorenz's goslings, I was imprinted early on by these stories and, for good or ill, I have been waddling flat-footed after them all my life. A good deal of the propellant in the rockets my uncles sent up came from explosions of vulgarity, the raw language of men who had knocked about and been knocked about, the vivid slang that the great demotic poet Walt Whitman called the "attempt of common humanity to escape from bald literalism, and express itself illimitably." I suspect that what my uncles were doing was disguising and transforming the illimitable horror of war in a wild, reckless language foreign to the polite proprieties of middle-class conversation of the 1950s. I have never lost my affection for the rude, vigorous tongue in which they expressed themselves. Many years ago, when the critic and poet Louis Dudek rather prissily dismissed me in *Books in Canada* as "a voice from the shithouse," I puffed up with unseemly pride, feeling as if I had inherited my Uncle Bàcsi's profane mantle.

In the course of time, I was sent to school. Before I went out the door to meet Dick and Jane and to be introduced to their lively suburban milieu, I was given a little coaching by my mother, a warning that there were certain words that you did not say in school. When I asked what these were, she provided me with a rather extensive list, words that I had heard my family employ as adjectives, nouns, and verbs suitable for enlivening any occasion. My mother also attempted a little academic coaching, her version of No Child Left Behind, and made an attempt to teach me my alphabet and hammer into my head how to count to ten before turning me over to the professionals. But being a hot-tempered, impatient woman, she soon gave that up as a bad business and I trundled off to school blithely illiterate and innumerate. Years later, my mother confessed to me that she had assumed that I was what was then delicately referred to as "slow," and that she had had very low expectations for my success in school. When I actually did surprisingly well in grade one, her hopes suddenly bloomed, inordinately so, and she decided that not only was she going to see that I finished high school but became determined that I would go to university. An idea that she grimly hung on to even in later years when my academic performance went into an alarming and precipitous decline.

I was an only child. My mother had been disappointed by life, and I became proxy for her own thwarted aspirations. I realize this is a cliché, but that doesn't stop it from being true. For her, an education was *the* way of escaping the small-town boredom and dead-end jobs that had been her lot, and she was determined I wouldn't share her fate. Needless to say, she was my biggest piece of luck.

The signal event of my first year of elementary school was learning to read. The fly in this ointment was that the summer before I entered grade one, the Esterhazy school had burned to the ground and with it, whatever library it had held. Except for texts mandated by the curriculum there were no books. All the town's resources went into the building of a school. The need for a new school was particularly pressing because a potash mine was being developed near the town, which brought in a flood of new-comers, more and more kids to be stuffed into the overflowing church basements where we were being taught. When the shiny new building opened the next year, there was nothing but empty shelving in the space optimistically referred to as the library. And there would be nothing on those shelves for some time to come.

Over the course of the next few years, I became a doggedly persistent scavenger of reading material. The local druggist was my biggest source of supply. In those days, unsold comic books had their covers torn off before being mailed back to the maga-zine distributor as returns; the comics themselves were supposed to be destroyed, but the pharmacist allowed me to carry off any copies I wanted. Fortunately for me, the least popular comics were the now defunct Classics Illustrated series, which were intended to expose reluctant young readers to "great literature." Reluctant young readers, however, recognized these comics were meant to be good for you and so they avoided them like Brussels sprouts, which meant I had an inexhaustible supply of unbought copies to choose from. The Classics Illustrated series was my introduction to *Kim, Michael Strogoff, The Hunchback of Notre Dame, The Man in the Iron Mask, Uncle Tom's Cabin, Jane Eyre, Oliver Twist, Two Years Before the Mast*, even *Hamlet*.

I'm sure that it sounds priggishly precocious of me, but it was reading these comics that put the notion in my head of becoming a writer. I can recall studying the potted author biographies that appeared in the back pages, poring over them in search of the secret that had made these women and men writers, believing that if I found the clue to that it might unlock my future.

Meanwhile, under the influence of Classics Illustrated, I began writing little stories. My grandmother was the town's seamstress and her days were spent sewing dresses for the wives of local businessmen, doctors, and lawyers, and doing alterations for a men's clothing store. On top of that, she had to babysit me after school because my mother had landed a job clerking in the town office. When school finished for the day I would scoot over to my grandmother's house, position myself on the floor near her Singer sewing machine, open a notebook, and begin to bombard her with pleas to spell the words that I wanted for my stories. This must have been particularly irritating for her because I had fallen deeply under the influence of the Classics Illustrated version of Julius Caesar's memoirs, and I was giving my characters monikers of my own invention, names that I imagined sounded authentically Roman such as Dufius, Gymnasiumus, and Auditoriumus.

At last, when I was around the age of ten or eleven, my desperate hunt for things to read ended when the frugal town fathers finally sprang for a municipal library. It was housed in the town office where my mother worked and was largely comprised of donations, the polite word for cast-offs. The library was hardly bigger than a broom closet, but it had the great advantage of being unmanned. Books were signed out on the honour system, and since there was no librarian supervising or censoring what I checked out, I was able to read anything that struck my fancy. My mother never raised any objections to what I was sticking my nose into because, as she would have put it, reading kept me from "running the streets like a stray dog."

My memory of my formal elementary schooling is rather foggy, but I can recollect with alarming accuracy many of the things I read during those years, probably because of my teachers' strenuous objections to some of the book reports I handed in. There was, for instance, a minor furor over my innocently turning in a review of Eugene O'Neill's play *Desire Under the Elms*. I'm sure the teacher had never read or seen this drama herself, but the title alone was enough to give her fits. I was even scolded for doing a report on the Reader's Digest condensed version of *To Kill a Mockingbird*, a novel so morally uplifting that high school students all over North America have been chain-ganged into reading it. The only explanation I got for its unsuitability was that it was "too old for you." I would have been twelve then, hardly of such a tender age as to have been irreparably damaged by Harper Lee's depravity.

I don't want to leave the impression that I was some precious prairie aesthete; I was simply indiscriminately pulling books off the shelves and devouring them. Eugene O'Neill's retelling of the Greek myth of Phaedra, Hippolytus, and Theseus was interspersed with Erle Stanley Gardner's Perry Mason novels and Albert Payson Terhune's dog stories. My problem was that I wasn't smart enough to figure out that book reports about dogs were a safer bet than reviewing a drama about infanticide and a son cuckolding his father.

Aside from these book-reviewing scandals, I was a pliable and malleable pupil—so pliable and malleable that it was decided I should be "accelerated" mid-year into the next grade, which only stoked my mother's ambitions for my further academic achievement. And I continued to write my dreadful juvenilia. I even embarked on what I grandly called a novel and which my mother volunteered to type in two-fingered hunt-and-peck style on the manual typewriter in the town office on her one day a week off. As I have already said, my mother was my luckiest break. Fortunately, I have no disturbing recovered memories of my first stab at novel-writing except for the fancy-pants name of my young English hero, Devon Malory, who was plucky and dauntless and voyaged the high seas in a noble ketch.

All this assiduous striving was followed by my disastrous high school years. Being so much younger than all the rest of my classmates because of my hasty acceleration through primary school, I arrived in grade nine as a beanpole-skinny four-eyes burdened with the reputation for being a "brainiac." This, you can well imagine, put me at a certain disadvantage. Unlike the plucky, dauntless hero of my novel, Devon Malory, I did not stand up to my persecutors, I ingratiated myself with them and succeeded in becoming a mascot to a number of bad companions who furnished a cordon sanitaire against gratuitous assaults from others with a taste for punishing easy targets. Add to this the toxic stew of adolescent hormones injected by the sudden arrival of puberty and I careered wildly off the scholastic rails. By the time I entered grade ten I found myself in 10E. My school followed a rigid policy of grouping students according to their marks and 10E was the end of the academic line; there was no 10F. The inmates of 10E were saddled with vocational classes such as Agriculture, where we lovingly swathed beans in wet blotting paper and sat around waiting for them to sprout. Aside from the bean experiment, I don't remember doing much else in 10E besides intimidating teachers, devising rigged hockey pools, and exacting money from the more defenceless members of the student body who were expected to make contributions to help pay the liquor fines that my classmates in IOE collected on their carefree weekends.

Somehow or other, a miracle occurred. Despite my atrocious marks, infractions of discipline, and general bad behaviour, the next year a hand came down from on high, plucked me from level E and deposited me in level B, where bean sprout surveillance was replaced by subjects that were prerequisites for university admission. I don't know how this happened. Perhaps my mother intervened with the school administration. She could be a stubborn and volatile woman, fierce as a mother grizzly in defence of her cub.

I staggered into grade twelve. My days of scribbling stories were far in the past. But then a remarkable woman, a teacher of composition, allowed me to forego the usual set essays of the How-I-Spent-My-Summer-Vacation variety if I wrote fiction instead. She sent one of my stories to the Saskatchewan English Teachers' Association's magazine, where it was published alongside the work of two young English teachers who were writers: Gary Hyland, a poet who later founded the Moose Jaw Literary Festival, and Bob Currie, another accomplished writer who became a poet laureate of Saskatchewan.

Still, my mother's hopes of me going to university were growing dimmer by the day. The final examinations for high school matriculation were set by the Department of Education; every grade twelve student in the province wrote the same tests that were marked in the capital, and these marks determined admission into the Saskatchewan university system. I had fallen so far behind in school that my chances of getting the 65 per cent minimum average for acceptance into the University of Saskatchewan were virtually nil, and I knew it. When it came time to sit the exams, the writing on the wall became clearer and clearer. Even the very best students were walking away from the tests white-faced with academic shell shock. As soon as I had undergone this trial by fire, I headed for British Columbia. My mother had let me know she was sick of the sight of me and, from the bloody look in her eye, I knew it was time to get out of Dodge.

And then came an inexplicable stroke of good fortune. The exams that year had proved so difficult that the results didn't accord with the way the bell curve was supposed to look. Radical adjustments were required to make the curve shapely again, and those adjustments boosted the marks of borderline students like me. When the results were mailed to my parents' home, my mother discovered that I had effortlessly vaulted the required 65 per cent with an average that stopped somewhere short of 66 per cent. She immediately filled out an application form for the University of Saskatchewan and phoned to tell me that if I was accepted, I was going, no ifs, ands, or buts about it.

As a matter of fact, I did manage to squeak into university and the world opened up for me. For the first time in years I went enthusiastically to work, determined not to repeat my mistakes in high school. A vague interest in history developed into a passion. A history professor became a mentor, one of those rare academics who could write and who cared about English prose. I remember him scolding me once, "There are so many buts in this paper that when I read it I heard an outboard motor in my head."

A university library provided me with access to books of a quality that I hadn't encountered before. I read voraciously, not just within my chosen discipline of study but outside it as well. I began to seek out books by Canadian writers.

When I consider it, my university years, the late 1960s and early 1970s, were opportune times for someone with hopes of becoming a writer. Remarkable books were appearing or had recently appeared in Canada. Fiction writers like Laurence, Atwood, Wright, Findley, Hodgins, Munro, Davies, Richler, Kroetsch, Wiebe, and Gallant were being read and talked about. There were many more, of course, but these were the ones who fell into my hands and whom I was reading with real excitement, a sense of discovery. A heady political and cultural nationalism was asserting itself. There were regional counterparts to this too. The Saskatchewan Writers Guild was formed in 1969 and the literary magazine *Grain* was founded in 1973. I read its first issue when I was a graduate student, promptly sat down and wrote a short story that I submitted to the new journal. The story appeared in the second issue of the magazine, which also carried the work of another fledgling writer who was to make a name for herself as an important and beloved poet, Lorna Crozier.

The summer before I entered grad school to do a master's degree, I married. I had scarcely turned twenty-one, and what on the face of it should have been one of those rash, regrettable decisions young people make that turn out badly proved to be one of the best things I ever did. My wife of nearly forty years, who died in 2012, was the perfect partner. A visual artist, she understood, encouraged, and supported my aspiration to write just as I understood and supported her desire to paint. Despite the financial hardships and inevitable disappointments that devoting yourself to the arts entail, it was a choice neither of us ever regretted.

By 1973, I had lost interest in pursuing a career as an academic historian, but my M.A. in history helped land me a job in the archives of the University of Saskatchewan library. I kept writing in my spare time. But after my initial success with *Grain*, my efforts were largely met with indifference or scarcely veiled scorn by the editors of literary journals. Yet I doggedly continued to send and resend my novice efforts. Eventually, most of these rejected stories made their appearance in my first book, *Man Descending*. Like most writers, I suppose, I retain a vivid memory of my most galling rejections. One editor, perhaps noting the unusual medley of vowels and clashing consonants in my last name, assumed I was a German speaker and suggested that I should consider writing in my first language.

Nevertheless, there were kind and supportive responses to my work. Robert Fulford at *Saturday Night*, while declining a story I had sent to the magazine, was encouraging. Darlene Madott, who worked there as an editorial assistant, passed on my name to Morris Wolfe, a freelance writer and editor who also wrote a column for *Saturday Night*. He took some of my work for the short-lived annual anthology of Canadian writing *Aurora*, published by Doubleday of Canada. A remarkable editor of the old school at Doubleday, Betty Corson, after very frankly informing me that Doubleday would never publish the novel I was working on, then went on to offer to make editorial comments on the book because she believed I had some talent. Do editors like that any longer exist? I was fortunate to have fallen into her hands. Like Blanche DuBois, I depended on the kindness of strangers.

By then I had gone back to university for a year to earn a Bachelor of Education degree and was teaching high school in a small Saskatchewan town. As a first-year teacher, most of my time was spent running in place, trying to keep up with marking and lesson plans, and spending many hours coaching basketball and track. Nevertheless, I forced myself to crawl out of bed early each morning to work for a few hours on the novel Betty Corson was reading in installments.

That year I sent a collection of short stories to Oberon Press. My wife, who had grown tired of small-town life and watching snow blow past the window, decided that she would like to go back to university and study art, so we packed up and headed back to Saskatoon. There was no chance of landing a full-time teaching job in a city school, so for the next few years I did substitute teaching. My wife and I were scraping along on our savings and the odd jobs that came our way.

Meanwhile, the manuscript that had been sent to Oberon was returned. I didn't know many people who could give me publishing advice but those I turned to said the wisest thing for me to do was to send it to a small press that had a record of publishing short stories. Instead, I sent it to Macmillan of Canada because its stable of writers included two of Canada's greatest short story writers, Mavis Gallant and Alice Munro. Expecting the string of rejections to continue, I thought it would be better to be refused by a house accustomed to publishing the best. I was looking for excuses for when I failed.

Months of silence followed. It was only after *Man Descending* was published that I learned the strange, lucky course my book had taken. A young woman from South Africa who was working at Macmillan and who hoped to become an editor had been told that, when her more mundane office duties had been dispatched, she could attack the slush pile—where *Man Descending* was gathering dust along with countless other unsolicited manuscripts. By chance, she pulled my manuscript out of the stack, read it, liked it, and then began a persistent campaign to get others to read it. As I waited in Saskatoon, impatiently twiddling my thumbs, my book was slowly making its way up the publishing ladder to the desk of the person whom George Bush would have called "the decider."

After about nine months, I wrote inquiring about the status of my manuscript. Following a long wait, I received a letter requesting more time to consider my book. I waited some more. I wrote another letter. Received a similar reply. I waited. Wrote another letter. Same response from Macmillan. I was getting very twitchy. I felt that the brass ring I had been chasing for nearly a decade might be within my grasp. Finally, I phoned and was put through to the publisher, Doug Gibson. Very calmly he explained the difficulty in arriving at a decision: short stories sold badly, I was an unknown, etc. I don't know what came over me, but something snapped in my brain and I issued a hotheaded ultimatum. I told Doug that Macmillan had a week to make a decision. If I did not hear from him by the next Friday, five o'clock Saskatoon time, I would withdraw the book and that would be it. Under no circumstances would I ever consider letting Macmillan publish it. At that moment, I meant every word I said. Of course, as soon as I hung up, I was appalled by what I had done. Who was I to draw a line in the sand, to set deadlines?

The next week was the longest week of my life. I hovered by the phone; I paced. It did not ring. Friday rolled around and I knew I was dead in the water. I couldn't stand the sitting around any longer, so my wife and I took a long hike across Saskatoon and splurged on a cheap lunch that we couldn't afford. I had burned my bridges and would have to start all over again. We got back home at around 4:45. I didn't have an answering machine so there were no messages to check. Then, at exactly five o'clock, the phone rang. I believe Doug may have been making a point with the nicety of his timing. He was on the line to tell me that Macmillan was going to publish my collection of short stories.

Doug does not remember things in this way. But believe me, I am certain this is what happened. When the book came out, I was thrilled to see that it carried blurbs from many of the writers I had been reading and admiring for a decade: Kroetsch, Wiebe, Hodgins, Wright, Munro. Reviews were generally good although there were some dissenters—there are always dissenters. It was shortlisted for the Governor General's Award and that was more than enough for me. As I have already mentioned, when it won the prize, I was rattled and thrown into despair. Somehow, I had pulled the wool over people's eyes and I was going to pay for it. Then Margaret Laurence's letter arrived, I took heart, and went back to work, hopeful that someday I might write a better book, one more deserving of praise and attention.

I have fared far better than I have deserved. For one thing, for most of my life I have been occupied with work that interests me. How many people can say the same? I constantly remind myself it might have turned out very differently. What if my mother had not been so determined to see that I got an education? What if I had not spent so many hours in smoky kitchens listening to my uncles tell stories? Or been given stacks of Classics Illustrated comics that my parents couldn't afford to buy for me? Or had access to a library without any conditions set on what I could read? What if the bell curve in 1968 had not been rigged in my favour? What were the chances that a young woman would pull *my* manuscript out of Macmillan's slush pile and take it into her head to become my stubborn advocate? What if Margaret Laurence hadn't given me the push I needed when I was overcome with self-doubt and seized by writer's block?

Of course, these questions are unanswerable. Maybe they are nothing but idle speculation. Maybe they are nothing but a web of preposterous fictions that I spin to try to see sense and meaning in the good fortune I have been blessed with. I hope you will excuse my self-indulgence. But after all, idle speculation and making up preposterous stories are lifelong habits for me, the way in which I have passed a very fortunate life. I only hope and wish that all of you, as I did, will get the luck you need, when you need it.

Margaret Laurence Lecture Series, Writers' Union of Canada
Annual General Meeting
St. John's, Newfoundland, May 8, 2014

Writer in Residence

AFTER TWENTY-TWO YEARS OF MARRIAGE, my wife Margaret and I recently became what real estate jargoneers refer to as "first-time homeowners." I am not sure how this reversal happened to our longtime and tenaciously held policy of avoiding owning property. We had always promised ourselves never to get mixed up in all that, mortgages, taxes, house repairs. Some previously undetected nesting instinct must have started to bubble deep down in our middle-aged brains. One day, one of us lightheartedly thought aloud: "What if we were to buy a house?" Like a bad smell, the question lingered. I caught myself asking friends, "Say a character in a novel, a fictional, entirely hypothetical character, were to buy a house? What steps would he need to take?"

"First, a prearranged mortgage," they all told me.

An appointment was made with a mortgage officer. With professional cheerfulness, he asked what I did. "I'm a writer," I replied. Did I work for the *Star-Phoenix*, the local paper? There was no fudging the truth. I conceded I wrote fiction. Tight-lipped, he turned to my wife. With any luck, she might turn out to be a registered nurse. When she confessed she was a painter—not of houses but of canvases—the writing was on the wall. He was dealing with *bohemians*.

His next inquiry concerned assets. I furrowed my brow. Assets, he explained, were things you owned.

I couldn't think of anything I owned.

"Do you own a car?" he asked helpfully. Immediately, I brightened. Yes, I owned a car. He brightened too. At last, something he could enter on the form.

"Year and make?" he asked, pen poised.

"1978 Ford Fairmont Futura."

For an instant, he appeared to be passing a kidney stone. "And what would that be worth?" he said finally. "$150?"

"No way," I said. "It's got to be worth at least $250."

He stared at me and I stared back. Slowly, he entered the figure.

After submitting several years of tax returns for the bank's examination, the implausible became actual: we got our pre-approved mortgage. This bit of fiduciary irresponsibility on the part of the bank prompted one of my more successful friends to declare he was divesting himself of all stock in that institution—immediately.

Sinking into the delirium of house-hunting, each and every day we scrambled into the Ford Fairmont Futura to scour the streets for For Sale signs. One morning, I suddenly swerved the car to a bungalow with white porch pillars, stained cedar siding, and a rack of deer antlers over the garage door. The spectacularly narrow driveway had its waist pinched by a set of wagon wheels sunk in cement, and more wagon wheels supported a rustic planter constructed from an old-timey seeder positioned conspicuously in front of the house.

I wrote down the realtor's number.

Touring the house a short time later, I discovered the western motif unflinchingly continued. A horse-head door knocker. A basement finished in imitation logs, wagon-wheel-shaped light fixtures, and plenty of ornamental horseshoes. A mural of a prairie vista, under glass, like a diorama.

The upstairs could have been decorated by Elvis if he had been restrained by a limited budget. There was a pink velvet valance, an acre of drapery and sheers, a genuine imitation fireplace set on a flashy slab of marble. A thick carpet and stippled ceiling that dripped meringue stalactites shrunk the height of the living room by a foot.

The real estate agent wanted my reaction. I enumerated deficiencies. No *real* fireplace. Small kitchen. Tiny bathroom. Then I said, "And the decor is a little eccentric."

"Eccentric?"

"Well," I said, "I can think of only three people who would really love this house."

"Who?" he wanted to know, sensing a possible lead.

"Little Joe, Hoss, and Pa Cartwright," I said.

We looked at other houses, but I found myself irresistibly drawn back to the Ponderosa. The newish furnace and hot water heater were ostensible reasons. It was also obvious that the house had been well-maintained—more—loved as passionately as the ugly child. We went back, did another inspection, agonized, debated. A day later we had bought ourselves a house.

Margaret declared that the carpets must go. Since I'm no Mr. Fixit, I asked a handyman friend to assist me. When the lethal-looking carpet knife slashed an incision between dining room and living room, I held my breath. We had been promised hardwood, and hardwood there had better be. Like a kid squeamishly peeling off a Band-Aid, I lifted the carpet to reveal … a suppurating sore. Below the living room window the wood of the floor was buckled and discoloured by water damage. In one of the bedrooms, somebody had glued the carpet directly to the hardwood. When it was torn up it left clots of rubber-backing stuck to the floor. They resembled fat, blood-sucking leeches.

My natural pessimism and paranoia were now burgeoning nicely. Every time I flushed the toilet, the pipes sang like castrati. To a renter, things going bump in the night are mildly disconcerting. As a property owner, they seemed to me to be a foreshadowing of doom: a furnace ready to explode, beams teetering on the point of collapse, sewage gurgling into the basement.

Early one morning, Margaret shook me awake and said tersely, "I hear water running." I heard it too. I checked the toilet—silent and still as a tomb. Dry-mouthed with dread, I careened downstairs—no thundering cataract evident. Had mischievous vandals laid the neighbourhood welcome mat by opening the outside taps? I threw on my clothes and trotted anxiously around the house. No.

Back inside, I methodically followed the sound to its source, a soft-water conditioner rented by the former occupant that had not yet been removed by the company that had leased it. The infernal machine had been programmed to recycle at three in the morning.

When not suffering night terrors, my wife and I stripped wallpaper, painted walls, anxiously oversaw the installation of venetian blinds, huddled in the basement gagging on noxious-smelling chemical fumes while the floors upstairs were being refinished. But all good things must come to an end. After a month of this, necessity dictated we abandon the truly surreal world of home renovation for a return to our far more solid worlds of imaginary characters and painted images.

A year and a half later, I ask myself, Why did I invest all this money in wagon wheels? The clue might lie in the year that the house was built, 1957. In 1957, I was six years old and potash had just been discovered near my hometown, Esterhazy, a tiny place of several hundred souls. With the mine came an influx of American engineers and managers, all of whom set about constructing the kind of houses they were familiar with in the

States: suburban bungalows and split-levels. For a town that had been sunk in permanent recession since the Dirty Thirties, and for a kid who had lived in a two-room shack with neither indoor plumbing nor running water, these very ordinary houses seemed the height of opulence. They were the kind of houses that symbolized domestic bliss and comfiness on fifties and sixties television: *Father Knows Best* houses, *My Three Sons* houses. Yes, even *Bonanza* houses.

For sixteen years, Margaret and I had hung on by the skin of our teeth, survivors in two of the most precarious of professions. Maybe I needed to close the journey from childhood to middle age with some small sign of success, my own Ponderosa. At forty-three, I bought the house I'd dreamed about when I was six.

Artists are quirky people, given to inhabiting a world of signs and symbols. Of course, sometimes these symbols clash. To Margaret, a visual artist, wagon wheels are embarrassing kitsch. But to me they are a poignantly endangered species. I fight hard to save them. This summer she also wanted to cut the roof off the wishing-well planter in the backyard, but I forestalled her by clambering up on a stepladder and painting it. Who destroys a freshly painted roof? Devious, perhaps, but would Pa Cartwright have allowed anyone to compromise the integrity of the Ponderosa?

My house has taught me that what begins in embarrassment may end in tepid affection. As I write this, I face a wall of verdant paper daisies, a relic of the former owner. A writer often accused of perpetrating a grim view of existence shouldn't have to labour before a wall of cheery, blooming daisies. But I do. Daisies are what I now argue with every day of my life. Existence, at its best, consists of just such weird Socratic dialogues.

Western Living, April 1996

Finding Home in Heule

A NUMBER OF YEARS AGO, when one of my books was translated and published in Holland, I received a telephone call from the producer of a literary program on Belgian television. He had recognized the Flemish origin of my surname and wanted to know from what part of Belgium my family had originated. I had no idea but, after rooting around in a few documents that had survived my grandfather's death, I discovered his mother's funeral announcement with an address scrawled on it. I sent this address to the producer and a few weeks later he phoned to inform me that the house where my grandfather had been born was still standing in what had once been the village of Heule, but which was now a suburb of Kortrijk, and the owner of it was a second cousin of my father's. Moreover, my grandfather's youngest brother Valere lived about a kilometre distant. The news that my great-uncle Valere was still alive came as a shock. No one in my family but my grandfather had written or spoken Flemish, so the last strand of communication with Valere and the family in Belgium had been severed when my grandfather George had died. Twenty years of silence had ensued, and everyone simply assumed that my grandfather's brother was long dead and buried.

The television producer wanted to arrange for me to pay a call on these relatives and film the meeting when I came to Holland to promote my book. He had already sounded out the Belgian Vanderhaeghes and they were enthusiastic. Was I interested?

Yes and no. I was and I wasn't. A family reunion conducted before television cameras struck me as artificial, absurd. However, if I visited on my own, there would be the language problem to overcome. The producer was ready to ease difficulties by paying for both a translator and a driver to ferry my wife and me from Amsterdam to Kortrijk.

Although I had been to the Netherlands several times before, I had never made the effort to take the short trip to Belgium; now a stranger was offering to put me in touch with my family, serve them up on a platter. Suddenly, I was eager to learn something of the history of a grandparent whom I had passionately loved, was intrigued by the prospect of seeing the house in which he had lived as a boy. Several friends and acquaintances had gone on similar pilgrimages and returned with glowing, emotional reports about their experiences in the ancestral homeland. One had gone to Scotland to criss-cross the country visiting clansmen. Another had gone to Jerusalem and had prayed at the Wailing Wall. Other people I knew were attempting to learn their grand-parents' languages before trekking off to Germany, to Ukraine, to Sweden. They had been rewarded, I was assured, with episodes of self-discovery, a deepened sense of ethnic identity. Everybody seemed to be beset with nostalgia for the first home, the roots of the family now adrift in the diaspora.

Banking on a similar payoff, I agreed to cooperate with the television producer. On a grey day in which the clouds were bunched overhead so near that I felt I could reach up and grab a handful of them, my wife Margaret and I set off from Amsterdam in a white Opel, accompanied by our driver, Frank, and the Dutch translator of my books, Ernst.

The journey, however, was not commenced without some degree of apprehension. I knew Ernst to be a fine man, but the fact that he was wearing a good deal of face makeup and eyeliner was sure to be remarked upon by my relatives and that prospect was causing me a little uneasiness. One of the few things that I knew about my grandfather's people was that they were conventional, fervent Catholics. My grandfather, on the other hand, bore some grudge against the church, and the moment he had set foot in Canada he had abandoned his religion. This had caused strains with the family overseas; year after year, until she had died, his mother had written to beg the lost sheep to return to the fold, something he had always adamantly refused to do, stubbornly standing his ground.

This wasn't the only thing worrying me. Before leaving Amsterdam, I had met with several of the Belgian film crew and they had prepped me about where I was heading. I learned that at the beginning of the twentieth century this region had been poverty-stricken, a place fled by immigrants determined to make their fortunes in the Congo or North America. It was the heartland of Flemish nationalism, an area which clung to a rich peasant dialect and cultivated long-held grievances against the French-speaking Walloons. Someone even provoked laughter by confiding that there was a famous folk song about my grandfather's village, "Tineke of Heule," which eulogized the perfect Flemish woman: prodigious cow-milker and scyther of flax, sweet-natured, copiously fertile, and every bit as contented as the cows she milked. He added that he sometimes sang this ditty to his wife, an art historian at the University of Antwerp, whenever he felt she was putting on airs. I had my fingers crossed that nobody would sing this salute to the ideal woman in Margaret's presence, or, if they did, would bother to translate it.

"Yes," this man mused aloud, "West Flanders is the Texas of Belgium." Recalling his words as the Opel hurtled across the flat Belgian plain, I couldn't help wondering how Margaret and the cosmetically enhanced Ernst were going to hit it off with the Texans of Belgium.

I didn't have a lot of time to cultivate anxiety, distances in the Low Counties being so short. In Ghent we rendezvoused with the television crew and ate lunch in a restaurant that had once been a windmill. Through its windows the house of the writer Hugo Claus was pointed out to me. In this part of Belgium, opinions were deeply divided about Claus. For some, he was a cultural hero who had overcome the disadvantages of an obscure language spoken nowhere else in the world to become something of a European literary celebrity. For others, he was an embarrassment because his most admired novel, *The Sorrow of Belgium*, anatomized the collaboration of Flemish nationalists with Nazi occupiers during the Second World War.

In Heule, our convoy came to a halt in a narrow street of brick row houses. The producer wanted the first meeting between Valere and me to occur in front of the sheds where he and my grandfather had worked side by side curing flax for the linen trade. A carefully choreographed theatrical touch. We all trooped out back and stood in a small courtyard to await the arrival of the car the producer had dispatched to deliver my great-uncle.

Within minutes, a vehicle pulled up and an old man and woman struggled out of it. At eighty-four, Valere was a dead ringer for my grandfather in the years just before his death. The same nut-brown skin; the same square, powerful body, and big round head settled solidly on a stump of neck. I couldn't take my eyes off him as we shook hands, nodding and smiling. He said something to me in Flemish. The television producer said Valere remembered me as a baby. This was wrong. I hadn't been born when he made his one visit to Saskatchewan; he was recollecting my uncle Dan's son, Garry. I am Clarence's son, I repeated over and over. Clarence. Finally, he understood. "Clarence the cowboy," he said in Flemish. Everybody laughed. At last, I was placed.

The old man wanted me to show him my feet. A little puzzled, I did. The feet aren't right, he declared scornfully. Vanderhaeghes have big feet. Proudly, he displayed his own, shod in black high-topped workman's boots polished to an anthracite sheen. Everybody crowded around to admire his tremendous feet.

We moved off to the house, where we were greeted by Joseph and his wife. I took a quick glance down at his feet. Nothing prodigious. More smiles and nods as we crushed into a narrow, cramped dwelling, dark as a Rembrandt painting. I was trying hard to imagine my grandfather and his six siblings, the only survivors of their mother's fifteen pregnancies, inhabiting these small and sombre rooms. But try as I might, I couldn't situate my grandfather here. The attempt to thrust the man I had known into this place gave me a strange feeling, Somehow, he wouldn't fit.

A table spread with a lace tablecloth was loaded with pastries and bottles of genever. The producer shooed all of the Vanderhaeghes, along with Ernst and Frank, into seats around the table while the crew propped themselves against the walls. In the confusion of the first meeting, Margaret hadn't been introduced as my wife. Consternation was general; the relatives hadn't known she would be accompanying me. *"Vrouw? Vrouw?"* Joseph's wife asked, pointing at her, voice rising in amazement. After her identity was confirmed for the second and third time, the woman went and stood by Margaret's chair, patting her tenderly on the head as if she were a baby.

The producer started to introduce the rest of the strangers. Abruptly, the old man interrupted him. He wanted to know who the Dutchmen were. We all shared a moment of guilty uneasiness, wondering who was going to finger Ernst and Frank, but they owned up to being Dutchmen on their own. The old man spoke again, squinting at them hard. The producer translated. "He says he remembers the Dutchmen from the days they came to buy the linen. They always ate too much and paid too little for the linen."

With this happy observation out of the way, we all attacked the food and drink. Valere unbent, grew jollier, more and more expansive. I had the strong impression that this had more to do with the genever and the presence of television cameras than it had to do with me. Given the circumstances, this was perfectly understandable.

To be truthful, the family reunion was a labour for all concerned. I kept prodding Valere for anecdotes about my grandfather's boyhood, but the lack of a common language made for difficulties. At one point, in his Oxbridge-accented English, Ernst whispered to me, "The old man is speaking some abominable dialect. I've never heard anything like it. I can hardly make out what he's saying."

Meanwhile, I was behaving with false animation, talking too loudly, asking too many questions. The more I strove to unearth some bond between us, the more discouraged I became. My outward exuberance was a sham, masking an inner detachment that regarded my play-acting for the cameras, for the relatives, with a cold and clinical eye. The epiphany I had come seeking was drifting out of reach. These were lovely, welcoming, kind people; there was no denying that. And I liked them. But my naïveté had deluded me into expecting more.

We continued drinking and gossiping, playing our roles until the producer discreetly signalled for the party to break up; the crew had a schedule to keep. Awkwardly formal, I presented the gifts I had brought from Amsterdam for my hosts, and one stage of the homecoming was concluded.

The crew escorted me out to be interviewed in front of the sheds where Valere, George, and, later, Joseph had prepared the flax to be used in linen-making. The interviewer questioned me about the old man's "earthiness." In my writing, he believed he could detect traces of the Flemish peasant's love of vulgarity, a similar deep attachment to the soil. Was this the case? Was there a link? I was supposed to say yes, but, in all honesty, I couldn't see this as the truth. I was so ignorant of Flemish culture and tradition that such a link could only have resulted from some mysterious transmission accomplished by blood, a notion I found bogus and distasteful. A successful TV program depended on my declaring my "Flemishness," but that I couldn't bring myself to do. As I squirmed my way evasively through question after question, the interviewer became more and more downcast and deflated. The interview concluded on a note of resigned and perfunctory failure.

There was one last journey to be made. The old man and his wife wanted us to see their home. When we parked outside it, I knew why. It resembled a suburban Canadian bungalow and was, by the standards of the village, a lavish house. Valere conducted us on the grand tour, with particular emphasis placed on the fact that it had two bathrooms. He led us to a hallway where framed photographs of John and Bobby Kennedy were hanging. By some photographic trick, the two brothers wore shimmering haloes of light. As we were admiring these, as we had earlier admired the old man's feet, Valere bustled off with the air of a man with an important errand to perform. My great-aunt seized this as an opportunity to spring the Big Question: Was I Christian? The last of my resolve to remain honest had evaporated during the interminable fencing with the interviewer. I said yes. Catholic? she asked, daring to hope. I shook my head. Ah well, she said without conviction, it's all the same, isn't it?

For a long moment of silence, we stared at the sainted Kennedys. Valere is a great Christian, she said at last. He spends hours upon hours on his knees in the basement, praying.

Just then we heard Valere clumping up the stairs from the basement, breathing heavily. Had he slipped below decks for a quick spiritual pick-me-up? Apparently not, because in his big, broad hand he clutched a brown envelope. This he thrust at me, growling something. The producer explained, "He has no children. He says he's going to die soon. You must have this."

The manila envelope was stuffed with photos. Quickly, I began to shuffle through them. They were pictures my grandfather had mailed back to Belgium, forty years of them. In the majority of them, he was posed beside a new piece of farm machinery: a binder, a hay rake, a threshing machine, a tractor. To his family back in Belgium the machinery established his credentials as a success. In the others, children and grandchildren were gathered in his arms or crowded around his knees. The children established his credentials as a patriarch.

In all these black-and-white snapshots, people squint into the stunning prairie sun; ebony shadows are stencilled on the earth; the prairie sky looms like a huge grey slate, cloudless, empty. Occasionally, a clump of poplars hovers on the edges of the photographs, the camera registering leaves molten in the glare of the sun.

Looking at these photographs, I had the small revelation I had been waiting for, recognized home, recognized my grandfather. The landscape and his attitude in it, cocky, a little defiant, defined him for me, would always define him. It was in this immense space he belonged, not the dark, brown, claustrophobic rooms I had just departed.

I turned over one of the snapshots and saw writing on the back. I couldn't read the words; they were Flemish. I might as well have been trying to decipher a rune. Passing the television producer the picture, I asked him what my grandfather had written. He studied it for a moment and said, "I don't know exactly. It's Flemish, but it's all wrong. A kind of English-Flemish."

Well, this was my grandfather too. The things he had forgotten or only half-remembered. Perhaps the writing on the photograph was the perfect metaphor for him, a bizarre mix of Flemish and Canadian, a record of loss and gain. I had often wondered how it was possible for him to forsake everything he had known, his country, language, religion. But the fact remained, he had *chosen* what to lose and what to gain. If he had any regrets, he had kept them to himself.

Nearly twenty years before, thinking about this loss and gain, I had written a short story about a Belgian immigrant overwhelmed, broken, because he had surrendered too much. But now I saw the source of the story was my own speculation: what would happen to me if I were ever forced to renounce everything I saw in the photograph, all that had been my grandfather's bequest to me, my place, my home?

My grandfather chose a home. And I have spent all of my life in the place he picked, everything familiar, easy, second nature to me. But one portrait of my grandfather given to me in Heule lets me see it fresh, anew. The one in which he stands, face to face with the sun, grinning.

In *Writing Home: A PEN Canada Anthology*, edited by Constance Rooke (McClelland & Stewart, 1997)

Grove of Solitude

IN 1955, MY FATHER bought 480 acres of land on the southern side of the Qu'Appelle Valley in Saskatchewan. Grove Park, as this district was known locally, had been settled by Finnish homesteaders, probably because the terrain recalled their homeland. However, my uncle had his own theory about this, claiming that "anyplace else would have been too easy for a Finn to farm."

It *was* inauspicious farmland. Covered with poplar, willow, birch, and gnarled scrub oak hard enough to dent an axe, wherever the hilly topography flattened out enough to sow grain it was also forbiddingly spiked with rocks. But my father did not intend to crop these heartbreak acres, only to graze cattle on them. Consequently, the few small fields clawed out of the bush were let go to grass, and nature commenced erasing all signs of human habitation. By the time I was ten, the Finnish settler's log barn and house had already weathered to a wasp-nest grey, the clay chinking was crumbling between the timbers, and the roofs had sagged to the point of collapse.

When I was a small boy, the short trip from my hometown of Esterhazy to this wilderness was the week's high point. Sundays, my father loaded the pickup with a saddle horse and we drove off to check on the cattle. I always strained like a dog on the leash for my first glimpse of the Qu'Appelle Valley. In early summer, a farmer might be seen discing bottomland, while the Qu'Appelle River, a silver, shining thread, spooled itself out as gulls kited the air and floated down to settle on the black earth like fat, lazy flakes of snow.

Then came the slow climb on a dusty road, the turnoff to the farm, the navigation of a narrow trail, tree boughs sweeping the sides of the truck and slapping the windshield. When we arrived at the decayed buildings, my father would set off on horseback to search for the cows and I would be left alone to await his return.

Grove Park was where I had my first brushes with absolute solitude, experienced both its delights and its terrors. Once, when I was seven or eight, I persuaded my father to let me tag along when he went to mend fence. The day was stiflingly hot, and clambering over deadfalls and fighting through dense thickets left me exhausted by midafternoon. My father perched me on a bare hilltop, exacting a promise that I wouldn't stir, vowed to be back in a half hour, and followed the fence line back into the trees. I sat on a rock, dreamily nodding in the sun as I watched red ants scurry around my sneakers.

Suddenly, I awoke with a start. Everything was still, so still that silence hummed in my ears. My eyes veered upward to a blank blue sky, dropped vertiginously to the motionless treetops at the foot of the hill. My solitariness, my littleness, sprang into focus. I lurched to my feet and screamed. Hearing that, my father came crashing out of the bush, frantic I would blunder off into the woods in a panic. I had only drowsed for minutes, but those minutes felt like I had been abandoned for an eternity.

But set against that moment of utter dread were others when I experienced a deep, calm connection with my surroundings. Sitting motionless, watching beavers fell trees at the creek. Standing in the old barn, listening to the wings of swallows swooping back and forth in the dimness, a foggy morning when a herd of ghostly deer drifted out of a stand of poplar and blithely picked their way across a meadow.

Last of all, a memory of water. The Finnish homesteader had told my father of a hidden spring in a ravine. One scorching August afternoon I set off with a shovel to find it. I tried a dozen spots, dug for what seemed hours, and the longer I dug, the thirstier I got. Then my spade turned up gravel, the grains of which wetly glistened; something bubbled, sighed, and a bright trickle slid down the bank. I threw aside my shovel, caught the water in the cup of my hands, and greedily drank.

The taste of it has never left me: achingly cold, sharp, sweet.

Canadian Geographic, May–June 1997

The Writer and Writing 1:
Thinking by Dreams

The Arts and
Urban Resilience

SASKATCHEWAN PEOPLE have always taken pride—some might say a pride verging on masochism—in their resilience, their ability to bounce back from steep economic downturns, appallingly severe weather, and the Roughriders' erratic play. Typically, Saskatchewan is Next Year Country and its cities Next Year Cities. Then, very recently, global demand for our natural resources gave Sleeping Beauty the prosperity kiss and she awoke to population growth, rising real estate prices, business expansion, and the scramble to deal with infrastructure deficits. But now, once again the boom appears to be waning. Which raises tonight's question, How do cities and communities build themselves to thrive in difficult times?

Unlike the other speakers this evening, I have no experience in government, business, public policy, or planning. A writer of fiction, I can only address this topic from the perspective of someone who has lived his entire life in and through his imagination and try to offer a flight of fancy about what role arts and culture might play in sustaining the thriving, vibrant, *resilient* city. Richard Florida's work on what he describes as the "creative class" has demonstrated that concentrations of artists of all kinds, of people engaged in the transmission of ideas, results in higher levels of urban economic development, a formula frequently seized upon by artists to justify their existence, proof that they aren't merely shiftless bums, but "good" for the economy.

The problem with this position is that it suggests that words like "vibrant" and "thriving" have no validity beyond what can be measured by a cost-benefit analysis. Still, what communities often fall back on in bad times are things that cannot be measured: shared values, a city's belief in its distinctiveness, its citizens' sense of belonging to a place and tradition. Linked to these is the identity that arises from the cultural capital that cities gradually accumulate, the architecture and monuments, the museums, the art galleries, the theatres that come into being over decades, a capital continually added to and elaborated upon by artists living in the here and now. It might be argued that, at least in part, New Orleans found its feet after the devastation of Katrina because of its rich musical heritage, a heritage that the city's musicians refused to let die, and that their efforts to preserve it helped bring the world back to New Orleans's doorstep. In the darkest days of World War II, a remarkable literary magazine, *Horizon*, was founded in London to champion the civilization that Nazism wished to destroy. In wartime Paris, the newspaper *Combat*, staffed by writers like Camus and Sartre, encouraged resistance to the German occupation. These examples of quixotic resilience can't be monetized because a dollar value cannot be assigned to a cultural tradition or a way of life.

Everybody applauds resilience but few people have anything good to say about failure. Yet you don't have one without the other. People don't boast about how they bounced back from a big success. Artists have a lot of experience with failure and so can teach us a lot about resilience. Often, they lose many times before they chalk up a win. Most Parisians loathed the design of the Eiffel Tower and expressed delight that it was slated for destruction when the 1889 exposition ended. Today the tower is *the* Parisian tourist site. James Joyce's *Dubliners* and *Ulysses* were banned in his native city; now tourists walk the streets of Dublin, his books in their hands, retracing the steps of Joyce's characters. Both Eiffel and Joyce ran big risks, courted failure, and helped to define their cities.

Despite a good deal of lip service paid to risk-taking, Canadians seem increasingly terrified of failing. Corporations sit on huge capital reserves, reluctant to invest under anything but fail-safe conditions. Politicians hew to "talking points," to "staying on message," for fear that any unscripted moment might expose them to political disaster. Everybody insists on playing in a risk-averse playground from which the teeter-totters and other life-threatening impedimenta have been banished. No one dares to profess a vision for our cities that goes beyond talk about property taxes and potholes because visions, by definition, are aspirations and aspirations can never be total successes. They will always fall short. Martin Luther King dared to announce "I have a dream" because to move things a little he was willing to permit himself to hope for a lot. Do we lack that capacity?

Let me make a truly radical, perhaps tongue-in-cheek proposal. To foster a little more resilience, maybe we ought to invite artists to participate in discussions about the future of our urban spaces. Artists are inveterate risk-takers, maybe because they have so little to lose. Most live on the margins, at or below the poverty level, covering the costs of making their art with badly paying jobs. In effect, their unpaid labour subsidizes the accumulation of cultural capital that benefits everyone.

Artists have a reputation, sometimes earned, for unconventionality, for saying and doing things that are the opposite of "staying on message." This may be why, while governments feel they have a duty to consult with business and union leaders, artists are hardly ever invited to the adults' table. What artists claim, that artistic expression deepens and broadens human experience, that it enriches the *quality* of life, and is an intrinsic *good* in and of itself, is seldom a topic of discussion in boardrooms, political caucuses, or union halls.

No one with a scrap of prudence would claim that economic issues are of no importance, but the question needs to be asked, Are they of *sole* importance to the life of vibrant, thriving cities? Most artists would say they aren't. Artists have historically tended—I use the word with reservations—*tended* to support free speech, human rights, tolerance, liberal education, open debate. Perhaps artists take these positions not because they are nobler, wiser human beings than their fellow citizens but because these things provide the soil in which art thrives. I would add that they also happen to be identified with good democratic practice, which right now could use a little pick-me-up. Maybe the time has come for Canadian urban centres to reconsider the seating arrangements around the decision-making table on the off chance that adding another chair to it, hearing another perspective, might help prepare us to more gracefully and humanely weather the hard times that are always just around the corner.

The Walrus Talks: "Resilience," Saskatoon, September 28, 2015

Novel Techniques: From Inspiration to Execution

I CAN'T TELL YOU how to write your novel, only give some indication of how I write novels and hope that you might be able to cherry-pick some observations from what I say that might prove useful to you. My advice is bare-bones and simple. I'm a simple-minded guy who tries to concentrate on a few things when working on a novel, things that provide me with a flexible and rough guide in navigating a narrative. Unfortunately, there's no detailed and infallible manual for something so daunting and difficult to execute as an extended piece of fiction.

Which brings me to the title of this talk, "Novel Techniques: From Inspiration to Execution." Inspiration means different things to different people. To me, it means writing the book you want to write rather than the book you think you should write. It's the opposite of calculation, such as *calculating* to please a publisher, supposed market, or audience. Being too concerned about placing a novel before it's written is putting the cart before the horse. I suppose this sounds naïve—I happen to believe it's the opposite—because unless you are intensely interested in what you're working on, unless you feel a deep and personal attachment to the subject that you are circling or to the characters that you are creating, you run the risk of producing something lifeless and robotic, something that superficially resembles a novel but is evidence of nothing more than your mechanically churning out something to gain acceptance from readers that you imagine looking over your shoulder. That's self-censorship of the worst kind.

Secondly, since the time required to write a decent novel is considerable, publishing fashions and orthodoxies may very well have radically changed before you have finished it. I suggest you write the book *you* would want to read. This may mean beginning with a character who interests you, a scrap of dialogue you have overheard on the subway, a dream you've had, an idea that obsesses you—novels often start in surprising ways or places. What matters is that the germ of your book feel important enough to you that you are willing to devote many months to exploring, developing, and mulling over how to bring it to fruition.

Once you feel you are inspired, how do you proceed? My advice is to test that inspiration. After all, there are as many false inspirations as there are false prophets. In my case, that testing means daydreaming the novel I hope to write, playing with it, imagining different approaches, different methods I might take in achieving it. At the start, I'm unwilling to commit anything to paper because once I set down something, black on white, it becomes too concrete, begins to feel set in stone. Doors close when I want to open as many points of exit and entry as possible. Psychologically speaking, throwing thirty or forty or fifty pages away is harder than disposing of what is essentially a reverie.

Which brings me to the point of planning. Anything as long as a novel demands at least some loose sense of where it is going, some loose sense of who the characters might be. Without that, a beginning is impossible. But I would caution against over-planning. There are people who advocate detailed character descriptions and highly choreographed plot outlines with everything that happens in each and every chapter prescribed and decided. Personally, I am leery about that approach. For me, that's too inhibiting, too likely to stifle a sense of discovery as you work through a book. Without a sense of discovery, you are likely to bore yourself, and a bored writer makes a boring book. If you are lucky, you will encounter happy accidents in the writing of a novel: your characters may do or say surprising things that you didn't expect them to do or say but which feel right or appropriate in the moment you see and hear them. To set the template too rigidly, too early, is to deny yourself and your imagination possibilities. If a novel is over-planned you may find yourself painting by numbers, simply filling in the blanks, and the result can be stale and inert. To tell the truth, I have never written a novel which went exactly where I assumed it would go when I began it. Characters that I imagined as central to the book often shrink and minor characters acquire more weight. They pull me in surprising directions. I negotiate with my initial plan and never follow it slavishly, but I repeat, some initial sense of direction is necessary.

I've put a lot of emphasis on inspiration, but I don't want to leave the impression that novels are the result of the divine afflatus dispensing a lightning bolt of genius that sweeps aside all difficulties. They aren't. Unfortunately, they are mostly the product of doggedness and an awareness, at least on some level, of techniques that you either consciously or unconsciously deploy to solve the problems you inevitably encounter in writing a lengthy piece of fictional prose. Flannery O'Connor once said that the question of whether the novel was dead, the assumption that the new media of her day such as television had written its end as an art form, didn't much concern her; all she worried about was whether the novel she was working on was dead. However, when you find your novel flagging (and you will), when it feels as if it is at death's door, don't give up on the patient too soon. You need to think about the means at your disposal that can resuscitate it and remember how, why, and where things can go wrong. Use those reminders to diagnose and cure the ills your book is experiencing.

One of the things that can defeat a novel from the very start is to fail to recognize what kind of story you are telling and what is the best way of telling it. Over many years spent reading the work of beginning writers, what has often struck me is that they haven't given this question very much thought. They tend to adopt the narrative strategy with which they are most comfortable rather than the one that will best serve the story. There is, of course, no hard and fast rule to deciding what the best strategy is, and there are many grey areas in between. But in my experience, writers who are most comfortable with writing in the first person are likely to veer towards this variety of "telling" because it is familiar and reassuring, even though it isn't the most suitable for the story they are embarking on, and writers whose immediate reflex is to opt for the third person are prone to the same problem. Perhaps a neophyte novelist has it in mind to create a work focused principally on a single character and that character's very personal story. Further, let us say the novelist has chosen to write that novel in the third person. Typically, this is a point of view which is likely to lend a novel a distant, somewhat detached perspective, and so the chance to make the reader feel like a quasi-confidant of the protagonist is missed. Think of novels such as *Huckleberry Finn* or *The Catcher in the Rye.* They address readers as if they are privileged listeners, conveying a sense that someone is speaking to you directly and intimately, just in the way a talented raconteur leans across the table in a bar or coffee shop and seduces you with his or her own voice, drawing you into their world and making you *hear* their stories in their own inimitable and original fashion. The way of expression *is* the character and, if a novel concentrates on a single figure, it might be wise to let that character engage the reader on the deepest level possible as a means of inducing the reader to identify with the protagonist.

On the other hand, sometimes novice writers who have grown accustomed to writing in the first person will embark on a novel peopled with many characters, many locations, and find themselves trapped after fifty pages because they can't shift the narrator to all the places he or she needs to be for the sake of the story. Their solution to this problem is often to use other characters to report information and incidents to the narrator, which she was not present to witness, in a clumsy, unnatural manner. To take this point about the limitations of first-person narration to the point of absurdity, imagine *War and Peace* told from a single perspective. It can't be done. I admit that this sounds obvious, but in my own case I haven't always recognized early enough the narrative blind alley I happened to be walking myself down. When they reach this dead end, many writers are inclined to give up on a novel because they feel the initial inspiration was flawed. Often the failure is because the means of realizing the inspiration proved inadequate to the task.

After you have an adequate sense of the direction your book should take, and a sense of how it ought to be told, you face beginning it. The first chapter often involves necessary housework. You will likely want to locate the reader in the story by introducing your protagonist, sketching the setting, etc. But I would argue it's important not to forget to give a gentle, or not so gentle, push of forward momentum to your novel as soon as possible, to elicit some smidgen of anticipation in the reader. Lay the groundwork for your plot as early as you can. To many writers, the word plot has a bad smell about it, suggesting something contrived and hackneyed. But in the end plot is closely tied to character; it's a matter of cause and effect: characters do something that has consequences, or face a situation that demands a choice, and their reactions to the situations they find themselves in set the dominos toppling, a cascade that plays out over the course of the book and has consequences in the protagonist's life. In saying this, I'm not arguing for the necessity of slam-bam action or earth-shaking events as the backbone of a novel. I believe this sequence of cause and effect is equally necessary for the most delicate and psychologically nuanced work that concerns itself with probing and dissecting the inner world of its characters. Without some sense of cause and effect, you are left with set pieces, and set pieces—no matter how charmingly or winningly written—aren't a novel. Any adequately realized novel has embedded in it a convincing sequence of actions that are a result of the characters' personalities and decisions. A link needs to exist between what characters do and what follows from what they do. There are many plot-driven novels that provide clever linkages between events, but which stint on the reasons why the people involved in these incidents are driven to act in the surprising ways they do. Their motivations are implausible or entirely absent. Characters are little more than pawns shoved about the board by novelists who think they are chess masters but soon reveal that they aren't.

Which is another way of saying that the heart of plot is inevitably tied to what the characters *want*. The best advice I ever got as a writer was when I made a brief foray into the theatre. The play I had written wasn't working, because the actors couldn't get a handle on their characters. The director said to me, "Guy, some of the actors can't play their parts because you haven't given the characters something to desire." I happen to believe if you know what your characters want and give them a chance to pursue it, to face obstacles that they surmount or fail to clear in chasing their bliss, you will inevitably give your novel forward momentum and have a better chance of finding out where it ought to head. And this is not just the case for your protagonist, but for every other character who is more than a supernumerary. The wishes and wants of characters lead to cause and effect, and cause and effect produces, or ought to produce, a compelling plot because the reader feels something is at stake, and that will inevitably provide forward momentum and energy to your book. It does something else. It helps you know and inhabit your characters more completely. If you give them the gift of a desire that they *need* satisfied, you humanize and individualize them, and you will avoid the stock, lifeless characters who appear only as symbols or embodiments of abstract virtue or vice, etc. Some very wise person—I can't remember who—observed that the villain is the hero of his own story. To understand why the villain thinks he's the hero of his own story you have to get inside the villain's skin.

What I am advocating is that writers allow their characters to embark on a journey and assume that if they know those characters well enough, the journeys these fictional creations take will carry them and the reader to a conclusion which will seem true and satisfying. For that reason, once I get my story going and happen to hit a rough patch, I resist the impulse to skip ahead to a later chapter that I think I can write with relative ease. I concentrate on the cause and effect because I believe that if I don't, I run the risk of losing the arc of the narrative. I know writers who are willing to leap ahead and return later to fill in the gaps they have left in the story, but in my case I feel it is necessary to solve the difficulties that confront me when they arise and not to shove them impatiently aside because I fear getting bogged down. That way, I don't lose my sense of following a train of events. The few times I have leapfrogged over a problem I found I soon lost my way.

As I said, these are the fundamentals I remind myself of when trying to write a novel. They are rudiments that will help get you from A to Z. Of course, once you get to Z you are going to have to run through all the letters of the alphabet again, making adjustments, adding nuances and shadings, paying attention to dialogue, writing the best sentences you can. But put bluntly, if you haven't made it to Z, you lose the chance to start all over again. And starting over is a novelist's lot in life.

Humber College, Toronto, July 11, 2011

The Outcast's Prayer

I'M GOING to seize this occasion to bandy about a few words on the subject of Art and Democracy ...

I happen to believe the health of a country's artistic community is a sign of the health of its democracy. If nothing else, artists are useful because they're a bit like canaries in a coal mine: when they begin to drop, everybody else is in danger. Think of Hitler's book burnings, his hatred of modern art and "un-Germanic" music, of the writers, painters, actors, directors, and musicians he either exterminated or forced to flee for their lives. Remember Stalin, Franco, and Mussolini. Contemplate all the tinpot dictators who continue in their glorious predecessors' footsteps. They agree with the great Nazi art critic, Hermann Goering, who is said to have robustly and manfully declared: "Whenever I hear anyone talk of culture, it makes me want to reach for my revolver." Which, I admit, may be another argument against strict gun-control laws, since unhindered access to firearms might help keep the population of poets in check.

In comparison to most artists in the world, Canadian artists inhabit a veritable Shangri-La, enjoying freedom of speech, expression, and thought. Nevertheless, artists who receive funding from governments and corporations are subject to subtle but real pressure to mind their p's and q's, to obsequiously tug their forelocks.

At the end of the culture-hating spectrum are those who argue artists deserve no assistance whatsoever. In a letter to the editor that appeared in the *Globe and Mail*, Mr. Greg Isberg writes: "If they had any talent, they would be able to make a living from [their art] without support. To me, funding the arts is just another welfare scheme."

Of course, Mr. Isberg's implication is that all welfare funding is bad; the poor and disabled should either sink or swim under their own power. But setting aside that Darwinian sentiment and turning to his contention that talent is inevitably rewarded with dough, then by Mr. Isberg's lights Vincent Van Gogh must have been a dreadfully bad painter since the only person he managed to sell a painting to during his lifetime was his brother. And if we got rid of artistic welfare, there would be so many more decorative beggars on our streets, removing the need for cities to fill vacant urban spaces with cute plastic wildlife, all those moose, buffalo, and deer currently beloved by Canadian metropolitan centres. Another cost saving.

Mr. Isberg's message is: Do whatever you want but pay for it yourself. Follow the example of the CPR and Peter Pocklington, sugar companies, Bombardier, and countless other businesses that steadfastly refuse to accept a nickel of government money. Produce your goods without grants, tax incentives, subventions, or government assistance of any sort just as entrepreneurs have been doing since the creation of this great country. Oh, they haven't? Really? Well, anyway, never mind that. Hey, you artists, stand on your own two feet. Which, I hasten to add, is what artists largely do. They wait on tables, groom golf courses, paint houses, and plant trees, all so they can keep doing in their spare time what they consider their real work, the work they love.

Despite the widespread impression that artists are always ravenously sucking the public tit, governments supply pitifully little money for cultural enterprises; grants are highly competitive and arrive infrequently. In reality, the infamous public trough is very shallow. Even factoring in the lavish wages that come from bussing tables or cleaning houses, the average income of writers in Canada is $11,000, a princely sum upon which to raise a family and keep the garret in bohemian splendour.*

Yet there is great antipathy to doling out even pittances to support the arts. This is particularly true when an artist produces a work somebody finds offensive. Then the troops rally and cry out, "Lord God Jehovah, smite the evil-doers hip and thigh, or divine intervention failing, let the government cut off their water!" Some years ago, a member of the Manitoba legislature found his hind legs and rose in that august assembly to demand a magazine have its funding withdrawn because a constituent had tipped him (Heaven forfend!) that it had published an erotic poem. This gentleman, who I'm sure had never read a poem since being lashed to his desk in high school and, kicking and screaming, being force-fed Wordsworth, knew bad art when somebody brought bad art to his attention, and erotic poems most definitely were. Wait until someone fingers biblical pornography such as the Song of Solomon to him. The nerve of poets who offend something called "community standards."

Which is to miss the point, because part of the job description for artists is to challenge our complacency and, in so doing, occasionally offend us. Most of the safely dead geniuses that we admire today certainly raised hackles in their time. Tolstoy, now widely regarded as an exemplary Christian, was excommunicated from the Russian Orthodox Church. James Joyce's books were banned in Ireland as immoral, and now the Irish Tourist Board cheerfully exploits Bloomsday as a drawing card for visitors to the Emerald Isle. The list of the naughty ones now rehabilitated

---

* This was roughly the figure circa 2000. According to The Writers' Union of Canada, present-day incomes of writers are actually in a steep decline.

goes on and on, which ought to make us remember: an artist is under no obligation to tell the public what it wants to hear; only to express with integrity and passion what the artist really thinks, feels, and believes. Otherwise, ventriloquists' dummies would serve our artistic needs very nicely.

I'd like to paraphrase Pierre Elliott Trudeau on this subject because I know with what warmth, affection, and admiration Mr. Trudeau has always been held here in Calgary, Canada's oil capital. Trudeau described bad artists as those who only want to please. Those who judge achievement by the applause they win.

Don't get me wrong. I'm not claiming that drawing a large audience inevitably damns the art as bad, or the lack of an audience signals a work of genius. How could I? Once upon a time I wrote a best-selling novel. I'm pointing out that audience approval is not a fail-safe proof of artistic merit. If it were, television programs like "Survivor" and "Who Wants to Be a Millionaire?" would be among the noblest masterpieces ever thrown up by Western civilization. Or maybe thrown up is an indelicate phrase.

The media, God bless 'em, have had a big hand in fomenting some of this ill-feeling. Let some character drop a load of bricks on a rat, or stow a crucifix in a jar of urine and call it art, and the press rub their hands in glee. What a story! The problem is that instead of presenting these types as a fringe element, it is often suggested that they are indicative of a general malaise prevalent in contemporary art. There is no denying that these loon balls are pathetic publicity-seekers, but there is also no denying that they also are not typical artists. In the face of the forces who crusade to stop publicly funded art, the fourth estate neglects to inform us that some of our most distinguished artists, writers such as Mordecai Richler, Margaret Atwood, Michael Ondaatje, and Carol Shields, got help from arts funding agencies at critical points in their careers. And some of them have paid it back many times over in taxes rendered to the public treasury.

I might confess in passing that I received money from both the Saskatchewan Arts Board and the Canada Council to assist in the writing of my novel *The Englishman's Boy*. Honesty also forces me to admit that this was not universally greeted as a worthy disbursement of public money. A rancher from the Cypress Hills apparently wrote Heritage Minister Sheila Copps demanding that I be stopped. The gist of his complaint about my novel was that the cowboys in it swore, and cowboys never curse. Perhaps this is a fact that Albertans are aware of since they are Canada's primary breeding ground for cowboys, but this news came as a great surprise to someone who has heard blue words pass the lips of my cowboy father and his friends. For a while, I was tempted to write to the minister of agriculture and demand that he stop the rancher, but decided I was unlikely to get any more satisfaction from him than my critic got from the minister of heritage. After all, as Westerners, we know that nobody in Ottawa ever listens to us.

As ridiculous as all this sounds, there is always a message in such controversies: behave yourself or get sent to your room. For the last decade, artists have wooed corporate support and donations from wealthy individuals to diminish dependence on shrinking government funding. As welcome as any support is in straitened times, nobody should think that assistance doesn't come with invisible strings attached. Chrysler Corporation recently asked an American magazine in which they advertise to submit articles to them for approval. And an American tobacco company had no qualms about bringing the TV news journal "60 Minutes" to heel with threats. If businesses dare to attempt to intimidate journalists (who have long wrapped themselves in their increasingly tattered rags of unbiased analysis and even-handed reporting), are corporate sponsors likely to allow artists free rein? Not in a month of Sundays.

So when the artistic directors of theatre companies or the heads of public galleries sit down to plan the upcoming season, do we seriously think that a still, small voice will not whisper in their ears, "But how will this go down with Firm X, or Mr. Moneybags Y?" Most corporations and rich donors hand out dough as a form of public relations and advertising; let's not pretend otherwise. And it's safer to put your logo on the backs of a fastball team than something as potentially dangerous as art. A few true entrepreneurs of spirit take risks with artists because they value art for itself. They think art a necessity and a public good, but such patrons are as scarce as hens' teeth.

It's up to artists to decide whether to buckle or stand firm against corporate expectations; the ultimate responsibility rests with them. Nobody is holding a gun to our heads, and a threat to our livelihoods is not the same thing as a threat to our lives. Artists, like everyone else, know the real world involves compromise, but it's necessary to recollect that some compromises are equal to silence. As free inquiry, free thought, and free speech are the very heart of democracy, so too are they the core of art.

We all have heard the old adage, "I do not agree with what you say, but I will defend with my life your right to say it." Do governments, special interest groups, patrons of the arts, enforcers of political correctness really believe this? Or are they merely paying lip service to an increasingly antiquated notion? As my father, that old cowboy who also happens to swear, would say, "Money talks and bullshit walks."

It's easy for a writer to exhort other artists not to bend, to stand firm, because all a writer requires is paper and a pencil. Not a heavy investment of capital. But those who work in symphony orchestras, in theatre, in film require substantial sums to make their art. And although I may sound like I'm preaching to others, I am also preaching to myself. I too have heard the voice of self-censorship nattering in my head when one of my plays got turned down because it was deemed politically incorrect, or when the librarian in my hometown refused to put my first book on the shelf because she wanted to spare the public the moral peril incurred in reading it.

The relationship of the artist to the larger society has always been uneasy, and in reviewing my own past I'm all too conscious of having smooched my fair share of bums. But I need to remind myself that the dead geniuses we now applaud were, like salmon, condemned by their natures to swim upstream. Everybody ought to remember that. It might give both artists and public pause. Because if artists drift with the current, cease the struggle, put their lips to the posterior of power too avidly, they become an entirely different kind of salmon, the kind which Bob Edwards described in *The Outcast's Prayer* as those that "glitter in the gleaming like a rotten dog salmon afloat in the moonlight." Then everybody loses. As Bob Edwards well knew, just because it glitters doesn't mean it's gold.

Acceptance Speech, Bob Edwards Award, Calgary Public Library Foundation, Calgary, November 7, 2000*

---

* Bob Edwards was an early-twentieth-century publisher of Calgary's *Eye-Opener*, a satirical newspaper devoted to lampooning politicians and prominent figures of the day. The Bob Edwards Award is supposedly given to individuals noted for "speaking their minds," so I found myself a curious choice for the honour given my reticence and mildness. The Bob Edwards luncheon is a fundraiser for the Calgary Public Library Foundation, and those granted the award are encouraged to be "provocative" when giving their acceptance speech. The year following my gentle talk, the 2001 honoree, Timothy Findley, got a little too provocative for the tastes of an audience that included oil company executives, whom he berated for polluting the environment and "behaving like terrorists." A number of Calgary's corporate elite walked out during his speech while others heckled him from the audience. Findley's talk was front-page news in several newspapers and confirmed the old adage, be careful of what you ask for.

Character and Circumstance:
Writing *August into Winter*

WHEN I WAS INVITED to deliver this talk to the Heliconian Club, the organizer suggested to me that one of the things that interested the members of the club was how and why a novel came to be written; what was the impetus for its creation. To be absolutely honest, when I first thought about this question, I wasn't sure I knew how to answer it, but when I began to review my novel's composition I came to feel that I was starting to see a little more clearly what were the often largely unconscious motivations that compelled me to write *August into Winter*.

So what were the beginnings of my novel? It started with a childhood memory that is now more than sixty years old. When I was ten, my mother and I paid a visit to one of my uncles who lived in Regina, Saskatchewan. On this trip my mother took me to the RCMP Museum located there. I remember as clearly as if it were yesterday her suddenly stopping before a glass display cabinet holding a Mountie's Stetson and a hammer. The Stetson had a deep dent in it that had been produced when the police officer had been struck on the head by someone wielding the hammer that lay beside it. My mother told me that the hat in the display case had belonged to a Mountie who had been murdered in my hometown of Esterhazy, Saskatchewan, when she was a teenager.

Of course, no museum today would dare mount such a display, especially since at the time the relatives of the murdered man were still very much alive and might have stumbled on the hat and hammer the way my mother and I had. Perhaps it was the macabre nature of the exhibit that fixed it so securely in my mind that the memory has lasted more than six decades. Or it might have been that a small boy's sense that something momentous, something worthy of inclusion in a museum had once occurred in the sleepy little backwater where he sluggishly waded through days of interminable boredom. This was something worthy of an episode on the then-popular television drama "Perry Mason," where murders were the crime *du jour*. I can't say why I carried the picture of the display case around in my head for all these years, but carry it I did.

It was only when I got a little older that I began to prod my mother and father to talk about what had happened that late summer day in 1939 when the police officer was killed. Both of my parents had grown up in the Esterhazy district and had indelible memories of the grisly incident and how it had shaken the town. Their answers to my inquiries weren't particularly detailed or specific, but certain elements of what they told me fastened in my mind as firmly as the museum display had. One of them concerned my father's brother, my Uncle Doug, a great favourite of mine. When he was in elementary school, he had often played with the future murderer, who I'll refer to as X. My uncle and X often hung out in a shed in X's yard that he had claimed for his personal use and had decreed off-limits to his parents who, strange as it may sound, didn't dare enter against his wishes. This outbuilding was the storehouse for items that X had pilfered whenever any opportunity arose to do so. It seemed that even at the age of ten, he was a confirmed kleptomaniac. Years later, as a young adult, he would be taken into custody for breaking and entering homes in Esterhazy and would kill the arresting officer as the Mountie was searching that very shed in which X had been secreting stolen property for more than a decade. My family had other tenuous connections to X and the infamous case. My Uncle Doug married a woman whose best friend was the wife of the police officer who died by X's hand.

The murder lingered in the memory of Esterhazy for a long time. Members of X's family still lived there when I was growing up and, in fact, occupied rather prominent places in the town. One of X's sisters was the wife of the highly respected town doctor and a pillar of the Anglican church. She was a leader among the wives of the town's businessmen and professionals, ladies who spent their time playing bridge and hosting tea parties. Another of X's sisters was the local postmistress, a stern and very strait-laced lady, who overawed nearly everyone who had any dealings with her. The postmistress lived in the home her parents had built sometime around the turn of the century when they arrived from England. It was one of the more imposing houses in town and nearly filled an entire lot that was surrounded by a brick wall topped with an ornamental iron fence. Stories still circulated about the murderer's parents who, when I was a child, had been dead for many years. They had had a reputation for being "odd," as the townsfolk charitably phrased it. Apparently, X's father had been a remittance man of some sort who had never worked a day in his life and had conducted himself rather like an English country gentleman who displayed an undisguised contempt for the local peasants. My mother didn't care for people who she thought were putting on airs and would often say of X's family, "Who are they to look down their noses at everybody else? Nobody in my family ever killed a cop."

My father had two other interesting tidbits concerning X. He told me that the son of the local squire had played accordion in a local band. When a dance was held in a one-room country school during the winter, X never drove to the gig or took a ride from anyone to get there. Instead, he insisted on running the five or six miles to the school, pulling his accordion on a toboggan behind him.

The second intriguing thing about the infamous murder case was that civilians were involved in running the murderer to ground. There was only one RCMP officer in Esterhazy in 1939, and when his corpse was found, a group of World War I veterans seized the initiative, armed themselves, and went off in pursuit of the killer. They cornered him in a poplar bluff and kept him there until they were reinforced by police from a detachment some distance away. My father told me that X had shouted to the men encircling him, "I killed one cop today. That's enough." Then he used the gun he had taken from the dead officer to put a bullet in his own brain.

Since you have read *August into Winter*, you will be able to see similarities between events in the novel and those that I have described, a passing resemblance between the fictional Ernie Sickert and Mr. X, as I've chosen to call him so as not to pick a scab off old wounds for his surviving relatives. The events concerning the burglaries in the fictional town of Connaught and the actual town of Esterhazy are roughly alike.

Nevertheless, what occurs in the novel is not reporting. What *really* happened has been magnified and heightened. The burglar who broke into homes in Esterhazy and murdered a police officer did not leave behind bizarre, troubling tableaux in the houses he burgled: brooms dangling in hangman's nooses, marbles staring up from the bottoms of egg cups, pornographic playing cards on pillows.

The real murderer, X, certainly behaved strangely—choosing to run through a frigid Saskatchewan night to play at a dance is nothing any sensible person would do. But Ernie Sickert's behaviour is much more bizarre, much more extreme. He runs *everywhere;* his need to run is a psychological compulsion brought on by his belief that his body harbours a dreadful being that will keep on growing and swelling inside him unless he can temporarily subdue it by expending the energy that he has in such abundance and which he is convinced this being is nourishing itself upon. To deplete this vitality, Sickert races everywhere, exists in a state of near perpetual motion.

The real X was an accordionist who, according to my father, pumped out passable polkas and schottisches on the squeeze-box, tunes good enough to keep the locals happily spinning around a one-room schoolhouse but which showed no evidence of remarkable musical talent. Ernie Sickert, on the other hand, is a jazz saxophonist with a gift that can root people to the spot, leave them awestruck by his musicianship.

And while the real murderer was responsible for a single death, in my novel Ernie Sickert chalks up six killings, wreaks enough havoc to put him in competition with the kind of monstrous, mythic serial killer with whom we have become distressingly familiar, a Son of Sam or Zodiac Killer, a Ted Bundy or John Wayne Gacy, murderers who have insinuated their way into popular culture and have become the dark familiars of our imaginations.

There are many more differences I could point to between what occurred in my hometown over eighty years ago and what unfolds in *August into Winter*. But the important point for me as a writer is not the list of differences that mark the boundary between what actually happened and what I imagined, but rather to note that tiny ember of memory that finally set the narrative afire in my head. There would be no novel if I hadn't retained a specific image for all those years, an image that I see with photographic accuracy, a picture of my mother standing and peering into a display case that contains a Mountie's dented Stetson and a hammer.

The mystery for me is why that image didn't fade like so many other things that I have seen or witnessed in my seventy-one

years on this earth. It must have emotionally and psychologically spoken to me in some profound way beyond my conscious
realization. I never lost that picture, nor did I forget the scraps
of information that I managed to glean from my parents about
the murder.

And then having said that, I have to wonder if the memory
that I have retained for so long might not be inaccurate or even
false. Might I have embellished and shaped it over the years?
Was that dent in the hat really there? Was the hat really there?
Quite likely it was, but I can't check my recollection because
the Stetson/hammer exhibit is no longer on display in the new
RCMP museum that I visited in Regina several years ago. But
the memory, whether it is a fact or not, *does* exist and that is what
put *August into Winter* into motion.

You don't make a novel out of a handful of facts. All that facts
can do is sting the novelist into action, nothing more. They lie there
inert unless they can be refashioned, transformed, and have some
semblance of life breathed into them. It finally dawned on me after
all those decades of hauling that memory around with me that the
"facts" of the case were little more than straws from which nothing
could be assembled unless they were added to and buttressed. The
question then became, What did I hope this fictional assemblage
to be?

What I first hoped to do with the weak straws of what I had
learned about Mr. X's case was to turn them into a short novel
of around two hundred pages, a swift-moving, lean, and action-
packed narrative that would have many of the features associated
with the crime novel genre. To this I wanted to add an under-
current of politics that would mirror the intense factionalism
that divides so many countries today. Over my career as a writer,
each novel I had written had progressively grown longer and
more structurally complex. I wanted a break from the burden of
manipulating multiple characters through a storyline with many

shifts and turnings. I thought of the book I was planning as a holiday from all that anxious effort.

Second, I was feeling nostalgic for the landscapes and places of my boyhood. I decided to set the action of the novel in the Qu'Appelle Valley, a place where my father had once owned three-quarters of a section of land on which he grazed cattle. The Qu'Appelle Valley was a district of which I was very fond as a boy and I wanted to revisit that place in my memory and celebrate its considerable beauty. I also happened to think that its heavily wooded hills, its river, and the lake near my father's farm would provide a suitable backdrop for a cat-and-mouse story about two World War I veterans who go after a man on the run and soon discover that the fugitive is more than a match for them. In my first thoughts for the novel, the pursued criminal, the prey, would become the predator and begin to stalk those who aimed to bring him to justice. I wanted a small cast of three or four characters who would inhabit a rather restricted area, the hills and valley that surround the Qu'Appelle River.

Again, readers of *August into Winter* will see traces of what I first sought to do in the section of the novel set in the Qu'Appelle Valley. The difference, of course, is that the novel expanded far beyond the limited cast and narrow confines of space to which I had hoped to confine it. My short novel turned into the longest book I have ever written. Its boundaries expanded outward from the Qu'Appelle Valley to encompass the battlefields of the First World War, 1930s Winnipeg, and the Spanish Civil War. It became something that bore little relation to my original conception. Why and how did this happen?

I can only answer this question in retrospect because it was only very gradually, after the book was finished, that I began to realize the reasons for why the novel had departed from the original conception. While I was writing it, I seldom considered how or why it was altering. I was immersed in the story I was telling myself, a story I hoped would resonate with readers, and that was my focus. What I want to emphasize is that in examining what likely led me to transform the shape and spirit of the novel, I don't wish to suggest that I was always cognizant of my motives for making the choices that I was making during the *writing* of the book. Sometimes what I did was the result of conscious, rational decisions, but most of it wasn't. I was simply pushing forward in the work, writing a scene that precipitated another scene, writing a character who demanded to be responded to by another character. All of this led me deeper and deeper into a different kind of book than the one I had once hoped to write.

But in some sense, this explanation begs the question. It avoids examining why the book travelled to World War I France and Belgium and then on to the Spanish Civil War. The reason this happened, I now believe, is that the majority of the novel was written during a time of great change in the contemporary political atmosphere. These changes preoccupied me to an unhealthy degree; I spent far too much time reading newspapers online, watching news on television, and listening to reportage on the radio, obsessing on the degradation of contemporary political culture.

Principally, I was troubled by the growing strength of the radical Right worldwide and, in particular, in North America. The electoral success of men like Duda in Poland, Orbán in Hungary, Erdoğan in Turkey, Duterte in the Philippines, Bolsonaro in Brazil, Putin in Russia, Modi in India, and Trump in the United States, the hostility to democratic norms and the authoritarian tendencies these men exhibited made me very nervous about the future. It wasn't hard to see similarities between the second decade of the twenty-first century and the third decade of the twentieth century. As the twenty-first century got underway, citizens of many countries were gripped by antidemocratic impulses. Many people were adopting hard-line, radical political positions that denied any possibility for political debate or compromise. The Right and Left were refusing to debate their positions and any alteration in their stances was beginning to look like an impossibility. Demonizing the views of political opponents was becoming "the new normal." Rational discourse was overwhelmed in a tsunami of bizarre conspiracy theories. The very idea that a fact or a truth could exist came to be seen as an increasingly quaint notion. On the Right, politics was flirting with armed force and paramilitary organizations were gaining recruits in almost every jurisdiction of the United States.

Once one group comes to regard another group of its fellow citizens as its irreconcilable enemies, the crushing of constitutional democracy and the rule of law becomes increasingly possible, even probable. The rise of "strong man" leaders all over the globe is a dangerous phenomenon. Strongmen need to flex and exert their muscles to demonstrate their strength. They do this not only to suppress dissent within their own countries, but also to direct aggression abroad by manufacturing enemies in an attempt to cement support at home. In a word, they need to invent threats to stay in power, just as a fire requires fuel to keep burning.

All this is illustrated by recent events in Eastern Europe. Although I cannot claim to have foreseen it, the territorial ambitions of Putin mirror those of Hitler; Ukraine, like Poland in 1939, has been turned into a bloody battleground on the whim of a dictator. A repetition of a World War II scenario of accelerating, uncontrolled conflict does not seem to be out of the question to me.

So as *August into Winter* moved forward, I found myself drawn to write about those great crises that marked Western civilization in the twentieth century, the horrors of trench warfare, the Depression that impoverished millions of people all over the world and drove them to look for relief of their troubles in political movements such as Fascism, Nazism, and Communism, all of which put great store in the "strong leader" and despised democracy. I felt compelled to use the example of the past to draw attention to present-day dangers. The warnings which I was issuing were oblique, or at least I hope they were, but I believed that alert readers were capable of recognizing that the past has something to say to the present.

But to do this effectively, it was necessary that I immerse myself in that dangerous past, and that required an enormous amount of research. Not only did I scour the pages of the *Winnipeg Tribune* for items that would become chapter headings that would illustrate what was happening in the world during the roughly four months covered by the novel; I also read widely in the literature of the Spanish Civil War. This included standard histories of the war, but also the eyewitness accounts of participants in it, particularly those of men who served in the Mackenzie-Papineau Battalion. I supplemented that eyewitness testimony with that of others who had been on the frontlines of the Spanish agony, journalists such as Arthur Koestler and George Orwell, whose *Homage to Catalonia*, widely denounced at the time of publication by those supporting the Republic, is now regarded as a classic record of Stalinist brutality in Spain. And I read writers who used their experiences in the Civil War to write novels: Hemingway's *For Whom the Bell Tolls*, André Malraux's *Man's Hope*, and the Spanish novelist Jose Mariá Gíronella's *The Cypresses Believe in God* and *A Million Dead*. But this list barely scratches the surface of my reading. I also pored over Communist pamphlets that circulated in North America in the 1930s, articles which postulated vast Trotskyist conspiracies at work in the Soviet Union and preposterously claimed that Trotsky sympathizers were introducing typhus into water supplies in Russia, blowing up coal mines, wrecking factories, plotting to assassinate Stalin, passing on state secrets to Japan, Germany, France, and Great Britain. All of these dark fantasies nearly as ludicrous as QAnon conspiracy theories about deep-state operatives and blood-drinking Satanists and pedophiles who run the entertainment industry and Silicon Valley.

Research for a historical novel generally falls into two categories. The first concerns facts that can usually be confirmed quickly and efficiently on the internet. How many combatants participated in the Battle of Teruel? How many days did the siege of Madrid last? But the rest of the research is often concerned with mood, texture, colour, and that is much harder to unearth, grasp, and convey. You aren't after facts but atmosphere. You are seeking a sense of how people talked, how they thought about the world, what worried them, what gave them hope. And discovering those details is a hit-and-miss proposition. You read hoping that you will find what you sense you need, but there are no guarantees that you will strike gold. And the process isn't an efficient one. I would say that less than 10 per cent of the research I did for *August into Winter* made its way into the text of the book.

As the novel developed, I also saw more and more clearly how the book dwelt on how we experience the presence of evil in the world. First, the intimate experience of evil, as when the little town of Connaught discovers it harbours a bizarre burglar in its midst, a burglar who metamorphizes into a murderer. How often do we turn on our televisions and hear someone say about some grisly event, "You could never have made me believe that this could happen here." But the novel also explored the phenomenon of evil on the largest stages, evil on a national or international scale, those arenas where territorial ambitions run amok, where wars are purposely fomented, where people's rights are ruthlessly trampled. I wanted to show that the perpetrators of evil on the small stage often share the psychology and character of the perpetrators of evil that has the greatest scope and consequence.

In saying these things, I might be making *August into Winter* sound like nothing but a political tract or history lesson. I would argue that in essence it isn't that at all, but a novel about characters, *people*, who are embedded in the everyday life which is the sum of history and who have to blindly navigate their environment in the same way that we have to blindly navigate the powerful forces, political and social, that are impinging on us today. It is a story about how people respond to the circumstances they cannot evade or escape, something which each one of us does moment by moment in our own lives, relying on deeply held beliefs and convictions that we don't ponder or ruminate about very often. These beliefs are simply there, in the same way that a novelist's deepest beliefs are the foundation of whatever they create. What a fiction writer creates is always more *felt* than *thought*. It is an expression of what they value and what they may despise.

I probably sound a little defensive on this point, but I wish to emphasize that I don't consider myself a didactic novelist, someone who is intent on teaching anyone anything. I only hope to invite readers to think. I have always considered myself a "character-driven" writer whose goal has been to depict human motivation and psychology in all its manifestations. When I went to university, I studied history—my interest in that discipline is clear in the pages of *August into Winter*—and it was in reading the Canadian historian Donald Creighton that I came across a remark that I later adopted as my touchstone for writing fiction. Creighton said, "History is the record of an encounter between character and circumstance … The encounter between character and circumstance is essentially a story."

I constantly remind myself that the kind of fiction that I am moved to write focuses on character encountering circumstances that test it. And because circumstances and character vary wildly, the permutations of story that these possible reactions can produce are legion.

A writer of my disposition needs to be a student of human nature, an observer. One of my late wife's most frequent complaints about me was that when we went out to dinner, she invariably caught me eavesdropping on a neighbouring table. Most writers have a tendency to snoop. Since childhood I have been a watcher and a listener, trying to figure out why people do what they do and say what they say.

I don't exempt myself from a similar analysis. I am continually asking myself: Why did I do what I just did? Is my explanation for what I just did true, or is it a lie I tell myself to quiet my conscience? Personal interrogation is the groundwork for interrogating the motives of my characters.

But I would also argue that observing people is only a start for a writer of fiction. Most of character creation isn't documentary, a record of what you have seen and heard. Characters come from imagining what it would be like to be the person you are writing about, even if that person doesn't resemble you in any obvious way. It is indulging in the sort of make-believe that we associate with childhood, pretending to be somebody you wish to be or whom you dread to be, somebody whom you would like to meet or somebody it would be your worst nightmare to encounter. In this process, reality and fantasy mingle in an alarming way, and quite frankly I often have trouble separating one from the other when I contemplate one of the characters this process has given rise to.

For instance, politics and war obviously play a role in the lives of many of the characters in *August into Winter*. They certainly bulk large in the lives of two of them, Dov Schecter and Vidalia Taggart. But even I can't be sure if their political passions are a product of their temperaments, their social circumstances, or whether the political positions they may have rationally adopted have actually transformed their personalities. In fiction as in life, people are hard to figure out.

Although we seldom acknowledge it, for some people politics plays an enormous role in their lives—and I'm not just talking about professional politicians. This was particularly true of the

1930s, which saw many people who would normally never have committed to political action deciding to devote a great deal of time, effort, and emotional capital to pursuing political goals. The same thing could be said today of many citizens of the United States who define themselves by their politics and who show an almost visceral, tribal loyalty to a political party or leader, loyalties that have been known to shatter families and friendships.

When I wrote Dov Schechter I did my best not to create a caricature of the kind of Communist who was a staple of the movies and television series I watched as a child and adolescent in the 1950s and 1960s, someone who was maliciously and malignantly intent on robbing people of their freedom and reducing them to nothing but robotic slaves of the state. Dov Schechter isn't that sort of Communist at all. He is an essentially good-hearted man who embraces Communism because he is genuinely disturbed by the widespread suffering provoked by the economic collapse of the 1930s. He is even more troubled by the rise of Nazism and believes that Communism is the only political force willing to actively try to defeat it. Dov volunteers to fight to preserve the Spanish Republic because he thinks that if the spread of Fascism is not halted in Spain the world will enter a long night of totalitarian darkness.

But those are not the only reasons Dov becomes a Communist. It is also in his *nature* to be a true believer. He *needs* to feel that some variety of salvation exists for this broken world. And the strength of his faith in the promise of Communism blinds him to the unflattering facts about the party and its activities. Like hundreds of thousands of other party members all over the world in the 1930s, he believes what he is told by the commissars and apparatchiks. He is an idealist who is incapable of recognizing that Stalin and his henchmen are capable of anything.

The fact that Dov is a Communist idealist and not any other sort of idealist might be a result of the milieu and culture in which he has grown up and which has helped to form him. For one thing, he is the son of Jewish immigrants and, like a significant number of first-generation Jewish Canadians and Americans, he rejects Orthodox Judaism in favour of an allegiance to a political doctrine whose stated aims are the eradication of all those things that separate people into exclusive categories of race, religion, gender, and class. The Communist goal of a classless utopian society of perfect equality is one in which, presumably, anti-Semitism will be forever banished, something that attracted a good many Jews to its ranks.

And Dov's hometown, Winnipeg, was the Canadian hotspot for radical left-wing politics. It made inroads there to a greater degree than in any other major Canadian metropolitan centre. This radical history begins with the Winnipeg General Strike of 1919 which, at least in part, owed something to the Bolshevik uprising in St. Petersburg in 1917. In the 1930s, Winnipeg elected two Communists to city council, Jacob Penner and Martin Forkin. And Joseph Zuken, also a Communist, served as a city councillor in Winnipeg from 1961 to 1983, which made him the longest-serving elected Communist party politician in North America. So Dov Schechter is part of the city's radical political traditions. And underlining the appeal that Communism had during the 1930s, it is important to remember that Dov's service with the International Brigades in Spain was not all that unusual. Canada, in proportion to its population, sent more volunteers to Spain to fight for the Republic than any other country aside from France, and France shared a border with Spain, which meant that volunteers from there could much more easily journey to Spain than those from North America.

While Vidalia agrees with the aims of Dov's politics, she can't subscribe to the notion that any political doctrine, or any other doctrine for that matter, can always be flawlessly and perfectly correct. She is the antithesis of the true believer. Nevertheless, she thinks the world can be made an incrementally better place if people exert themselves to make it so—this is what she is teaching her students at the end of the novel—but she also believes that the world cannot be significantly reformed if people resign their independence of thought and do what they are told to do by a purported higher authority. And why does she think this way? Maybe it is because she's a woman and being a woman in 1939 likely means that you have been submitting for most of your life to what men decide is right for you. Vidalia is tired of that. She wants to forge her own way, even if that means opposing the man she loves. She is as much of a feminist as a woman can get away with being living in the place and time she does. And it's her feelings that push her into assuming positions traditionally associated with small-l liberalism rather than any programmatic political doctrine. For Vidalia to be able to think for herself is a *necessity,* and because the Communist party frowns on anyone who departs from its ideology, she can't surrender to it. In part, Vidalia is patterned on my own tough-minded mother, who taught in a one-room Saskatchewan school and then, when war broke out, enlisted in the Canadian Women's Army Corp, where she rose to the rank of sergeant major. Service in the army gave her a wider view of the world, but it also made it difficult for her to return to the domestic duties women were expected to resume at the end of the war. She spent a good part of her life champing at that onerous bit and looking back on a time when she had been assigned responsibilities once reserved only for males.

Again, I need to emphasize that although much of what I am saying may leave the impression that these characters were constructed as symbols that exist simply to illustrate an abstraction, this certainly wasn't what I was thinking about as I tried to bring them to life on the page. I was simply trying to write believable people who would strike the reader as complex human beings shaded by both good and bad attributes, who acted in understandable, plausible ways. For me, Dov simply wasn't just a generic Communist. I needed to attempt to see him as he would see himself, and human beings resist seeing themselves as simple formulas or the embodiment of a principle.

Beyond setting my characters in a social context, I also wanted to portray the presence of evil in the world and have them confront that fact. There is, for lack of a better description, what I have earlier described as the intimate experience of evil, the sort of anxiety that is produced in a small community when it realizes that there is someone in its midst, one of their own, who is dangerous in a fashion that is random, unpredictable, irrational, and inexplicable. And then there is the sort of global insanity perpetrated by political madmen whose actions appear every bit as impenetrable as Ernie Sickert's, leaders who have the potential to pitch entire nations into wholesale warfare and to destroy the lives of millions. "The death of one man is a tragedy. The death of millions is a statistic" is a statement that has been attributed to Stalin. Even if he never said this, it clearly exemplifies the attitude of totalitarian leaders to human life. For Hitler, six million Jews was a statistic, the higher the death count the better. For Stalin, the Ukrainian famine he created, and the gulag death camps he engineered, the countless people who died in both, all those victims were nothing but a statistic, faceless numbers.

Set against the events occurring in the fictional town of Connaught are the momentous events in the larger world. That is the reason I decided to begin each chapter in the novel with a news clipping from the *Winnipeg Tribune*.* I wanted to remind the reader that before war broke out, people thought that it might be averted, and then when the war commenced and, for a time, lapsed into what was dubbed the "phony war" because nothing much was happening on the western front, people drifted into complacency.

---

* The *Winnipeg Tribune* was a newspaper published from 1890 to 1980.

While the twenty-first century reader knows what the eventual outcome of the attack on Poland is—the estimated deaths caused by the Second World War are between forty and fifty million—the person who picked up a newspaper in August or September or October of 1939 knew nothing of the carnage that was waiting just around the corner. This is one of the lessons of the historical novel, a reminder that we are no more capable of foreseeing the future than Oliver Dill or Dov Schechter were and, because we aren't, we ought to weigh very carefully the potential actions of those we choose to lead us.

Which brings me to the character of Ernie Sickert. A question I often face from readers of *August into Winter* is, Where did the monster Ernie Sickert come from? One woman who is a good friend said half-jokingly to me, "How can I ever invite you over to dinner again now that I've seen what goes on in your head?"

The best answer I can give—and it is an incomplete one—is that Ernie Sickert is a projection onto the page of my greatest fears. What truly terrifies me about Sickert is how completely incapable he is of seeing things in any fashion that doesn't relate to him and his skewed, terribly twisted take on reality. There is no way for any other human being to reach Sickert and shake his conviction that he is right about absolutely everything. Along with this comes an inability to accept that anyone besides him deserves any consideration whatsoever.

Sickert's narcissism, his megalomania, demonstrates his assurance of his limitless capabilities and talents. He could be a world-famous dance band leader. If he was given the opportunity, he could be instrumental in winning the war for the Allies. But coupled with his overweening arrogance and invulnerable self-assurance is a paranoid streak. Ernie is sure that his magnificent gifts are resented by lesser beings, and these inferiors are bent on persecuting and destroying him.

These are personality traits that totalitarian leaders have in abundance. They believe that their genius sets them far above those it is their destiny to rule. But they are also tormented by the idea that they are surrounded by enemies, fear popular uprisings by the people whom they oppress, and harbour suspicions of palace intrigues and plots hatched by their minions who profess loyalty, but secretly conspire to seize the throne.

Writing Ernie Sickert was difficult because living with Ernie Sickert made me confront my own fears. Not long after I turned *August into Winter* in to my publisher, my editor sent me an email in which she wrote, "Do you know who Ernie Sickert reminds me of? Donald Trump."

When I read that, I saw it was true. In some way, I had been unaware that Trump had supplied the model for much of Ernie Sickert's personality. All through Trump's presidency I had been anxious about the next disaster that might result from his monumental self-certainty and unmerited self-confidence. Trump's infamous declaration that he was "a stable genius" could have come straight out of the mouth of Ernie Sickert. The fact that both the adjective and noun were unearned, that they contradicted reality, was evidenced by the president's impulsive, feckless, childish behaviour. Trump's petulance when things did not go his way and his willingness to do anything to correct the perceived injustice of things not going his way were completely in sync with Ernie's sense that everything and everyone were destined to orbit him. My editor's comment made me aware how stealthily and insidiously the fears that Trump had engendered in me had inexorably bled into the character of Ernie Sickert.

Now Trump is not a serial killer like Ernie, but on reflection, I can't shake the feeling that he is not the man to be left with his finger on the nuclear button. Nor is he the man to be left in charge of a democracy. Like Ernie Sickert, Trump believes nothing should ever curtail his desires or his actions. Because he ought *not* to lose an election, that means he *can't* have lost an election. If the law tells him he cannot do what he wants to do, then the law is corrupt and rigged against him. Only days ago, just as I was writing this, Trump declared that the Constitution of the United States should be terminated if it presented obstacles to overturning the election of Joe Biden as president of the United States. Ernie Sickert and Donald Trump imagine themselves exempt from rules that apply to others.

If the nature of evil and the rise of radical political extremism lurks in the background of *August into Winter*, something else does too. The ending of the novel is strongly influenced by the Covid pandemic. Like everyone else, the pandemic threw me off course for a considerable length of time. The book halted in its tracks as my partner and I attempted to make the necessary adjustments to cope with a new way of life.

But after a bit, I told myself that it was necessary to get on with matters as best I could. In saying that, I need to admit to my own good fortune; I never fell sick, nor did I experience the loss of anyone near and dear to me. As a part-time university instructor, I didn't lose my job, as thousands of others did.

My stroke of luck moved me to consider how comparatively well-off Canadians of my generation had always been. We had not gone to war like our parents did, nor had we experienced the severe economic disruption or devastating droughts of the 1930s. In terms of the hand that history can deal you, we had been pretty lucky. The pandemic was our first large, pervasive crisis.

When I returned to my novel, I was determined to end it on a hopeful note. I wanted to imply that people in the past had suffered immeasurably more than we had but had still managed to keep going. In the novel, as Oliver and Vidalia stagger through a life-threatening blizzard, Oliver spots the light of a farmhouse in the distance and says to Vidalia,

"You see it? We're almost there. Nearly there. We keep
going and we get to it. We get to that light."
And they did. They put one foot in front of the other and
at last they reached it.

In the end, I suppose that plain-spoken quotation sums up
what I wanted *August into Winter* to be about, a story about people
putting one foot in front of the other, people struggling to make
sense of their world, trying to overcome its injustices, trying to
come to terms with guilt about their pasts, people searching for
love, losing and finding it, and ultimately constructing the best
life they can.

I hope I succeeded, just a little, in doing that.

Speech to the Heliconian Club, Toronto, January 18, 2023

What Is Art, Anyway?

CERTAIN QUESTIONS seem only to exist to embarrass those who attempt to answer them: What is the meaning of life? And this evening's challenge, What is art, anyway?, certainly stands very high in the set-yourself-up-for-humiliation category. But God hates a coward, so here goes nothing.

About the time that I began to mull over my thorny homework assignment from *The Walrus*, the Republicans, the Grand Old Party of Abraham Lincoln, had for all intents and purposes completed the long, bloody presidential primary march, leaving the wispy-maned realtor arguably within strolling distance of the White House. And, for me, this threw the question What is art, anyway? into a new light. I began to ask myself, Isn't art both an activity *and* a way of *thinking*—and mightn't this way of thinking, maybe, possess something of intrinsic value for civil society? As the campaign proceeded with all its attendant horrors on full display, it struck me that as far as I was aware no reports of any artist commenting about the crude political comic strip dominating the news had garnered any significant attention in the news. I am not surprised by this; I only note it. The last American novelist to speak on public issues and attract considerable media attention was Gore Vidal. Remembering Vidal, coiner of the memorable phrase "the United States of Amnesia," brought to mind George Orwell, who also wrote bitingly and coruscatingly about the cant, hypocrisy, and pious lying that characterized the politics of his time.

Feeling in need of a palate cleanser after gorging for weeks on a diet of CNN, I revisited Orwell, hoping he might provide new insight on the gruesome spectacle of politicians scrambling up what Disraeli tellingly called "the greasy pole." But instead of providing comfort, Orwell gave me a shock when I read this disturbing assertion made by him: "All art is propaganda," he announces in one essay, a statement reiterated in several more pieces written in the same decade. This claim brought me up short, forced me to say, No, Mr. Orwell, sir, please excuse me but you are *wrong*. Art is exactly the *opposite* of propaganda, and any artist worth her salt is the very antithesis of a spin doctor or message-massager. Propaganda refuses to entertain the idea that any of its claims are challengeable; it admits no reflection and aims to silence discussion. Art, on the other hand, feeds and sustains itself on free inquiry and if it doesn't, it dies.

Anton Chekhov made this argument in a letter to A. S. Suvorin. "You are right in demanding that an artist should take a conscious attitude to his work," he writes, "but you confuse two things: *the solution of a* problem and *stating a problem correctly*. It is only the second that is obligatory for the artist."

For Chekhov, stating a problem correctly meant that the artist needed to view her subject from as many perspectives as possible. He did not mean to suggest that artists are not permitted to have their own points of view, only that they must entertain the notion that other points of view exist and that they, too, have a right to speak in a work of the imagination.

That multiple points of view are helpful in understanding people and problems is an idea that seems to be overlooked in political circles and, in general, goes largely unrecognized in a world increasingly addicted to binary thinking, to the notion that everything can and ought to be reduced to an either/or proposition. I am sure that Mr. Trump's charming nickname for Ms. Clinton, "Crooked Hilary," is not a knowing wink to Immanuel Kant's famous dictum that "out of the crooked timber of humanity no straight thing can be made." Because that would mean that The Donald was acknowledging that he too is—as are we all—just another imperfect, misshapen board in society's lumber pile. It would be an admission that differing perspectives are not aberrations but essential facts of life.

In 2013, *Scientific American* reported on a study by a social psychologist at the New School in New York City. Excerpts from popular fiction, nonfiction, and literary fiction were given to participants to read while other members of the study read nothing at all. Then they were tested on their ability to infer other people's thoughts and emotions. Any gains in this respect for nonreaders, readers of popular fiction, and nonfiction proved to be negligible. However, it was noted that test results for empathy among readers of literary fiction improved markedly.

If this is true, then it supports my conviction that the ways in which people think have important consequences for society. Maybe the erosion of arts education in our schools, the historic aversion of all levels of government to providing adequate arts funding, and the recent tendency for university liberal arts departments to wax increasingly illiberal have contributed to the distressing manifestations of intolerance that characterize political discourse, the arrogant assumption that there are only two choices confronting us: to be right or to be wrong. And while there is nothing inherently misguided in seeking solutions, if we refuse to ask essential questions before trumpeting results then the body politic loses something vital to its health.

What kind of thinking may provide an antidote to this? Let me call it open-ended thinking, thinking by dreams. I admit that putting the words *thinking* and *dreams* together in the same sentence might strike some as paradoxical. But for many artists, the dream is the starting point for the What if? question, a question that doesn't assume it has already arrived at an answer. This question operates with great latitude or it cannot operate at all. Once posed, it is pursued by stumbling down blind alleys, by fumbling for unexpected openings, by exploring, by selecting and discarding, by observing and listening, by circling a question born in reverie to regard it from every possible angle. It is thinking that refuses to view the world and human beings as simple propositions; it is thinking that is suspicious of prepackaged solutions and of those who bellow declarations or claim to solve complex problems in 140 characters. It insists on relentlessly questioning every position. Thinking by dreams, artistic thinking, is essentially *democratic* in its nature. At the present moment, both at home and abroad, a little more exposure to it can't be such a bad thing, can it?

The Walrus Talks: "What is Art, Anyway?" Calgary, May 30, 2016

Books and Writers 2

Life Imitates Hollywood

FOR CANADIANS, the title of Rick Moody's new novel *The Diviners* will surely bring to mind Margaret Laurence's much-revered work of the same name. But Canuck readers of a certain age beware: a sea change of sensibility, which divides and defines literary generations, is writ large between *The Diviners* then and *The Diviners* now. Laurence's take on the world was nothing if not passionate, high-minded, and serious, while Moody's is cool, hip, and wickedly funny.

His *Diviners'* length, choice of historical moment, and brazen announcement of themes are signs that usually signal a Big Book. The novel begins with the heading "Opening Credits and Theme Music," succeeded by a provocative observation: "The light that illuminates the world begins in Los Angeles." For the next ten pages, in a pyrotechnic display of virtuoso prose, Moody tracks the course of this light as it spills across the Pacific, gilding Japan, Tibet, China, Afghanistan, and Europe, until it arrives in New York City, "Morning, just after the election, year two thousand." At this fraught moment in the history of the United States, amid a contested election and a looming constitutional crisis, Gotham rouses.

But despite the political teaser, what really occupies centre stage in Moody's novel is a soap opera charting the trials and tribulations incurred in mounting a multigenerational miniseries called "The Diviners." The focus of action is Means of Production, a film company led by Vanessa Meandro—better known to her browbeaten staff as Minivan because of her weight problem—a highly respected producer of indie movies that prompt audiences "to overthrow a despot or to work for the legal aid society or maybe just make a film."

Moody's cast list is epic, hilarious, and quirky: Thaddeus Griffin, action star of *Single Bullet Theory* and *Single Bullet Theory II*; his lover, Annabel Duffy, a young African American woman who along with her brother, Tyrone Duffy, former artist and now possibly murderous bipolar bike messenger, were adopted by a socially conscious, white Congregationalist minister and his psychologist wife. It is Thaddeus and Annabel who conceive of the miniseries, a history of dowsers through the ages who are also members of oppressed minorities such as Jews, Gypsies, and Mormons and whose aim is to slake thirst and promote world peace and understanding.

For various reasons, neither Annabel nor Thaddeus admits to originating a certain story idea, one that has apparently "sprung into being without an author." Authorial anonymity only feeds excitement about this red-hot property, whirling more and more players into the mix: the Sikh limo driver Ranjeet, who assumes the role of guru of "theory and practice of TV"; Len Wilkinson, bigwig at the entertainment division of the conglomerate Universal Beverages Corp., revered for coining the phrase "inspired by a true story"; celebrity publicists the Vanderbilt sisters; the one-named pop star Lacey; et al.

These characters' histories intersect and collide in surprising and ingenious ways, resulting in an intricate, arresting plot. A prodigiously talented writer, Moody—author of the novels *Garden State*, *The Ice Storm*, and *Purple America*, as well as two books of stories and an award-winning memoir—offers a multitude of pleasures. His edgy prose is superb; his comedic talent produces, at a bare minimum, a giggle a page; his immersion in popular culture never compromises an acute, acerbic intelligence. Nevertheless, somewhere around page 300, I became uneasy, began to feel I was spooning my way through a bathtub full of whipped cream in the hope that if I only reached bottom I would be rewarded by a bite of something more substantial. I grew increasingly suspicious that, for all its brilliance, *The Diviners* had been set roaring down a dead-end road. Was it possible for a satire of 492 pages to dodge repetition, avoid flagging? Especially one aimed at such an easy target? Evelyn Waugh's *Decline and Fall*, Voltaire's *Candide*, Jerzy Kosinski's *Being There* make savage points swiftly and just as swiftly retire from the field of combat. Their protagonists, naïfs adrift in the carnage, have the virtue of eliciting some small spark of sympathy because of their guileless innocence.

Unfortunately, innocents are in short supply in *The Diviners*. The novel's principals are monotonously ambitious, narcissistic, and shallow. Admittedly, Moody does not exempt them from suffering: they number among themselves victims of random assault, toxic parenting, mental illness, self-mutilation, and sexual addiction. Jeanine Stampfel, a burn victim, observes that the nationwide success of her colleagues' favourite television program, "The Werewolves of Fairfield County," is not due to "the richness of its screenwriting, nor through able performance, but by virtue of the simple human tendency to see one's vulnerabilities in others."

Yet it is only as the conclusion of *The Diviners* looms that Moody's characters are capable of recognizing vulnerability in anyone else, television werewolves excepted. Then, as if a sad second act in American lives would be too terrible to contemplate, characters perform amazing about-faces. Finding herself pregnant by Thaddeus Griffin, Annabel Duffy decides, "Love is the idea of the little mixed-race baby…" Minivan, while location scouting, stumbles upon illegal Mexican migrants in the desert. Confronted by their misery, "The Diviners" miniseries is drained of its earth-shattering importance, and Vanessa implausibly decides to aid them. Somebody once defined sentimentality as unearned emotion, and these greeting-card illuminations fit the bill. Such transformations seem somehow fuzzily linked to the notion of divination, and to Americans' raging thirst for meaning and fulfilment. Minivan's pitch to Jeffrey Maiser of the Universal Beverage Corp. (UBC) beats this drum ferociously, emphasizing the need for "a spiritual renewal that fully recognizes the importance of carnal appetite."

What of the presidential election that perilously hangs on hanging chads? It barely registers on anyone's radar except for Minivan's mom, Rosa Meandro, an alcoholic summarily tossed into rehab by her daughter. Rosa hears voices in her head that discuss the progress of her daughter's miniseries and pass on cellular phone traffic from Washington that is attempting to influence the outcome of the election. This is the closest Moody comes to establishing a connection between the making of "The Diviners" and the making of President George W. Bush by judicial decree— that is, until "Epilogues and Scenes from Upcoming Episodes" arrives on the scene as the concluding chapter of the novel.

Here, in a clumsy *deus ex machina*, an unnamed right-wing jurist at the Supreme Court meets with his old school chum, Naz Korngold, head of UBC. Naz wishes to radically restructure UBC and kill "The Diviners" project, but he has a small problem. Will markets stabilize in the near future and justify his putsch? In other words, will the right man assume the presidency? The distinguished jurist answers the question to Korngold's satisfaction. "Weakness has no business in the future that begins today, friend," he intones prophetically. "Weakness is a relic of a past."

So the curtain falls on the miniseries and the election of 2000, the disparate threads of the novel knotted, although not in any particularly convincing way. Does *The Diviners* aim at being more than a spirited, side-splitting romp through the scorpion-ridden wastes of U.S. showbiz? The author drops plenty of hints that he is aiming higher. As entertainment, *The Diviners* gives full value for money, but if "the light that illuminates the world" was meant to expose the present ills of American civilization, Moody sheds a lot more heat than light on the matter.

Review of *The Diviners,* by Rick Moody (Little, Brown, 2005)
Globe and Mail, October 28, 2005

The Woman of La Mancha

PETER HANDKE'S *Crossing the Sierra De Gredos*, set in an unspecified time in the twenty-first century, is a beautifully hallucinatory, eerily compelling novel. In it, Handke, a leading figure of the Austrian avant-garde and a rumoured contender for the Nobel Prize, relates the story of an anonymous woman living in an unnamed port city of northwestern Europe.* She is a powerful banker, equally admired and hated, the subject of countless profiles, a strangely opaque celebrity, yet notorious enough to be recognized, insulted, and threatened in airports all over the globe. Handke invests this "queen of finance" with a gift not typically associated with money managers: an extraordinary receptivity to images, which come to her in flashes of illumination and are the mysterious source of her worldly success.

The banker decides to commission someone to write her biography, and she makes a quirky choice, a reclusive writer of fiction living in the Spanish town of La Mancha. I confess Handke's invocation of Cervantes gave me a twinge of momentary alarm.

---

* Almost exactly twenty years after this review appeared, Handke did win the Nobel Prize for Literature, an award that created great controversy because of Handke's stubborn apologetics for Serbian war crimes committed during the breakup of Yugoslavia. The perennial question was passionately debated: can a person whose politics are reprehensible also be a splendid writer?

However, fears that still another novelist was clutching the hem of greatness, hoping the long stride of the illustrious predecessor would drag both author and story along in a cloud of borrowed glory, proved unfounded. Handke's novel is no ham-handed rehash of *Don Quixote*, and his allusions to Cervantes are so delicately respectful, so unobtrusive, that they resonate all the more powerfully because of their discretion.

The banker sets off across the Sierra de Gredos of Spain to keep an appointment with the writer. Over this harsh mountain landscape, which she traverses by bus and on foot, a threat hovers: "The darkness of a prewar period had closed in again." Everywhere she encounters signs of an undeclared, unacknowledged war, flights of military aircraft, refugees huddling in queer, makeshift shelters, and cities whose inhabitants manifest bizarre psychological traumas.

As one might anticipate, this journey is a spiritual pilgrimage. The "queen of finance" has lost, or is estranged from, everyone dear to her and seeks to repair the wounds of love and yearning. The trip also provides the occasion for a meditation on the current state of global affairs. References to a detention centre known as the Institution for Implementation of Justice, to the World and Universal Bank, to a planet that boasts it has no borders yet is beset with "restrictions and prohibitions as perhaps never before," and comments on how the murderous impulses that once were the prerogative of history's mobs are now incarnated in the world's leaders all spark uncomfortable recognition. Handke's novel skips, darts, and strikes sidelong blows. By turns, it is a novel of ideas, a satire, a poetically sensual evocation of the natural world, and a hymn to longing.

Unlike many recent novels set in the future, it is also curiously hopeful. The banker insists that her life story takes place in "a transitional period when there were still, and once again, surprises." The surprises she places hope in are authentic and personal images that "seemed, in the face of the transitoriness and destructibility of the body, indestructible," but which are being displaced by "ready-made and prefabricated ones, images controlled from the outside and directed at will."

Handke's dismissal of modern media is hardly new, but the intensity of his repudiation of it is. The "alternative images" this book offers, lovely epiphanies of the inner life, transcriptions of the shimmering, transcendent quality of an external world we fail to see, are striking contrasts to the vapid electronic fog that surrounds us. The novel issues a fervent call to look again, both inward and outward.

Handke's goal, I take it, is to produce a work where it is not "the purely external surprising, astonishing, and unusual happenings that provided material," but one that relies on "the astonishing and unusual juxtapositions of external and internal, the interactions and indeed the resonances" appropriate to the time and era, a book capable of "'lighting the way' (like the rose in the old poem)."

These snippets of quotation from the novel not only announce the extent of Handke's literary ambition but also indicate his marriage of style to purpose, conveyed gracefully by Krishna Winston's translation. While a master of riveting, specific, and detailed description, he also makes use of philosophical abstractions, aphorisms, and question marks that liberally sprinkle every page. Seemingly straightforward declarations are summarily denied, qualified, or interrogated. At first, I found this annoyingly evasive, as if I had been handed a fork to eat soup—and not just any soup, but a dauntingly large tureen of consommé. Yet gradually, I came to understand these were not simply stylistic tics but an attempt to prod perception, and that this wonderful, profound novel asked more than the suspension of disbelief, it demanded attention and patience, "a reading," as Handke's narrator says, "that was neither skimming nor poking around nor devouring, but a reflective tracing, in places also spelling out and deciphering."

Glittering bit by glittering bit, Handke creates a brilliant mosaic that justifies the ecstatic affirmation with which he concludes his novel, an affirmation that bears comparison with Molly Bloom's in *Ulysses*. Great writers teach us to read anew. Perhaps Handke is one of them.

Review of *Crossing the Sierra Gredos,* by Peter Handke, translated by Krishna Winston (Farrar, Straus and Giroux, 2007)
Washington Post, July 29, 2007

Who Snickers Last?

JÖEL BRENNER's *The Emperors of Chocolate* opens ominously. It is July 31, 1990. In Amsterdam, Theo Leenders, an executive of Mars, anxiously awaits a phone call from the company's manager of operations in the Middle East, who has mysteriously gone missing. For three weeks, Mars Electronics, the company's intelligence unit, has monitored developments in the Gulf and been fed information by contacts in the State Department. Then, unexpectedly, Saddam Hussein invades Kuwait. Candy's cloak-and-dagger dudes are caught off guard! The tocsin sounds! The warriors of Mars and Hershey rush to battle stations!

The ensuing tale is both laughable and sordid. Hershey and Mars scramble to market a bar capable of withstanding a temperature of 140°F (60°C). *Life, People,* and *Newsweek* publish photos of troops munching Desert Bar, Hershey's heat-resistant chemical breakthrough. Meanwhile, Mars is speeding its unmeltable treats to the battle zone, having convinced U.S. Army Command that "Snickers bars are just as necessary as weaponry."

The Pentagon issues a call for bids to supply 6.9 million chocolate bars. Mars wins the contract. Hershey appeals to the U.S. General Accounting Office, claiming Mars candy will melt at temperatures below 140°F. Mars threatens to sue Hershey for defamation. Hershey threatens to sue Mars for misrepresenting its chocolate.

The facts that Brenner relates are enough to create the impression that these cutthroat and ludicrous chocolate battles are an absurd Armageddon orchestrated by Willy Wonka and Monty Python. Recipes are guarded like missile secrets, competitors manufacture knockoffs of each other's product, and a request to speak to a company representative is met with, "I'm sorry, we don't do that."

Brenner traces this bizarre rivalry, this kooky corporate culture, back to Milton Snavely Hershey and Forrest Mars, Sr., men of differing but imposing eccentricity. Of the two, Hershey is easily the more attractive personality. The son of Pennsylvania Mennonites who made up for his rudimentary education with a passion for experimentation, by 1913 Hershey dominated American chocolate manufacture. The backbone of his business was the iconic five-cent Hershey bar, a sweet the American public relishes, but which Europeans describe as "cheesy" and "barnyard." When a factory was built in Smiths Falls, Ontario, even Canadians, usually so enamoured of things American, couldn't be induced to eat the stuff.

Milton Hershey was interested in utopian dreams more than in mere money, and he used the profits from his confections to help finance a model town for his workers. Hershey, Pennsylvania, had every imaginable amenity: 150-acre park, zoo, swimming pool, community centre, model housing, trolley service, schools, and a junior college with free tuition. Nor did Hershey stop there. He also established an orphanage that became the sole beneficiary of his estate, and the Hershey Trust now provides homes for children from inner-city neighbourhoods: $35,000 a year is spent on each resident; 80 per cent of the children go on to college. Its most successful alumnus is William Dearden, who became CEO of the Hershey corporation in 1976.

Hershey's benevolence had another enduring legacy. Because the trust was financed by company profits, management avoided risk-taking, fearing to jeopardize its wards. Besides, after years of supremacy, Hershey assumed its position as America's number-one chocolate maker was unassailable. It was not until 1970 that they broke with tradition and advertised their products.

Enter Forrest Mars, Sr., a man determined to knock Hershey off the pinnacle of the Big Rock Candy Mountain. As a child of six, after his parents' divorce, Forrest was sent to live with grandparents in North Battleford, Saskatchewan (Brenner calls it North Brattleford and claims it is a mining town, which it isn't). Later, Forrest completed his high-school education in Lethbridge, Alberta, but his sojourn in the Bland White North seems to have had no influence in shaping him. In Brenner's book, he emerges as a fellow with a proclivity for spectacular tantrums rivalling those of the Austrian paperhanger and postcard *artiste*, Hitler.

Since Mars was a family-owned business with no obligation to report to shareholders, its leader's mania for secrecy could be indulged. On the surface, the corporate style Forrest Mars, Sr. initiated was strictly egalitarian. Everyone at Mars is referred to as an "associate." Everyone, including the owners, punches time clocks and flies coach. All desks are the same size and there are no separate offices. Everyone's paycheque is tied to company performance. Cleanliness and quality control are obsessions.

Despite all of this, Forrest Sr. was unashamedly dictatorial. He browbeat and humiliated "associates" into achieving Stakhanovite production quotas, berating employees by phone at 4 a.m. and sending them scuttling back to the factory. An early partner who helped finance M&Ms, one of the company's most successful lines, was forced to report daily sales figures to the great man. When they fell short of expectations, he scribbled "Failed" on them, and posted them in the washrooms. Mars's salesmen from Forrest Sr.'s glory days gloatingly report "accidentally" knocking

Hershey product to supermarket floors or shunting it to the back of stores.

In times of stress, Forrest Sr. had Richard Nixon's predilection for prayer. Once, in a meeting with executives, he announced himself a religious man, sank to his knees, and intoned, "I pray for Milky Way, I pray for Snickers..." No one dared to move or indulge in a snicker themselves. Forrest Sr. was also known to order his son to the carpet to solicit divine aid from the Higher Power during advertising conferences.

Forrest Sr.'s traditions seem to have survived under the stewardship of his children. Like Mao, Forrest Sr.'s thought is codified in a company handbook, *The Five Principles of Mars*. In company headquarters, a butcher block is displayed with a charming plaque attached to it. "Head on the block responsibility," it reads. Mars's challenge, in time, forced Hershey to respond with similar ruthlessness. The two companies are now neck and neck in a bitter race to dominate the American candy market.

There are plenty of riveting anecdotes and arcane chocolate trivia in *The Emperors of Chocolate*. Brenner, a reporter for the *Washington Post*, proves herself a diligent researcher and adept at making business strategies and structures comprehensible. However, in a recent article in the *New Yorker*, Clive James made the point that how journalists say something counts for everything. It is in this department that Brenner fails conspicuously and is conspicuously failed by her editors. Her book is marred by needless repetition, clichés, and grammatical errors. At best, her prose can be described as workmanlike. At its worst, it can be downright embarrassing, a treacly mess:

> Candy. The word itself is magic. A sweet invitation to childhood. To days of hide-and-seek and ABCs and sugarplums that dance like fairies in your head.

Never mind that you've never tasted a sugarplum. It's
the fantasy that counts. That mystical, mesmerizing
pull of licorice and lollipops, peppermint and chocolate
drops. They beckon from the shelf like children from the
playground…

Etc., etc. Brenner's artless writing so dampens the potential of
this fascinating material that in the end *The Emperors of Chocolate*
earns only a tepid adjective: interesting.

Review of *The Emperors of Chocolate: Inside the Secret World of
Hershey and Mars,* by Jöel Glenn Brenner (Random House, 1999)
National Post, January 30, 1999

Brand Name vs. No-name: The Western Canadian City in Fiction

Not far from the centre of the American Continent, midway between the oceans east and west, midway between the Gulf and the Arctic Sea, on the rim of a plain, snow swept in winter, flower decked in summer, but, whether in winter or in summer, beautiful in its sunlit glory, stands Winnipeg, the cosmopolitan capital of the last of the Anglo-Saxon Empires – Winnipeg, City of the Plain, which from the eyes of the world cannot be hid. Miles away, secure in her sea-girt isle, is old London, port of all seas; miles away, breasting the beat of the Atlantic, sits New York, capital of the New World, and mart of the world, Old and New; far away to the west lie the mighty cities of the Orient, Peking and Hong Kong, Tokio and Yokohama; and fair across the highway of the world's commerce sits Winnipeg, Empress of the Prairies. Her Trans-Continental railways thrust themselves in every direction—south into the American Republic, east to the ports of the Atlantic, west to the Pacific, and north to the Great Inland Sea.

WITH THIS FLOURISH of un-Canadian immodesty, Ralph Connor began his novel *The Foreigner*. Published in 1909, the book ushered the prairie city into Canadian fiction. A world away, while Connor composed *The Foreigner*, James Joyce happened to be inquiring of his brother Stanislaus, "Is it not possible for a few persons of character and culture to make Dublin a capital such as Christiana has become?" Lying behind Joyce's question was the uncertainty that every artist situated outside the great centres of cultural production is likely, at one time or another, to anxiously confront. Can the local eccentricities and raw life of a remote, provincial city such as Dublin or Saskatoon be transmuted into artistic gold? Is there hope for great art outside New York, London, Paris? Joyce was encouraged by the success of the dramatist Henrik Ibsen, who, despite writing in a little-known language, Norwegian, had nevertheless become the most discussed and admired playwright of his day, a man who had brought Christiana (present-day Oslo) front and centre on the stages of the world, bathing it in the limelight. With Ibsen's reassuring example before him, Joyce wrote *Dubliners*, *A Portrait of the Artist as a Young Man*, and *Ulysses*, works in which "dear old dirty Dublin" was exalted into mythic status, a city fit to host the reincarnation of an ancient Greek hero. It might require genius to do it, but Joyce was convinced that the backwater could be made an all-embracing ocean.

The Joycean solution to creation on the artistic margins was one which western Canadian writers in the half-century following *The Foreigner* were blind to or responded to with an almost palpable ambivalence. For writers up until 1960, the representation of prairie cities was not only a problem of how to characterize the infant metropolises, but also one of even acknowledging their very existence. Connor's initial burst of tub-thumping was to be succeeded in the years following by mostly silence and hesitant diffidence on the part of writers who aspired to "artistry" and "seriousness." It was a long time before any other novelist would dare to emulate Connor's unbridled civic enthusiasm.

Neither Calgary, Edmonton, Regina nor Saskatoon ever found themselves thrust into a paragraph where they were made to brashly rub shoulders with London, New York, Peking, Tokyo, or Yokohama.

Ironically, Ralph Connor, probably the least artistically gifted of the handful of prairie novelists writing about western Canadian cities in the first half of the twentieth century, was the writer who succeeded in achieving one of the most striking depictions of early urban life. Several factors were responsible for this. Chief among them was that the writing of *The Foreigner* coincided with a wave of national self-confidence propelled by rapid industrial progress and relentless development of the West, a confidence which found its most famous expression in Prime Minister Wilfrid Laurier's claim that "The nineteenth century was the century of the United States. I think that we can claim that it is Canada that shall fill the twentieth century." In a time of burgeoning nationalism, a panegyric to a city held to embody so many national hopes and aspirations seemed perfectly natural.

Second, Connor, a Presbyterian clergyman with a social conscience, had discovered that a dose of "facts" mixed with Victorian melodrama exactly served his aims as a writer. The darling of the earnest, book-buying, church-going public, Connor saw novels primarily as a means of attracting attention to pressing social, religious, and political issues. *The Foreigner* was a titillating concoction of slums, wicked villains, social activists, even a Russian Horatio Alger character who also happened to be the son of a dangerous nihilist. However, underneath the cloak of "cloak and dagger," at the heart of the book was a debate central to the emerging nation. This debate concerned Eastern European immigration and what it meant for Canada. Many Canadians may have resigned themselves to such immigration as an unfortunate necessity, the only way of filling up the vast spaces of the West. But others saw it as an insidious danger, suspecting that the very foundations of Canadian government, Canadian political liberty, and the Canadian legal system were being undermined by ignorant, uncouth foreigners to whom centuries of despotism had taught nothing but a fear of the knout.

Connor, however, welcomed the despised eastern Europeans, arguing that a policy of education and benevolent assimilation would turn them into good citizens. To illustrate his conviction, he wrote *The Foreigner*, a novel which chronicles the transformation of a young Russian boy, Kalman Kalmar, into a worthy Canadian. In telling this comforting and uplifting story, Connor offered readers glimpses of Winnipeg street life, Galician weddings, and unsavoury immigrant housing, a world which many of his contemporaries were scarcely aware existed, and of which there is not the slightest hint in Sara Jeannette Duncan's coy report on Winnipeg to the *Montreal Star* in 1888:

> Another thing that one does not expect in Winnipeg, for
> some inexplicable reason, is the artistic modern wooden
> house. Why Eastlake and the reign of Queen Anne should
> be shut out of one's western conceptions does not readily
> appear, perhaps because the shanty of the pioneer is so
> intimately associated with prairie architecture, but they are
> shut out; and chairs of "antique oak," tiled fire places and
> Kaga vases, strike one oddly for a while.... Tennis lawns
> there are and boat houses on the rear grounds that slope
> down to the water's edge. Past them six canoes abreast,
> full of young men and maidens, singing as they float down
> the river in the clear moonlight of the prairies, often make
> an idyllic picture on a summer evening.

Against Sara Jeannette Duncan's genteel, respectable cameo of Winnipeg society, Connor pitted a darker, grimier portrait of immigrant life.

There they pack together in little shacks of boards and
tar-paper, ... crowding each other in close irregular
groups as if the whole wide prairie were not there inviting them.... All they ask is bed space on the floor or,
for a higher price, on the home-made bunks that line
the walls, and a woman to cook the food they bring
to her; or, failing such a happy arrangement, a stove
on which they may boil their varied stews of beans or
barley, beets or rice or cabbage, with such scraps of pork
or beef from the neck or flank as they can beg or buy at
low price from the slaughter houses, but ever with the
inevitable seasoning of garlic, lacking which no Galician
dish is palatable. Fortunate indeed is the owner of a
shack, who, devoid of hygienic scruples and disdainful of
city sanitary laws, reaps a rich harvest from his fellow-
countrymen, who herd together under his pent roof.

The Foreigner, despite being a heavy-handedly didactic novel,
nevertheless broke virgin ground in the representation of the western Canadian city. The desire to have fiction serve practical ends
led Connor to deal with new realities, the accelerating urbanization of Canadian life and the changing ethnic composition of the
country, which other writers who aspired to serve "higher," "purer"
aesthetic ends were unwilling to engage with. Although his char-
acterization of eastern Europeans would by today's standards be
judged racist or, at best, patronizing, nevertheless Connor was
one of the first writers to recognize the immigrants' existence in
fiction and recognize also that they would change the country
in ways that could scarcely be anticipated. In the preface to *The
Foreigner* he wrote:

In Western Canada there is to be seen to-day the most
fascinating of all human phenomena, the making of a

nation. Out of breeds diverse in traditions, in ideals, in speech, and in manner of life, Saxon and Slav, Teuton, Celt and Gaul, one people is being made. The blood strains of great races will mingle in the blood of a race greater than the greatest of them all.

Winnipeg was the scene of a great national experiment, the laboratory of this auspicious beginning.

Connor's concern with communicating the seriousness of the social crisis caused him to muster a wealth of sociological detail to "prove" his points. From this distance, it is impossible to vouch for the accuracy of these details, but there is little doubt that the focus on the textures of city life, the hectic bustle of the streets, the turmoil of the train station, the grit and squalor of the slums, help mark *The Foreigner* as one of the earliest Canadian novels to possess that intangible—a truly urban feel.

Despite this beginning, in the four decades that followed *The Foreigner*, the city largely disappears from sight, and the life of the farm and the small town dominates the imagination of western writers, a not-surprising development when it is remembered that the region remained overwhelmingly rural. Nevertheless, the extreme one-sidedness of the picture is worth remarking. Why is there such a nearly total neglect of cities? Particularly when they were the sites of any number of dramatic and stirring events. Why no novel of the Regina cyclone which devastated the city, killed twenty-eight, injured two hundred, and left five hundred buildings destroyed? Why no novel of the Winnipeg General Strike of 1919, or the Regina Riot of 1935?

The answer may simply be that writers were at a loss how to represent the prairie city. They lacked appropriate models of how to do it. Art, more than most artists would like to admit, relies on imitation. Writers in western Canada could depict small towns confidently because a satisfactory model of representation had been worked out earlier in the fiction of the American West. With minor adjustments in regard to weather and landscape, Willa Cather's Hanover, Nebraska, and Sherwood Anderson's Winesburg, Ohio, offered useful blueprints.

"The town is, in our tale, called 'Gopher Prairie, Minnesota,'" wrote Sinclair Lewis in *Main Street*. "But its Main Street is the continuation of Main Streets everywhere. The story would be the same in Ohio or Montana, in Kansas or Kentucky or Illinois and not very differently would it be told Up York State or in the Carolina hills." Or, one might be tempted to add, in Manitoba, Saskatchewan, or Alberta. The fictional North American small town had evolved into a place where interchangeable false-fronted buildings lined interchangeable Main Streets, and if christened with some innocuous and characterless name, such as Riverview, Horizon, or Crocus, wore an air of comforting anonymity.

This strategy was useful when representing a small town because the reader possessed no counter-image to contradict the one the writer offered. If a novelist claims to depict Chicago, the Chicago written about has to stand up to comparison with the "real" Chicago. On the other hand, no one has a picture of the *real* Horizon to conflict with the one that Sinclair Ross paints. But when drawing on a city for a setting the writer has two choices: use an existing city—as Connor did with Winnipeg in *The Foreigner*—or invent a city as Sinclair Lewis attempted to do in *Babbitt*.

> The towers of Zenith aspired above the morning mist; austere towers of steel and cement and limestone, sturdy as cliffs and delicate as silver rods. They were neither citadels nor churches, but frankly and beautifully office-buildings....
>
> Over a concrete bridge fled a limousine of long sleek hood and noiseless engine.... Below the bridge curved

a railroad, a maze of green and crimson lights. The New York Flyer boomed past, and twenty lines of polished steel leaped into the glare.

... Cues of men with lunch-boxes clumped toward the immensity of new factories, sheets of glass and hollow tile, glittering shops where five thousand men worked beneath one roof, pouring out the honest wares that would be sold up the Euphrates and across the veldt. The whistles rolled out in greeting a chorus cheerful as the April dawn; the song of labor in a city built—it seemed—for giants.

Despite the fact that Lewis's description is arresting, I would argue he has a problem. Novels that hew to realism operate on principles of verisimilitude. Zenith poses a nagging problem in this respect. It invites readers to ask the question, "This city built for giants, why haven't I heard of it?" Zenith cannot be accepted on faith the way Horizon or Gopher Prairie can, places so tiny and insignificant that they can easily escape notice. Zenith, this hive of industry and progress, cries out to be identified, invites the reader to play a version of the *roman à clef* game, to demand, "Which city is Zenith *really*? And if Zenith is really Detroit, or Chicago, or Cleveland, why not name it in the first place?"

The reluctance to name the city (if it happened to be Detroit or Cleveland) might have had something to do with the fact that as the century wore on, Hollywood movies became the chief shaper of North American perceptions of urban life. Increasingly in American film, a few cities (New York, Chicago, Boston, Los Angeles, sometimes Philadelphia and San Francisco, or an exotic and romantic locale such as New Orleans) became the paradigm of "real" cities, places where important things happened, or could be expected to happen. It's unlikely that any Hollywood producer in the 1930s and 1940s would have considered setting a story within the city limits of Duluth, Pittsburgh, Cleveland, Des Moines, or, for that matter, Edmonton. These cities were by unspoken agreement disqualified as worthy settings for modern urban dramas.

Dick Harrison has suggested that the effect the potent image of the Hollywood Mountie had on the popular imagination prevented the development of a fictional version of the Mountie in western Canadian writing. If Hollywood could refashion such a quintessentially Canadian symbol as the Mountie, and smother competing interpretations in the cradle, one can only guess what a debilitating effect the movies had on the confidence of western Canadian writers when it came to portraying cities of the region. The movies were firmly fixing the images of the contemporary city in the public's mind, and the images they were fixing were the arresting images of New York, Los Angeles, and Chicago.

Still, some western writers, because of situations and themes they wished to explore, found themselves compelled to use urban settings. When they did, most showed an extraordinary unwillingness to identify which cities they were writing about, as if they feared that putting a name to them would court derision. The result was the city *qua* city, a bare-bones sketch of the urban with most distinguishing features eradicated, a place faceless and bland and, above all, nameless.

Even in those novels with small-town settings, western Canadian novelists avoided identifying the larger centres which acted as magnets for disgruntled characters eager to escape into a wider, freer world. In Sinclair Ross's *As For Me and My House*, Mr. and Mrs. Bentley leave Horizon to become proprietors of a secondhand bookstore in a "little city" where they used to live. The little city has a university and is two hundred miles southeast of Horizon, but what city is it? Geographical evidence suggests it can only be Winnipeg, but Winnipeg is never named. In a similar fashion, while there is passing mention made of Calgary and

Edmonton in Edward McCourt's *Music at the Close*, where Neil Fraser attends university is never stated, nor is the site of the riot of striking coal miners in southern Saskatchewan given as the small city of Estevan.

When a city is named, it is likely for comic purposes, as in Paul Hiebert's *Sarah Binks*. There, the Sweet Songstress of Saskatchewan's visit to Regina with her paramour, Henry Welkin, is described at length.

> … Sarah and Henry Welkin visited all the places of
> interest. Twice they went to the opera. Again and again
> they rode on Regina's street car. The cafes, Chinatown,
> the Botanical Gardens, the Union station—Henry
> Welkin was eager that his young *protégée* should drink
> life to the full. He took her to the aquarium and to the
> public library, and together they studied what fish and
> what manuscripts were available at these places. They
> made the rounds of the art galleries; they visited the
> parliament building and studied its geology. Nor was the
> world of commerce neglected; together they visited the
> department stores, the groceterias, the banks, the freight
> yards, and the big implement warehouse of the firm
> which Henry represented and which he was particularly
> anxious for her to see. Sarah drank it all in. She was
> eager and she had youth…. From Willows to Regina
> was a far bigger step than she had anticipated.

Now this is, after all, humour painted in broad strokes. It goes without saying that there was no opera in Regina in the 1940s, no Botanical Gardens, no aquarium. For Hiebert, the thought that anyone might think there might be is, in and of itself, ridiculous. Now it is possible to take all this a little too seriously, but it is also possible to detect certain assumptions underlying this comedy.

The writer's comic representation of Regina coincides with what is already a firmly established assumption, that cities like Regina are cultural wastelands, which makes any suggestion that a visit to them might provide a modicum of intellectual stimulation hilarious. This despite the fact that by 1947, the date of the publication of *Sarah Binks*, Regina had earned a reputation—if for nothing else—as a centre of advanced social thinking and innovative public policy.

By the 1950s, some prairie writers had begun to react to the work of novelists such as Ross, Frederick Philip Grove, and W. O. Mitchell and attempt new approaches. Edward McCourt, for one, had come to feel that the main characteristic and limitation of prairie fiction was a preoccupation with the overwhelming physical environment of the prairies, which distracted from the real business of writing, which was to bring people to life. Accordingly, when he came to write *The Wooden Sword*, published in 1956, he placed his protagonist, a university professor, in a city on the prairies. And, tellingly, his protagonist detests the prairies. The fact that McCourt was himself a professor of English at the University of Saskatchewan might lead one to assume that the story unfolds in Saskatoon; yet if McCourt's university professor is located in Saskatoon there are few clues to confirm that; the city is drawn in a way to avoid positive identification. To anyone familiar with the University of Saskatchewan, McCourt's depiction of the institution might be vaguely familiar, but no more than that.

> The University in sight now. Grey stone battlements clear against the sky. Dreaming spires like lonely uplifted fingers, signposts of culture, symbolic of the vision of the founders. Skeleton girders everywhere. Somebody always building something. For years now, Steven reflected, he had been competing unsuccessfully against the noise of riveting machines, bulldozers, cement mixers. Here no holy hush of cloistered halls.

All McCourt's descriptions in this novel are equally attenuated, abstract, and unspecific. Readers are launched into the unnamed streets of an unnamed city with an unnamed river flowing through it. Unfortunately for McCourt, his aim of bringing people to life is defeated by his reticent approach. Fictional people, like real people, draw life from their surroundings, are coloured and influenced by their milieu. Living in a ghost city, McCourt's characters are condemned to being ghosts too, floating in a grey, amorphous limbo.

Adele Wiseman's *The Sacrifice*, published in 1956, the same year as *The Wooden Sword*, is unquestionably the most artistically complex, assured, and mature of the prairie novels of this period, a reworking and updating of the biblical story of Abraham and Isaac which, in that respect, has something in common with Joyce's reworking and updating of the story of Ulysses. However, unlike Joyce, who brought his native city Dublin to the forefront of the telling of his myth, Wiseman leaves the city of her birth virtually invisible. While a rich rendering of Jewish immigrant life might lead one to presume the city of *The Sacrifice* is the city (Winnipeg) in which Wiseman was raised, the evidence to support such a contention is nonexistent.

As the novel opens, a train slows on the outskirts of a city. Abraham, the patriarch of a family of newcomers to Canada, impulsively decides that he has had enough of travelling, this is where he will settle. In a variety of languages, Ukrainian, Yiddish, Polish, German, he asks the conductor the name of the city he is entering. The uncomprehending trainman can give no answer because he cannot understand the question. And when the conductor does announce the next stop to the rest of the passengers, Wiseman handles the moment by a single sentence that divulges nothing to the reader. "The conductor called out the name of the city."

If anything, Wiseman's setting is even more shadowy than McCourt's in *The Wooden Sword*. One short passage places the city in an undulating landscape, with a clear division between heights and flats, and a double-humped mountain bearing a brooding lunatic asylum on its back. None of which suggests Winnipeg. Where are we? It is impossible to know.

With John Marlyn's *Under the Ribs of Death*, published in 1957, we come full circle and return to a novel that lives and breathes Winnipeg. His novel, like Connor's, is about Winnipeg, the gateway to the West for thousands of European immigrants. It is a book which resounds with names familiar to every Winnipegger: Henry Avenue, Salter Street, Selkirk Avenue, College Avenue, Portage and Main, Logan and Main, Alexander Avenue. In fact, the city of Winnipeg itself rises to the status of a character, its topography a reflection of the inner world of the novel's protagonist, Sandor Hunyadi, son of a Hungarian immigrant. For Sandor, the North End represents everything that is to be rejected and fled from; the South End where the "rich English" live, everything that is to be sought and pursued. The contrast of South End luxury and privilege with North End poverty and disadvantage is symbolized by the streets themselves. When Sandor Hunyadi is interviewed by a WASP businessman, he realizes that he has made a mistake by mentioning that his father lives on Selkirk Avenue.

> The silence in the room was edged with old fears that set him trembling, with suddenly remembered North End talk of discrimination beyond the invisible barrier of Portage and Main, talk which he had always disregarded as having no possible reference to himself, but only to half-qualified, dime-a-dozen clerks. For nine years Nagy had been beating it into his head that this kind of prejudice was a luxury no business man could afford, and he had come to believe it, even though he still found it distasteful to deal with North End people.

Under the Ribs of Death shares more with Ralph Connor's *The Foreigner* than just a willingness to root a story in an actual place. Its theme is also assimilation, this time from the perspective of the immigrant. Sandor Hunyadi, like Connor's Kalman Kalmar, becomes a business success and, like Kalman Kalmar, he becomes "English," even to the extent of changing his name to Alex Hunter. But *Under the Ribs of Death*, unlike *The Foreigner*, is shot through with regret for what has been lost in the journey to respectability and acceptance. The difference in the authors' attitudes is best illustrated by the party scenes involving immigrants. Connor, the outsider, typifies the celebrations of foreigners as drunken, brutish, and violent. Marlyn, the insider, depicts them as warm, exuberant, and loving rather than dangerous.

> The food arrived, the hot steaming fragrance of it filling
> the room, savoury and varied and as spicy as an adven-
> ture, rich with treasured cooking-lore of the whole of
> Europe. Crumb by crumb the women had garnered the
> skill and details, the piquant flavours and the subtle
> aromas from a thousand sources—small ingenuities that
> came from poverty, recipes taken from the vanquished
> and imposed by the conquerors, graciously given to
> neighbours or stolen from friends, handed down from
> mother to daughter so that at last in Frau Hunyadi's
> kitchen there came to fruition an age-long process,
> proudly, lovingly, and painstakingly fulfilled.

Under the Ribs of Death is concerned with the loss of identity, and identity is ultimately wrapped up in whatever sets the individual apart, with differences of every kind, including minute differences of place and atmosphere. The no-name generic city, the blank backdrop could not have served Marlyn's purposes. Writing the history of one immigrant boy, Sandor Hunyadi, became the writing of the history of immigration in Winnipeg. This demanded a great deal of sociological detail, but the detail was married to a comprehensive artistic vision in which the city itself became the symbolic map upon which a young man's spiritual and psychological pilgrimage may be traced. Marlyn's *Under the Ribs of Death* may be no *Ulysses*, but it nevertheless answered Joyce's question with an emphatic yes, suggesting that acknowledging and celebrating origins may make better aesthetic sense than disavowing and disguising them.

For fifty years, the western Canadian city scarcely made an appearance in fiction and when it did, the representation was usually an uneasy compromise between what had to be said because plot demanded it, and the desire not to divulge where you were really talking about for fear that its location might be a strike against a novel. Simply put, the root cause of this was a lack of confidence, confidence of every kind. To begin with, western Canadian writers, like the Irishman Joyce, had doubts about the material on hand. Could it really be the stuff of art? Added to that, as the century matured, whatever initial economic optimism and pride the new western cities had excited tended to wear away as two world wars, Depression, and a decade of drought stunted their growth and frustrated their promise. It was one thing to sing the praises of a prospective "capital of the last of the Anglo-Saxon Empires," but when that city failed to deliver the goods, failed to live up to expectations, that gave pause. It was hard to be enthusiastic about failure without looking ridiculous.

The lack of a model to guide the representation of small, provincial cities also proved to be a problem. Moviemakers concentrated on a few great cities as embodiments of urban sophistication and dynamism, exacerbating those feelings of self-doubt and inferiority that had always been present in the citizens of less cosmopolitan centres. Either consciously or unconsciously, writers accepted the implicit message, big things happen in big cities.

This left the novelists of the region who wanted to tackle urban issues in a quandary. If the place where they lived failed to meet "world-class" standards, what was to be done? The most frequent way of dealing with the problem was to create a no-name city, a city that tried to earn a pass by pretending not to be what it really was. As a strategy, this was in most cases self-defeating, giving a strange air of unreality to novels which were written in the tradition of realism.

In the years following the publication of Marlyn's book, the growing urbanization of the West has encouraged prairie writers to turn to the prairie city as a subject and a setting more often. The cultural nationalism of the late sixties that demanded Canadian writers emphasize the distinctiveness of their country was, in a sense, an endorsement of Marlyn's example, and was increasingly taken up by regional writers. This subtle change in attitude is best illustrated in the work of a writer whose career encompasses both periods. Adele Wiseman's *Crackpot* is much more clearly and unambiguously situated in North End Winnipeg than her earlier novel *The Sacrifice*.

Yet some of the old uneasiness about daring to particularize western cities still appears to persist. This may be because the image of the city presented in pervasive popular culture is still being manufactured outside the borders of the region, and its psychological power is still a threat to regional literary representations. The no-name city has not been irrevocably consigned to the dustbin of literary history, as I well know. When I came to write my first novel *My Present Age* in 1984, a book with an entirely urban setting, something prevented me from naming the city whose geography played as large a role in the psychology of my protagonist as Winnipeg's had played in Sandor Hunyadi's. What seemed an insignificant matter to me then, does not, with hindsight, seem so insignificant now, but rather a retreat into evasion, a failure of artistic nerve, and a refusal to assert the validity of a

place and a voice. It seems that for artists on the margins, auton-
omy can only be bought at the price of vigilant self-awareness.
   Mea culpa.

From *The Urban Prairie*, Mendel Art Gallery and Fifth House
Publishers, 1993

Always a Master,
Never an Apprentice

AFTER A CAREER of five decades' duration, the monumentally prolific John Updike can tot up over fifty volumes of memoirs, book and art reviews, poetry, short stories and novels, a bibliography longer than most of his literary rivals' arms. Of all American writers, it is John Updike who most clearly can lay claim to that old-fashioned, nearly defunct title: Man (or Woman) of Letters. Now he offers a collection of 103 stories spanning the first production of an *enfant terrible* of literature and concluding with the author's toe barely touching the threshold of middle age.

Despite the fact Updike chose not to arrange these stories chronologically, instead grouping them geographically (Olinger Stories, Tarbox Tales) and topically (Out in the World, Married Life, Family Life, The Two Iseults, Far Out, The Single Life), the meticulous index he provides precisely dates completed drafts mailed to editors, allowing a diligent reader to trace his growth as a writer, as well as mark the sea changes that swept middle-class America away from the guarded, sunny optimism of the We Like Ike days to a furious distaste for Tricky Dick Nixon.

As with all significant writers, opinion divides on Updike. I remember passing a mildly favourable observation on his work to a woman at a cocktail party in Vermont that prompted a full-throated, indignant dismissal of "that hateful, right-wing misogynist!" On the other hand, in *U and I*, Nicholson Baker confesses to feeling that "for [Updike] to die would be for my generation's personal connection with literature to die."

At this point, it would be best to come clean and admit that for me, as for Nicholson Baker, Updike has always been a magisterial presence. I first stumbled on him as a naïve teenager, lured by jacket copy on *Rabbit, Run* promising a novel about an ex-high-school basketball star. It came as rather a shock to find that Rabbit Angstrom had few similarities with, say, Scott Young's plucky fictional hockey players, but the author's thorough descriptions of female anatomy were definitely an educational plus, helping to mitigate any initial disappointment of expectations.

Hoping for more of the same, I went on to read Updike's early collections of stories, *The Same Door, Pigeon Feathers, The Music School, Museums and Women*, which the chaste editorial eye of the old *New Yorker* had left bereft of the explicit copulatory incidentals of *Rabbit, Run*. Nevertheless, by then I was hooked on Updike, dimly realizing that he was not simply about sex, but also about art and religion, what he once described as "the three great secret things."

In his foreword to *The Early Stories*, Updike restrains from alerting the reader to his obsession with these "three great secret things," restricting himself to comments on minor revisions to the originals and listing his influences. Some of these are obvious, chief among them John Cheever, James Joyce, and Vladimir Nabokov. The one surprise is Ernest Hemingway, who showed him "how much poetry lurks in the simplest nouns and predicates." Still, Hemingway's bare-bones ghost is scarcely detectable, with the exception of the very earliest stories such as "Ace in the Hole" (1953), "Friends from Philadelphia" (1954), and "The Kid's Whistling" (1955). Yet these leaner, meaner novice efforts demonstrate that Updike's unmistakable voice was already present and testify to the preternatural accomplishment of a writer just entering his twenties. These are not stories that should fall into the hands of creative writing students; their example would be too discouraging.

With the Olinger stories, set in rural Pennsylvania, Updike embarks on an exploration of subjects that recur again and again in his mature work. In one of his most famous stories, "Pigeon Feathers," young David is pitched into a crisis of faith after reading H. G. Wells's *The Outline of History*. On a late-night trip to the outhouse, the boy is "visited by an exact vision of death: a long hole in the ground, no wider than your body, down which you are drawn while the white faces above recede." Weeks pass in a scouring anxiety until his grandmother requests he exterminate the pigeons that are fouling the barn. Armed with a .22 Remington, David launches into a wholesale massacre of the birds, the story ending with an elaborate Joycean epiphany as he contemplates the corpses. "And across the surface of the infinitely adjusted yet somehow effortless mechanics of the feathers played idle designs of color, no two alike, designs executed, it seemed, in a controlled rapture, with a joy that hung level in the air above and behind him."

It's a sight that leaves David "robed in this certainty: that the God who had lavished such craft upon these worthless birds would not destroy His whole Creation by refusing to let David live forever."

Although this final statement is not without irony, winking at David's likely self-delusion, it is echoed in much of Updike's later work. Like Gerard Manley Hopkins, Updike sees the earthly world as numinous, a script written by the hand of divinity, the one visible manifestation of a Protestant God otherwise remote, beyond apprehension or comprehension. Here certainly lies the source of the Updike penchant for fine description that some have found irksomely self-indulgent. But the material world—women's bodies (and men's), dirt paths, leaves, the sea, the stars—all are an antidote to his characters' terror of extinction. In Updike's formulation, "The world is the host; it must be chewed."

Few of Updike's stories lack an overt or covert reference to religion, although not all are as tentatively comforting as "Pigeon Feathers." In "The Christian Roommates," Orson Ziegler, an uptight Methodist from North Dakota, finds that after a long and hilarious struggle with a Harvard roommate who is an annoyingly pacifistic, draft-dodging, Gandhian, self-converted Episcopalian, Ziegler becomes a man who never prays. Populated by stoical, dogged church deacons; theology students; adulteresses with church affiliations; St. Augustine's mistress; even the unresurrected Jesus living out his final days in Japan, Updike's fiction has little in common with writers who treat religion as a quaint anachronism. For him, it is a crucial existential choice.

The sections following the Olinger stories are largely devoted to subjects most often thought of as Updike's typical fictional terrain—sexual love and adultery. A series of stories follow Richard and Joan Maple's agonizing march towards divorce, showing how this slow progress plays out excruciatingly in their and their children's lives. The mood of these and other stories that revolve around philandering couples is one of sadness, nostalgia, and scorching guilt. But coupled with these sombre feelings are expressions of ecstatic love for the affected children. A father gazes fondly at a son whose "sleep is so solid he sweats like a stone in the wall of a well." Another wryly observes, "A father is like a dog—he needs a boy for a friend."

As husbands and wives prove faithless, Updike sings his faithful love song to America. His America may be narrow in scope—white, middle-class citizens most at home in Pennsylvania and New England—but what writer's country isn't equally limited? Updike's antennae quiver to the smells and sounds of the United States. Richard Maple "seems to love, perhaps alone in the nation, President Johnson, who is unaware of his existence." Returning expatriates are grateful to be back in the arms of the Republic, and an American host offers a reproof to a critical English visitor in a taxi. "'You're afraid,' Luke said loudly, so the cabbie, democratically, could hear, 'of our hideous vigor.'" For Updike, "America is a vast conspiracy to make you happy."

Any attempt to comprehensively convey the amplitude and range of these stories is a mug's game. Rereading them after so many years, I am struck that the anthologists have got it mostly right, frequently giving the nod to "A & P," "The Bulgarian Poetess," "The Happiest I've Been," "Pigeon Feathers," "When Everyone Was Pregnant," "Your Lover Just Called," et al. But it must also be said that a score of other stories could come off the bench to substitute without diminishing Updike's reputation.

Inevitably, some stories feel slighter, less successful than others. Several of these are the most "far out" of the Far Out section, stories which Updike admits are "unduly precious to me." And cloyingly precious some of them are. "During the Jurassic" describes dinosaur amours, "Under the Microscope" places the spotlight on a pond-life cocktail party, and "The Baluchitherium" involves an interview with an extinct mammal. All would have fared better in the hands of Italo Calvino. Still, these are minor quibbles.

The real problem in focusing on any one aspect of this collection is that it immediately invites a departure. Did I mention that many of these stories are gloriously satirical? Or that Updike's intelligence has no apparent bounds? Or that few writers can balance a labyrinthine sentence with his effortless assurance and grace, or carve an epigram as incisively?

For those who wish to revisit and savour the pleasures Updike once provided them, or for those who would like an introduction to the cunning old master, there is no better place to start than the stunning *Early Stories*.

Review of *The Early Stories, 1953–1975*, by John Updike (Alfred A. Knopf, 2003)
Globe and Mail, December 13, 2003

John Brown's Dark Angel

MOST LITERARY HISTORICAL NOVELS are as concerned with the now as the then, reflecting our own faces back to us out of the past, as in a glass darkly. This is certainly true of Russell Banks's *Cloudsplitter*, which deals with the fiery abolitionist John Brown, whose life can be seen as a simulacrum of modern anxieties about race and political terror. Brown was the driven advocate for a second American Revolution that he hoped would win blacks full and equal citizenship in the republic, and he did not hesitate to wade through blood in his attempt to achieve this end.

The novel opens in the 1880s; the narrator is Brown's third son, Owen, an elderly hermit on a hilltop in California, shaken out of his long-kept silence by an appeal for information for the magisterial biography of his father finally published by Oswald Garrison Villard in 1910. The researcher's request unleashes a flood of memory in the old man, prompting an anguished confession concerning his role in the events that culminated in the debacle of Harpers Ferry, West Virginia, where his father led a raid on a federal arsenal in 1859. In this account, the son plays Nick Carraway to his father's Gatsby, one figure in the novel circling and commenting on its mysterious hero.

One of the great strengths of *Cloudsplitter* is the recognition that public acts are often rooted in private life. Owen Brown maintains that "the universe is like a desert, and each of our lives is a grain of sand that touches three or four adjacent to it, and when one grain ... is moved or adjusted even slightly, those next to it will move also ... until over time a great storm arises and alters the face of the planet." It is his belief that even a great storm such as the American Civil War is not solely the result of impersonal economic and political forces but owes something to the domestic shifts and adjustments within the Brown family itself.

All the public acts that made John Brown one of the most admired and hated men of his day are recounted in Banks's novel: his work as a conductor of the Underground Railroad in North Elba, New York; his career as a feared guerrilla leader in Bloody Kansas; his quixotic bid to foment an armed slave insurrection in the South by attacking the federal arsenal at Harpers Ferry. But coupled with these sanguinary and spectacular exploits are Owen's reflections on a man who was a business failure and a monomaniac on the question of slavery, too often prepared to neglect his family's welfare for the cause but nevertheless a tender, loving father whose virtues bound his children to him with chains of love and respect. It is these chains that help create a revolutionary cadre in the Browns' front parlour. Private life and public events freeze together in an indivisible mass that inches fatefully toward Harpers Ferry with a glacier's monumental, inevitable advance.

The Brown family's slow progress to their tragic destiny is lit by a series of brilliant, lightning-like insights into the tormented mind of Owen Brown. One of the most powerful occurs in an African American church in Boston, where he is swept up by "the beautiful Negro voices pealing like heavy, dark bells," and experiences a mystical convulsion accompanied by a swelling, oceanic peace. But this transcendent communion with the congregation is merely temporary, an expression of Owen's guilty longing to achieve the kind of identification with Blacks his father so easily manages. The son desires their friendship, even their love, but senses that colour is an insurmountable obstacle for both races, the consequence of "the long, savage war between the white race and the black race on this continent." He brutally confesses that his shame at failing to bridge this gap makes him wish that "Negroes did not exist—as if their very presence in our country were pestilential and the disease of race-consciousness were their fault and not ours."

Race-consciousness is the nettle in *Cloudsplitter*. Even those like Owen, who recognize and grasp the depth of their own preju- dice, are forced to endure its torturing sting. His clumsy overtures of friendship to a Black associate of his father's, Lyman Epps, lead only to frustration and humiliation. Relations between the two men deteriorate until the day Lyman is killed when Owen negli- gently hands him a cocked pistol. Technically, it passes as an acci- dent, but gazing at the bloody corpse, Owen realizes that he had wanted Lyman dead because death is the only thing that obliter- ates race, and only with that final, terrible obliteration could he bring himself to love him. Owen is shattered by his most despair- ing thought: "My nature was fully formed; and it was a killer's. And only by cleaving strictly to Father's path would I be kept from killing men who did not deserve to die."

Only in killing men whom his father has taught him deserve to die—slavery sympathizers and slavery advocates—does safety reside. Owen becomes his father's dark angel, the man respon- sible for the Pottawatomie Massacre, an incident in which five pro-slavery men were killed in revenge for the sack of Lawrence, Kansas. Owen is also the son who goads John Brown to launch the attack on Harpers Ferry that results in the death of twelve of Owen's comrades-in-arms, among them his father, two brothers, and a brother-in-law.

Owen Brown dominates *Cloudsplitter* with his anguished presence. He is a man given to harrowing self-reflection and troubling self-knowledge, "a man of another time: a man of the future I suppose, a modern man." It is the familiarity of the voice of Owen Brown, a voice from our own time, that kindles sympathy and recognition in today's reader.

Which brings me to John Brown, whose portrait I find not nearly as compelling and persuasive. For anyone coming fresh to Brown's story without history's baggage, this may not be a problem. After all, as Banks makes clear in his author's note, *Cloudsplitter* is fiction, not a version of history. Nevertheless, the novelist who chooses a historical figure as much written about as John Brown must compete with earlier, entrenched versions. Exploding them can sometimes be a risky artistic enterprise.

It may be that Banks simply decided to transfer some of John Brown's darker motivations and psychological complexity to his son. For instance, he ascribes Brown's shady business dealings (even thefts) to naïveté rather than the self-righteous justifications of a man busy with the Lord's work who feels himself entitled to the worldly goods necessary to let him do it. In Banks's interpretation, Brown's famous secrecy is a policy dictated by circumstances, where others have argued it was that and more, a symptom of paranoia and exalted egomania.

Banks is more convincing on the subject of Brown's religion, drawing a picture of a man whose days were marked with observance and belief. Yet he seems to miss the urgency, the anxious mental exertions to divine the will of God that characterized so much of nineteenth-century Protestantism, at least the variety of it to which Brown adhered.

However, these are minor reservations about an important, timely novel likely to be much discussed and debated. There is so much to admire here: Banks's complex portrait of Owen Brown; his brave dissection of race-consciousness; the skill and compassion with which the Browns' long march to Harpers Ferry is described. Anybody interested in a thoughtful and illuminating look at both the past and present will find it in the pages of this rich, disturbing novel.

Review of *Cloudsplitter,* by Russell Banks (Alfred A. Knopf Canada, 1998)
Globe and Mail, February 28, 1998

"Novel History" Is a Success— as a Novel

THE BOOK JACKET of *Gabriel Dumont in Paris* announces it as "a novel history" rather than employing the more diffident description "historical novel," which suggests, however imprecisely, that the writer's paramount allegiance is to the art of fiction. If the word *novel* is meant to be an adjective, it is not apropos, since I can detect nothing that distinguishes *Gabriel Dumont in Paris* from conventional historical fiction. If it is a noun, the suggestion seems to be that equal attention has been given to the demands of both disciplines.

In his afterword, Jordan Zinovich hints that this is the case, writing, "Throughout this book I have attempted to cling with some tenacity to the historical documentation." For a non-specialist like myself, his ample bibliography buttressed my assumption that the letters and first-person recollections of historical figures such as John Kerr, Norbert Welsh, Archbishop Taché, Auguste-Henri de Trémaudan, John Donkin, Edward Blake and a host of others were either transcriptions from memoirs and documentary records or a faithful précis of them.

That is, until I encountered two passages attributed to Francis Dickens, son of Charles Dickens and an inspector of the North-West Mounted Police from 1874 to 1886. Returning to the bibliography, I discovered an entry for Eric Nicol's *The Astounding*

Long-Lost Letters of Dickens of the Mounted. Nicol's book is an unabashed tongue-in-cheek hoax, featuring the invented correspondence of the hapless police officer addressed to Minerva, wife of "the owner of a bar in which Frank dissipated much of the legacy bestowed on him by his long-suffering father."

Yet Zinovich reproduces a nearly verbatim quotation from this farcical fraud that relates an encounter between Dickens and Dumont. I was perplexed. Was Zinovich gulled by Nicol's transparently comic take on the period, or is *Gabriel Dumont in Paris* a postmodern historical novel that emphasizes the irony and irreverence of the "transgressive text" which introduces fabrications and falsifications to remind us that all narratives, historical or otherwise, are human constructs with a tenuous relationship to "the Real"?

Without the time or the inclination to pore over the rest of the cited works or make a trip to ransack the Provincial Archives of Manitoba, I concluded that Inspector Dickens's letters had been taken without a grain of salt and abandoned fussing and fretting about the author's intentions. After all, the historical novel may drape itself in the garments of the past but the only judgment that really matters is whether such a work succeeds as a novel and nothing but a novel.

On that score, Zinovich pretty well clears the bar. The prologue attributed to the Montreal historian A. Trémaudan states that what follows is Dumont's story as told to the Parisian M. Demanche during Gabriel's year of exile in the City of Light, a narrative bolstered by Trémaudan's own research into the Métis leader's life.

The tactic of first-person narration by Dumont, alternating with the voices of his admirers and enemies, creates an arresting picture of a people with a radically democratic political tradition, a nation comprised not only of stereotypical warriors and buffalo hunters but also farmers and traders who speak Indigenous languages as well as several European languages which they are capable of both reading and writing. There is more in Dumont's house on the South Saskatchewan than the infamous billiard table commandeered by the British expeditionary force; it also boasts a copy of Shakespeare's plays, well-thumbed by Dumont's wife, Madeleine. The detailed description of this multilingual, multicultural, multiracial society is as exhilarating as its destruction at the hands of a wilfully obtuse government is tragic.

In Zinovich's hands, Dumont's career is a reflection of the sad history of his people. In 1851, Gabriel is a young boy fighting the Sioux at the battle of Grand Coteau, which marked the zenith of Métis military power on the plains. He courts and marries Madeleine and for a brief time lives the traditional free life, pursuing herds of buffalo so immense that they drink rivers dry. But the herds dwindle, Métis land on the White Horse Plain is handed to Mennonite immigrants, and many of his people retreat to the South Saskatchewan to salvage what they can of their cherished way of life.

By now Dumont is a respected leader, a man to be reckoned with, growing prosperous as a merchant and ferryman, becoming what the priests had always urged him to be, settled and stable. However, the advance of white settlers from the east imperils Métis land rights; the Métis petition the government in Ottawa for redress of their grievances. When the politicians fail to listen, Dumont rides to Montana, returning with Louis Riel. After that, the cataclysm.

The drama of these events is obvious, and the actions of Dumont, as recorded in his own words and those of onlookers, are equally so. Competing voices offer conflicting interpretations of an imposing figure: unparalleled military tactician; sometime drunkard and gambler; mystic; a man generous to a fault, compassionate, yet prepared to murder wounded prisoners after the battle of Fish Creek.

Trémaudan's prologue issues a challenge: "Who was Gabriel Dumont? I cannot completely answer that for you—you must find the Truth of him yourself, if that is your concern." Zinovich, the writer lurking behind the conceit that the story is told by others, bears the ultimate responsibility for leading us to some understanding about what the "Truth" of Dumont is. His version is nearly convincing. The problem is that while the man of action is carried off with verve, the inner Dumont is not nearly as compelling. His voice can be passionate, even lyrical, when describing the battles, the prairie landscape, and the death of the old life, but the character of the Métis leader is not as vivid as the circumstances to which he must respond.

For instance, Dumont's relationship with Riel is rather perfunctorily drawn, a mere sketch in loyalty. Was Gabriel's only reservation about Riel's leadership that he meddled disastrously in military matters? And what did he make of Louis David's brand of chiliastic revolution, or his bizarre ethnological theories (South American Indians were descended from Egyptians, North American Indians from Jews). Or Riel's fantasy of transporting Jews and European Catholics to the New World to intermarry with the Indigenous populations and swell the Métis nation? Was Dumont himself a true believer or a troubled doubter of all this?

In the public's mind, Dumont has always played second fiddle to the charismatic prophet, Riel, but second fiddles can harbour thoughts about the conductor and the music they are ordered to play. When it comes to Dumont's interior life, Zinovich's "novel history" reads more like history than a novel and Dumont is more of an archetype of his people than an individual with his own perplexities and anxieties. As Trémaudan says in the prologue, "Do all our plans and best intentions decide any *real* aspects of our lives?" This is the question Dumont never asks himself, and one the reader can never apply to him without a deeper entry into the mind of the man who is not only a character occupying the historical stage but also one who has to command our attention in a novel.

Setting aside this reservation, *Gabriel Dumont in Paris* achieves a rich evocation of a time and people. Métis songs, petitions, poetry, illustrations from nineteenth-century magazines and the voices of dozens of participants in events that determined the shape of Canada crowd the page, jostling for the reader's interest, creating a powerful collage of what the West was then and, by implication, what it might have become if certain short-sighted decisions in a far-off capital had not been taken.

Review of *Gabriel Dumont in Paris*, by Jordan Zinovich
(University of Alberta Press, 1999)
The Canadian Forum, December 1999

Sylvia the Gardener

WHEN I RECEIVED THE INVITATION to write something about "Sylvia Legris the gardener" (who also happens to be my domestic partner), a memory flickered in my mind of "Chance the gardener," the protagonist of the movie *Being There*, based on Jerszy Kozinski's novel of the same name, the story of a gormless innocent whose banal observations about gardening are taken for profound political punditry, a man whose simple-mindedness triumphs in every situation he hazily ambles through. A character, I might add, in whom Sylvia takes great delight.

Linking Sylvia with gardening also led me to speculate about whether sensibility is a constant. What might be the connections between gardening and poetry? In some instances, are poems germinated and tended like gardens and, in turn, gardens like poems? Of course, once you set out in search of similarities you are likely to find them. I plead guilty to that.

Despite being a reluctant gardener myself, most of my life has been passed in the company of enthusiastic horticulturists. My mother and father were practical country people who always maintained an enormous vegetable plot and displayed a mild disdain for those who wasted their time growing anything that couldn't be eaten. My wife, a painter, was of an entirely different stripe, a passionate cultivator of inedible blooms. Her flower garden was an action painting: a wild spattering of poppy and daylily, daubs of chrysanthemum and daisy, dribbles of flax and coneflower, streaks of cosmos and pansy mingled with the brushstrokes of many other flowers, the names of which I never learned.

My wife's failing health and final illness slowly reduced this vivid canvas to an overgrown and desolate patch. After her death, my bleak apathy encouraged more weeds, more desolation. By the time I finally mustered up enough will to attack all the rank growth, my way of dealing with it was slapdash, perfunctory. I took a spade to the jungle, indiscriminately digging up both flowers and weeds, intent on taking the easy way out by starting from scratch, by sowing low-maintenance vegetables such as potatoes, carrots, beets, and onions.

In the time before Sylvia and I became a couple, the garden was, even at its best, the sort of "large, loose, baggy monster" that Henry James deplored. An apartment dweller for most of her life, Sylvia's botanical pursuits had always been a tidy business restricted to the usual houseplants and a few zucchinis raised in captivity on a balcony. My unkempt patch came as a shock to her orderly urges and she immediately volunteered to help me clean it up.

The root of the continuing disarray went back to my first crack at rehabilitating the garden. I had been hasty, given to shortcuts, hadn't sifted the earth for daylily rhizomes, hadn't pursued the lateral roots of Canada thistle wherever they led, hadn't torn up the far-reaching root systems of the Siberian elm or paid enough attention to eradicating each and every Shasta daisy. So each spring, last year's problems repeated themselves.

Sylvia might have been a relative novice when it came to gardening, but unlike me, she is very good at detail, fanatically meticulous. Unwilling to settle for dirt that was less than pristine and immaculate, she crawled about on her hands and knees hunting down and uprooting every scrap of unwanted stolon, tuber, bulb, root, and rhizome that my spade dislodged.

I think that was when Sylvia first got hooked on the reality and notion of *garden*. All through that first summer, she grew more and more diligent about keeping the vegetable plot in a healthy and flourishing state. She sought advice from friends who were experienced nurserymen and nurserywomen and surfed the internet looking for answers to her questions concerning plants. Above all, she learned by doing, by gaining experience through trial and error. Maybe she was less willing to sacrifice herself to the demands of the garden than I've suggested. Maybe it was simply witnessing my slipshod and slovenly ways that drove her into action, but whatever the reason, genuine interest or desperation, Sylvia was taking charge of the garden and, little by little, making it her own.

With hindsight, I can now see that something else was occurring. At some deep and profound level, gardening began to exert an influence on her poetry. In *The Poetics of Space*, Gaston Bachelard said it better than I ever could: "When a dreamer can reconstruct the world from an object that he transforms magically through his care of it, we become convinced that everything in the life of the poet is germinal." Substitute "she" for the masculine pronoun and Bachelard might have been describing how Sylvia's immersion in the world of the garden was germinal to her work; how her burgeoning sensitivity to weather, soil, and the still, quiet pageant that marks the slow changes in the life of plants was also becoming stealthy, subterranean preparation for her next book.

In an interview with *Freelance*, the magazine of the Saskatchewan Writers' Guild, Sylvia stated, "I don't seek out the focus of a project but progress towards it quite organically. Each of my collections has evolved in some way out of the previous one. While working on *Pneumatic Antiphonal* ... I had immersed myself in so much information about the human body, yet I had barely made it beyond the lungs! Everything about anatomy is ceaselessly fascinating—how could I quit? The transition from *Pneumatic Antiphonal* to *The Hideous Hidden* seemed both logical and instinctive." And the transition from *The Hideous Hidden* to *Garden Physic*, the collection that she is at work on now, appears to be both logical and instinctive, perhaps even inevitable.

The Hideous Hidden, a wide-ranging collection that takes as it subjects the work of early anatomists and the depiction of the universe of the human body by linguistic means, was not yet completed when Sylvia first stepped into the garden. Years later, I can recognize hints of her new work, *Garden Physic*, in the offhand comments that she began to drop then, in comparisons drawn between raw human viscera and the plant life that lurks below the earth, in the similarities of appearance she noted between a knot of daylily rhizomes and a tumour, in her description of the tenacious root system of the Siberian elm as "a circuitry of veins," a phrase that also happened to be the title of Sylvia's earliest collection of poetry. One thing was naturally leading to another. Past and present were preparation for the future.

As far as I could see, the way Sylvia approached gardening didn't differ much from the way she approached her poetry. In an interview that she gave to the University of Saskatchewan's *MFA in Writing News*, she urged beginning writers to "pay attention," and went on to say that

> the practice of looking at artwork (in its broadest definition: painting, sculpture, installation, performance, film, etc.) honed my ability to look at things closely, from different perspectives, to pay attention to minute detail and to how changeable one's perceptions can be depending on elements like light, sightline, etc.

Such care is a hallmark of both Sylvia's gardening and of her poetry. Rows of vegetables march in good order. Lines and stanzas do the same on the page. Even in the rough draft of a poem, Sylvia will take pains to kern text so that it "looks right."

The garden receives the same scrupulous attention. Stakes marking vegetable rows are plumb-line straight. Seed trenches are dug to the depth mandated on the seed envelopes. Seeds are sown with precision and deliberately spaced according to recommendations. While I'm inclined to carelessly dribble small seeds such as carrots into their beds, Sylvia painstakingly introduces them into the soil, one by one.

I know all this sounds a little Virginia Military Institute–like, but that's because I haven't gotten around to mentioning the other side of Sylvia; I haven't drawn attention to the goofy grace notes she insists upon insinuating into her garden. Pattern and form are disrupted by gaudy pinwheels spinning in the wind and dollar-store plastic frogs that the manufacturer claims are equipped with motion sensors that supposedly trigger a chorus of croaking when intruders are detected. The frogs, however, remain mute as they contemplate rabbits pillaging the chard.

Like many artists, Sylvia's work is a product of the tension between opposites, in her case a tug of war between minimalist and maximalist urges, between Bauhaus and Baroque. A taste for the austere walks hand in hand with lavish eloquence. Gravity encounters absurdity. Sylvia the gardener sends a knowing wink to Chance the gardener.

The same sort of zany embellishments crop up in her poetry. When Sylvia's research uncovered the fact that the ancient Greek botanist and physician Dioscorides believed medicinal properties existed in grime that could be scraped from public bathhouse walls and collected from wrestling schools, this was information she couldn't resist. Here are a few lines from her poem "Grime from the Wrestling School."

Duck the high crotch leg setup (heralds
the wizzer, levels the lower body takedown).

Quick freestyle turn, back-flat, the mat rolls
a gazzoni, grunge-prone, rub A535-exposed.

Back-arch analgesic it, the tight waist, the cross-face,
the barrel roll-Voltaren, the lift, the switch, the sit out.

In this madcap and exuberant outburst of language, a poem
where brand-name muscle-pain relievers collide with technical
terms from the sport of wrestling and a cascade of verbal dominos
is precipitated by a pharmacopeia created in the first century CE,
we see Sylvia's fascination with all aspects of language, her pure
pleasure in the way words sit in the mouth and then sing, her
allegiance to the idea of poetry as resonance, reverberation, pure
sound, and her belief that research into any subject has the potential to expand, vivify, and enrich poetic language, her conviction
that etymological sediment harbours many treasures.

She has discussed all this in respect to the writing of *The
Hideous Hidden*:

In order for me to probe deeper into anatomy—to look
at the history of dissection—I had to cut deeper into
its attendant language. What draws me to any material
is evocative and unusual language, the sound of it, the
look of it, with medical language the sheer historical
capaciousness of it.… Because anatomical and medical
language has gone through countless permutations over
the centuries, in a contemporary context this language
is layered with history and is etymologically rich—a
linguistic motherlode if you're a poet.

The Notes and Sources section appended to *The Hideous Hidden* reveals just how widely she has delved into that linguistic motherlode. Sources cited include the writings of Virgil, Hippocrates, Aldous Huxley, Vladimir Nabokov, Da Vinci's notebooks, as well as the work of other early medical researchers and scientists such as Galen, Robert Willan, Sir Astley Cooper, Bartholomei Eustachi, Andreas Vesalius, and many, many more.

Just as medical Latin played a large role in the composition of *The Hideous Hidden*, botanical Latin has been equally important to *Garden Physic*. The botanical corpus that informs *Garden Physic* is as varied and wide-ranging as the literature of anatomy that animated its precursor. A short list: Dioscorides' *De materia medica*; Nicholas Culpeper's seventeenth-century. *The Complete Herbal*; the long eighteenth-century epic poem *The Botanic Garden*, composed by Erasmus Darwin, grandfather to Charles Darwin; the correspondence of Harold Nicolson and Vita Sackville-West that discusses their Sissinghurst Castle garden; the visual representations of plants and flowers in the fabrics and wallpaper of William Morris and in the highly magnified photographs of the German artist and sculptor Karl Blossfeldt, plant portraits that imbue their subjects with an architectural monumentality.

With her usual avidity and persistence, Sylvia has combed this literature to create her own striking and arresting lexicon of botany, much of which relies on the striking names which centuries of farmers, shepherds, herbalists, and gardeners gave to the plants that were so much a part of their lives, all rendered in the beautifully metaphoric and imagistic language of the common people. Sylvia has compiled these in her own offbeat taxonomy, dividing them into categories such as: Blasphemes & Oaths (Bastard Rocket! Good Laurel of Caesar! By the Seed of the Lotus! Homer's Moly! Pig Nuts!); or Odds, Sods & Improbabilities (Pudding Grass, Candy Carrot, Ass of the Priest, Sticky Willy);

or Menagerie (Adder's Tongue, Dog's Mouth, Dragon's Arum, Lion's Paw Cudweed, Snake Bryony).

It is hard not to think of Sylvia as a resurrectionist, a modern-day body-snatcher who lifts long-dead and dormant language out of the grave to enrich contemporary poetry with the strange and lovely locutions of the past, with different ways of seeing and paying attention to the world. This doesn't mean she is some stodgy antiquarian, far from it. She's a poet who tilts and disrupts our expectations of what contemporary poetry is or ought to be, someone who jams archaic vocabulary up hard against the body of the language of the present, invites contemporary speech to sassily talk back to its own history while relentlessly reminding it of an older, more elaborate music.

This is what makes Sylvia's voice unique. She is one of a handful of writers in whom influence is not readily apparent, a quality that is the mark of a truly individual and radical talent. Her work has always been Janus-faced, a complication of tensions, poetry that is charged with nervous expectancy and is always eccentrically inimitable.

As I write this, the year is one week short of the winter solstice. In the backyard, the garden that five years ago Sylvia saved from my delinquent husbandry and went on to resurrect, sleeps, sheeted in white. While it waits for spring, Sylvia is writing it into a new becoming.

Music and Literature, January 2019

Recollections 2

My Adventures
in the Screen Trade

IN 1996, I PUBLISHED *The Englishman's Boy* which, in part, tells the story of the corruption of a Hollywood writer by a ruthless studio head. So there was certainly more than a tad of irony when I signed on to adapt my novel for the screen. The crossing guard was about to gambol in the traffic.

Collisions between moviemakers and novelists would seem inevitable. Writing a novel is a solitary, unsupervised job. Like Mao, a novelist is used to playing the Great Helmsman, but a movie carries the fate of so many souls, and so much is invested in the cargo, that steering by your own stars is clearly out of the question.

I understood this in theory, but changing old habits is not easy. Luckily for me, Minds Eye Pictures decided to buffer my ego. Initially, all criticisms were channelled through the story editor, minimizing friction and confusion. Second, at an early stage I worked with the director, who helped me to write pictures, not words. And both director and story editor were also wise enough to let me discover my mistakes on my own. After a second draft that had me pretty chuffed, neither offered comments. Instead, a reading of the screenplay by actors was arranged. Minutes into it, the fine speeches had me cringing. By the next morning's meeting I had performed my own post-mortem.

Which is not to say that my grasp of what was expected of me was ever perfect. For the life of me, I still can't grasp the necessity for a treatment, except as an exercise to satisfy funders. Grudgingly, I did as instructed, scrupulously writing to the length demanded, only to be told that it "felt thinner than the novel." Yes, I thought. The elimination of three hundred pages, a weight loss of 90 per cent, is bound to leave any story anorexic.

To make generalizations after writing one screenplay may be unfair, but it's also fun. Unlike publishing, I found there is a wonderful directness in the world of film. It's bracing to be told something is "shit" and to reply that "your head is up your ass." The director couldn't stand the last scene of my script, which he thought (my words, not his) was highbrow wanking. I had my huff, thought about it, and finally concluded he was right: the picture should end with an appeal to the heart, not the head.

I'm not sorry to have written a screenplay. I learned plenty. For one thing, working on a movie recalled to me the delights of clean, energetic storytelling. I also learned that often three heads are better than one.

For years, moviemakers have shunned the novelist whose books they are eager to option. Maybe they think they are not worth the trouble. It's true that working with novelists can create sparks, but they might just be the kind of sparks which fire stronger, quirkier, more unpredictable pleasures.

Montage, Fall 2000

Cowboy Camp

THE SUMMER OF 2006, a miniseries adaptation of my novel *The Englishman's Boy* went into production in Saskatchewan. Since half of the drama is set in the American and Canadian West of 1873, it was decided that a crash course in equitation was necessary for the actors. When I learned this "cowboy camp" was being convened in the Qu'Appelle Valley, north of Regina, wild horses couldn't have kept me away. For males of a certain age who galloped their mothers' brooms over backyard ranges in the fifties, holstered cap guns flapping against their thighs, the fantasy of playing cowboy is irresistibly attractive.

On the first morning of instruction, I arrived wearing a pair of boots I had bought in Dallas fifteen years before and worn only once or twice since. My middle-aged feet had spread like the rest of me, forcing me to mince about camp in a most unmanly fashion. The wranglers in charge of teaching horsemanship were former professional rodeo riders and ranchers—laconic, leathery types given to unfathomable stares, most of which I felt were directed my way.

The first course was a safety primer, covering topics such as how to approach a horse from behind without getting kicked into the bleachers, or what to do if you find yourself on a careering runaway. For instance, don't scream. It might further panic the horse. Next, each actor was assigned a mount and was instructed to spend time currying and feeding it and performing other ingratiating services meant to encourage it to, if not like you, at least tolerate you. While this went on, I lingered hopefully on the fringes like a kid awaiting the call to join a pickup football game. Invitations were not forthcoming.

By the time the actors were engaged in learning the rudiments of steering, stopping, and accelerating their new four-legged friends, I was in a desperate state of unrequited desire. Making meek, supplicating motions, I approached a wrangler and identified myself as the writer. Like Richard III, I abjectly begged for a horse.

"Take mine," he said and, dismounting with catlike grace, left me to claw myself aboard, joints grinding and creaking. This was a mistake. Wranglers' horses are not like the ones assigned to actors. Actors are provided with the most docile horseflesh available, because injury to the talent would be a catastrophe. But what happens to the writer is not a cause for concern. On the ensuing trail ride, the grin soon melted off my face as I wrestled to restrain my high-spirited steed. If it bolts, I reminded myself, resist the urge to shriek. Better to die in silence than disgrace myself.

In the next few days, I found myself aching in places I didn't know I owned and walking like an animated wishbone. Meanwhile, the actors were soldiering on, growing ever stiffer, sorer, and more chafed. They were also learning that horses, like thespians, sometimes exhibit quirks, foibles, and temperament. One morning at breakfast, I asked one of the actors, who sat morosely stirring his fruit cocktail, what was the matter. He blurted out, "My horse hates me. He knows I'm from Toronto and I'm wearing pantyhose." It was a charged, confessional moment. Only later did I learn that all the other actors had also donned pantyhose. The wranglers had given them a "tip." Hosiery minimized saddle friction, preventing flesh from getting rubbed to the state of freshly ground hamburger. They had descended on a womenswear store to get outfitted.

Too soon, I had to leave, despairing at having notched only a single ride. When I returned weeks later, all the actors from Vancouver and Toronto had developed a blasé competence around horses and were now being glamorously referred to as "the posse." As a Westerner, I seethed at the unfairness of it all. But one afternoon, when an actor was somehow occupied and his horse needed to be ridden to a location, I was called upon. "Guy, take Michael's horse. Go with the posse."

Michael happens to be considerably shorter than me, but there was no time to adjust the stirrup lengths. Off I went, an overweight, superannuated jockey, knees hovering near my armpits. At the top of a hill, I halted to take in the scene. By squinting my eyes, I was able to banish the craft-services vehicle and other cinematic impedimenta below. In the valley, teepees glistened in glaring sunshine. Raked by a breeze, a grove of poplars flashed silver. Insects hummed in the heat. The posse filed down the slope, costumed and armed. I drank it all in. By marrying movie illusion with psychological delusion, my fantasy was fulfilled. At age fifty-five, better late than never, I had become a high plains drifter.

The Walrus, July 12, 2007

An Innocent's
Excellent Adventure

ALMOST EXACTLY FORTY YEARS AGO, I paid my first visit
to Toronto. It was Canada's Centennial Year and as part of
the official celebrations the federal government had launched
a program for high school students called Young Voyageurs.
The motivation for this venture seemed to be a conviction that
strewing teenagers higgledy-piggledy across the country would
promote national understanding and pride, which at some future
date would lead to a pandemic of Canadian patriotism.

To this end, I and approximately twenty other Saskatchewan
students who had been raised in the resentful certainty that
Toronto was the place where the sweat of the honest tillers of the
soil was wrung out and turned to gold by the fat cats in Bay Street
counting houses were optimistically dispatched to learn how to
come to love and admire the Great Satan.

We travelled eastward by train. Rail transportation then was
every bit as erratic as it is now; our contingent of Young Voyageurs
might have reached Toronto more quickly if we had paddled there.
Arriving nearly a day late, at two o'clock in the morning, we staggered out of Union Station to the sight of the Royal York, then
still a commanding presence on the Toronto skyline, and were
met by a group of bleary-eyed families who had volunteered to
billet us. My hosts were Mr. and Mrs. X and their son, to whom

I'll assign the name Tommy. Mrs. X was a fount of chipper welcome. Her son was pleasant, but somewhat wary of the hayseed;
think of how Ned Beatty eyed the hillbilly rapists in *Deliverance*.
Mr. X simply shook my hand, and then swiftly shunted us into the
car to make the drive home to Etobicoke.

Soon we Young Voyageurs were swept up in a whirlwind
of activity, visits to City Hall, the Art Gallery of Ontario, the
Royal Ontario Museum, and Casa Loma, all of which left me
gobsmacked. There was a ride on the new subway system, a picnic
on Toronto Island, as well as excursions to Niagara Falls and the
Stratford Festival, where I saw Alan Bates play Richard III.

All of this was certainly enlightening and broadening, but it didn't
compare to the enlightenment shed by the X family, my first contact
with bourgeois bohemianism. They were the first self-consciously
"artistic" and "socially progressive" family I had ever collided with,
utterly strange and exotic birds for someone like me, raised in a
rather hardscrabble, keep-your-nose-to-the-grindstone atmosphere.
Mr. X worked in an advertising agency, a profession whose demands
on his imagination had left him a tortured insomniac. At all hours
of the night I could hear him padding about the house, trying out
new slogans *sotto voce*—although I admit a trick of memory may be
embellishing his late-night prowls with whispered jingles.

His son, Tommy, strummed the guitar and wrote obscurely
poetic songs. Amazingly, this did not elicit shame and scorn in
his parents as it would have in mine; they actually *encouraged*
him to share his product with them, which he did seated cross-
legged on the broadloom, crooning teenage angst while his parents nodded encouragement and, post-concert, offered thoughtful
critiques of his lyrics. Tommy, perhaps sensing some resistance
on my part to his tunes, found it necessary to undertake my
musical education. Exposed to nothing but Top 40 radio playlists
back in Saskatchewan, Tommy's playing of Gordon Lightfoot's
Canadian Railroad Trilogy was revelatory for me. Having nothing

but thinly veiled contempt for performers who didn't write their own material, he decided I needed to be exposed to more of those who did. Much to the annoyance of organizers and chaperones, Tommy and I started to dodge some of the scheduled events on the Young Voyageur itinerary. For instance, we evaded a dance held in a church basement so we could see Joni Mitchell play the Riverboat in Yorkville.

In 1967, Yorkville was an intriguing hippie haunt, not a roofless high-end mall. It didn't take much to persuade me to forsake a demure church sock hop for the Riverboat, but if I had resisted his blandishments, he probably would have abducted me. Joni Mitchell was from Saskatchewan; I was from Saskatchewan. In Tommy's fevered, scheming mind, nothing could be more natural than for me to accost Joni and lure her into reminiscing about wheat fields, endless skies, et cetera. With the ice broken, I could then introduce her to another up-and-coming singer-songwriter. While I sat mute and sulky, Tommy tried to thrust me out of my seat in Joni's direction at the conclusion of each of her sets. I stubbornly refused to budge. To relieve his pent-up frustration at my balkiness, he ended up scribbling "I love Joni Mitchell" in three-foot-high letters on the bathroom wall of the coffee house. I believe he may have also left his phone number so Joni could contact him.

The second excellent musical adventure Tommy and I had came when we attended a Jefferson Airplane and Grateful Dead concert. An anticipated late return from a Young Voyageur junket to the Stelco plant in Hamilton would have meant missing the opening act, but Tommy's indulgent parents concurred with our opinion that Art trumped Steel and raised no objection to our missing the smelters.

The venue for this gala evening of acid rock was the O'Keefe Centre, which Tommy assured me had a very strict dress code.*

---

* The O'Keefe Centre has had many rechristenings in the more than fifty years since 1967 and in its most recent reincarnation is called the Meridian Centre.

He said we would be turned away from the door if we weren't wearing jackets and ties. I had neither, but Mr. X lent me one of his blazers and a very proper striped tie, something that looked as if it might have a private school or regimental provenance. On arrival at the O'Keefe Centre, Tommy and I were astonished to find ourselves in the midst of a tie-dyed, headbanded horde, not a lounge suit in sight. We quickly stuffed our ties in our pockets, but sports coats could not be easily disposed of, so we ended up sitting on our shame to hide it, two slightly elevated pillars of mortification. Meanwhile, an amoebic light show queasily pulsed behind the bands as the crowd gaily festooned the stage by flinging rolls of toilet paper at it.

Shortly after this Happening, which was breathlessly described in various newspapers as a seminal cultural event in the life of the city, the Young Voyageurs were returned to Saskatchewan. In retrospect, I now see that this government program of reverse Pol Potization (temporarily emptying the countryside into the cities) did achieve some of the effects that the government had hoped it would have. It might have been too much to ask a Westerner to love Toronto, but during my short stay there in 1967 I developed a great fondness for it. First impressions, like first kisses, are the most memorable. For me, the city will always reflect the spirit of the family that welcomed, astounded, and startled a naïve stranger four decades ago. In every subsequent visit, I have found Toronto to be as large-hearted, as charmingly self-obsessed, as earnestly progressive, as amiably decent, and as endearingly dotty as anyone could ask a megalopolis to be.

Globe and Mail, June 6, 2007

Parasaurolophus

WHY IS IT THAT the image of *Parasaurolophus walkeri* produces something akin to nostalgia in me? As far as I can recall, the fifties and early sixties, the years of my childhood, were pretty much free from the dinosaur obsession that causes today's kids to vibrate like tuning forks. A quick flit through the internet provides evidence that there was some ancient reptile-creep into pop culture during those decades: the first plastic, mass-produced dinosaur toys appeared; Godzilla was wreaking cinematic mayhem in Japan; "The Flintstones" was a hit on ABC in 1960; and, apparently, gleeful children were digging dinosaur toys out of the bottom of cereal boxes. Maybe living in the rural gulag of Esterhazy, Saskatchewan, quarantined me from terrible lizard fever, but my excavations in the arid rubble of breakfast-cereal boxes unearthed nothing but baking soda–powered frogmen, submarines, and plastic GIs. No dinosaurs.

In elementary school, nothing much was said about primeval reptiles. I have a vague recollection of teachers dismissing them as lumbering dolts that had lost the evolutionary race to more nimble and quick-witted mammals, which, it was implied, had reached their apotheosis in us, a bunch of crewcutted, pigtailed nose-pickers for whom a fabulous future awaited as long as we knuckled down, studied hard, and got more *mammalian* so we could leave those reptilian Russkies in the dust.

The tone of pedagogy in the fifties was frantically sanguine. Sure, the first half of the century had experienced some setbacks: two world wars, the Holocaust, and now the threat of nuclear annihilation was hanging over all our heads, but hey, look at these neat artists' illustrations of what's just around the corner: Towering skyscrapers looped by superhighways that will hurtle you to your destination in automobiles that don't require human guidance. Vehicles that will allow the man in the grey flannel suit to sit back, relax, enjoy a martini on his way home to the nuclear family without risk of a drunken death. And see, here's a magnificent city under a glass dome with a perfectly controlled climate, and in that metropolis, nutritionally balanced meals will be available in convenient pills that gyroscope-commuters can pop on their way to work, etc.

The never-stated but clear implication of all this was that dinosaurs were *losers* and losers were what none of us should ever be.

This hectoring, aggressive, competition-fuelled optimism continued into high school, peaking in 1967, Canada's Centennial year, perhaps the most aggressively upbeat year in the history of the country, a time when Bobby Gimby's bouncy tune became the insidious earworm of an entire nation ("CA-NA-DA, One little two little three Canadians"). This was the year I paid my first visit to Toronto and the ROM, an institution that charmed and awed me.

I was pretty much impressed with everything in the ROM, but the dinosaurs take first rank in my memory. I recall the weird fossils and skeletal reconstructions emanating a ghostly presence that no artist's cheesy renderings of dinosaurs could ever match. I must have encountered *P. walkeri* then, although I have no recollection of it, probably because an adolescent male was more likely to be fascinated with T-Rex, whose potent demeanour and wicked-toothed grin better meshed with never-to-be-realized adolescent male fantasies of total physical awesomeness awaiting you just around the corner—once you lost the pimples and packed some beef on your own skeletal frame.

Now, however, I find *P. walkeri* far more compelling than T-Rex. Probably, this is a function of age. By sixty-two, television and newspapers have fed me so much vicarious carnage that I have come to develop a more favourable opinion of herbivores. And *P. walkeri* has a particularly gentle and vulnerable look to it, that droopy canopy of ribs, that curve of neck that somehow seems too fragile to support that big head and bizarre cranial crest. It's hard to see *P. walkeri* as anything but a *memento mori* with a 73-million-year provenance, a reminder that both winners and losers end up as just one more deposit in another sedimentary layer of our madly spinning earth.

Frankly, these ruminations are afterthoughts. To come clean, my first reaction to this image was, Man, this is one goofy-looking dino. And a nanosecond later: God, he reminds me of Daffy Duck! I admit this is a big stretch. A duckbill in common and a generically goofy appearance are very weak links between a cartoon character and a long-dead saurian, but the longer I gazed at *P. walkeri* the stronger my conviction grew that somewhere, sometime, I had seen something that was prompting me to stuff them into the same mental envelope.

I confess a childhood attachment to Daffy. Daffy's inflated ego, his loudmouthed bluster and expostulation, his haplessness, his put-upon air were far more *simpatico* to me than Bugs Bunny's smooth, streetwise mammalian savvy, which allowed the was-cally wabbit to overcome every obstacle. An impulsive trawl of the internet to renew acquaintance with my favourite duck turned up something intriguing, a posting of a 1939 Loony Tune called *Daffy and the Dino*. Watching it, I had a powerful sense of déjà vu. If that feeling was justified, I must have seen the cartoon on television, which had possibly acquired this outdated product to entertain the preschool crowd.

In this early incarnation of Daffy he is more *P. walkeri*–like than in subsequent versions, his neck frailer and more serpentine, and although never achieving the same Porsche 930 turbo spoiler look of *P. walkeri's* cranial crest, in 1939, Daffy's prominent head feathers swept outwards from the back of his skull rather than assuming the more familiar tufty, feather-foliage silhouette that later jauntily rode the top of his head. The family resemblance between Daffy and *P. walkeri* was marked.

Here was the explanation for my fond feelings for *P. walkeri*. *Daffy and Mr. P were brothers in loserdom!* Dinosaur and duck were everything my teachers had warned me against and that I secretly identified with, which created an affection that I still haven't been able to shake, a fondness for the gloriously maladapted, the misfits, the also-rans of our blue, blue planet.

In *Every Object Has a Story*, Royal Ontario Museum (Anansi, 2013)

Remembering Avie Bennett,
a Charming Rascal

IN 1985, MCCLELLAND & STEWART, publisher of many of Canada's most illustrious and popular writers, was teetering on financial collapse. Then Avie Bennett, like one of those folkloric "Broadway angels" who step in to resuscitate a cash-starved musical, bought the company and kept the house lights burning brightly at M&S for the next fourteen years. In 2000, he donated 75 per cent of his shares in M&S to the University of Toronto, with Random House acquiring the remaining 25 per cent, marking the end of a curious interval in publishing history in which a highly successful real estate developer proved he could navigate, with verve and panache, the often closed and hermetic world of Canadian letters.

Avie Bennett was not only a boon to Canadian literature, he was a longtime supporter of the National Ballet of Canada and the Art Gallery of Ontario, as well as a committed citizen deeply engaged in education and public policy. Over his long career he served as chancellor of York University, chair of the Historica Foundation of Canada, president of International Readings at Harbourfront, honorary chair of the Board of Trustees of the Art Gallery of Ontario, and co-chair of the Canadian Democracy and Accountability Commission that issued a stinging report urging greater social responsibility on the part of corporations.

In recognition of his public service and unstinting philanthropy, Avie Bennett was awarded a Companion of the Order of Canada, an Order of Ontario, three honorary degrees, and many other distinctions.

Sometimes, however, honours obscure the individuals they decorate, reducing them to a type, cookie-cutter "distinguished Canadians." There is no denying that Avie *was* a truly distinguished Canadian, but he was also a quirky, larger-than-life character, a grand original with a razor-sharp mind, a savage wit, and an irresistible sense of fun.

I first met him when I became part of an author exodus that saw writers such as Alice Munro, Robertson Davies, W. O. Mitchell, Mavis Gallant, and Jack Hodgins depart storm-tossed Macmillan of Canada for the more serene shores of M&S. My introduction to Avie was a cursory one as far as I can recall, no more than a handshake and a perfunctory how-do-you-do. It was only when David Staines was appointed editor of the New Canadian Library and he invited Alice Munro, Bill New, and me to serve on the advisory board of the NCL that I came to appreciate firsthand Avie's remarkable character, to witness his fierce sense of honour, to relish his nimble intelligence, his passion for the literature and history of this country, his delight in mischief-making, and his blunt, oh-so-blunt way of taking on the world.

What I liked best about Avie was that he was a bit of a charming rascal. He loved the fact that as chancellor of York University, he kept Mordecai Richler surreptitiously supplied with Scotch onstage while Richler awaited an honorary degree in a lengthy convocation ceremony that slowly and inexorably trudged ever onward. But Avie was equally amused when I made a short speech at a dinner held in his honour at York University and referred to him as the Iron Chancellor, adding that in my experience he was a man who hid an iron fist in a glove of steel, my small revenge for his habit of jumping on me with the wry observation "And you call yourself a writer" whenever he detected me making an ungrammatical slip of the tongue.

There were times when Avie and I bumped heads—sometimes that's what writers and publishers do—but I never doubted that he was a man of the utmost integrity, someone whose word was his bond. Avie Bennett had no time for unethical people, frequently saying he couldn't do business with anyone he wouldn't invite home to dinner, a rather stringent standard of commercial conduct in today's business climate. His honesty and fair dealing earned him the respect of his writers and often their friendship. When Avie left M&S, I made a point of keeping in touch with him. Feeling somewhat guilty for having eaten so many dinners at his expense, I invited him to lunch. His response was, "Great. It's been some time since I dined beneath the Golden Arches."

Yet Avie's flinty manner shielded a tender heart. When my wife Margaret was dying and I was struggling to look after her at home, Avie frequently called me, lending calm and practical counsel. Sensing my increasing desperation as things grew more and more dire, he made an astounding proposal. He told me he would happily pay for Margaret's stay in a private care home. This was an offer I could not accept, but it is one that speaks eloquently of Avie Bennett's great compassion and generosity. For me, of all the things about this unforgettable man this remains the most unforgettable. Avie Bennett was much more than a publishing icon and distinguished Canadian; he was a *mensch*.

Globe and Mail, June 9, 2017

The University and the River

HAVING TOTTERED INTO my golden years, the sight of my portrait superimposed on an aerial view of Saskatoon leaves me awash in nostalgia. I don't mean naughty French *nostalgie de la boue*, but the basted-in-rosy-memory sort of nostalgia that writers are supposed to refrain from. But looking at this painting, I realize I am viewing the background to my writing life. Fifty years ago, I arrived here, a seventeen-year-old kid from a small Saskatchewan town for a trial run at the University of Saskatchewan, a run that, given my dismal academic performance in high school, I was certain would prove a headlong sprint to failure. I was only a college student because my mother had discovered that, somehow, I had met the bare minimum requirements for admission at the U of S and had enrolled me there while I was off in British Columbia trying to figure out my life. What I thought would be a very short stay in Saskatoon turned into a half-century sojourn, my loyalty to the city due to the fact that the university had awakened in me an interest in writing fiction and, later, had given me part-time employment.

I remember wandering the stacks of the old Murray Memorial Library as a freshman, stopping whenever a title caught my eye, and thinking, "If I want to, I can read that." I had grown up in a town where the school and town libraries were stocked with the sort of books that you find at church jumble sales, books that manage to be both excruciatingly life-affirming and agonizingly mind-deadening. Suddenly, I had stumbled on writers who spoke of a world that I had never imagined existed. With that accident, everything changed for me.

In John Hartman's painting, the university sits just a little farther back from the third bridge off my left shoulder. But in the picture I carry in my head, the university always sits squarely in the middle of the city because that's how it sits in my mind. After all, the university gave a centre to my life, became the hub around which my aspirations began to turn. There I was taught how to *really* read, the first step in becoming a writer.

The South Saskatchewan River has also left its mark on me. It meanderingly bisects the painting, but while the river physically divides the city, it also draws it together. On the banks of the Saskatchewan, people come to jog and walk and cycle, or simply to lollygag and soak up sunshine. During my student years, I seldom lived more than a few blocks from this sinuous, beautiful, liquid chord that pulses through the city's heart. Walking Saskatoon's bridges, I have seen the river smoke with winter cold or flash scales of eye-aching light under the hot summer sun. I have sat on its brushy east bank, a young man with an old Audubon bird book in his hand, birds darting and chittering around me. A moment of peace so piercing that now, during sleepless nights, I feel I must have dreamed it.

So, the university and the river. A sappy, nostalgia-drenched greeting card addressed to myself.

In *Many Lives Mark This Place: Canadian Writers in Portrait, Landscape, and Prose,* by John Hartman (Figure 1 Publishing, 2019)

The Writer and Writing 2:
History and Literature

The Wars

AFTER THIRTY YEARS, I can recall with unlikely and surprising clarity when I first read Timothy Findley's glorious novel *The Wars*. I was on the last leg of a long bus trip, the coach clattering over a rough rural road on a dark winter night, the wan beam of the overhead reading light skittering back and forth on the page, the book shuddering in my hands at every bump, and a case of motion sickness threatening. Yet I could not stop reading. At intervals, I would look up to rest my eyes on the surround of blackness pressing against the window, then plunge back into the story of Robert Ross, his family, his friends, and his comrades-in-arms as they whirled helplessly in the maelstrom of the Great War, the war that was supposed to end all wars and didn't. I arrived at my destination with the book finished, strangely exalted and disturbed by an encounter with a novel harrowing and uplifting, a novel that was both a marvellous work of art and a passionate indictment of the first cruel idiocy of the twentieth century.

A few years later, I attended a reading given by Timothy Findley. When it was over, I insinuated myself into a group of admirers gathered around him and lingered hopefully until a lull in the small talk gave me the opportunity to blurt out my enthusiasm for *The Wars*. In short order, I heard myself erratically veering here, there, and everywhere like one of those shopping carts with a wonky, ungovernable wheel, trying desperately to touch upon everything I thought wonderful about his novel. With his typically graceful touch, Findley tactfully intervened, saving me from the embarrassing babble in which I was drowning and steering me out of the unfathomable depths of *The Wars* and into safer, shallower conversational waters. My one attempt to tell him what this book meant to me ended in miserable failure.

Now, many years later, having reread *The Wars* many times, I am still unable to find the words to adequately express its greatness. The more acquainted I become with it, the less I *know* it, the more enigmatic, unfathomable, and profound a work it becomes. I am left with nothing but vague intuitions and haphazard guesses about the magic Findley worked to create a magical book.

For one thing, at every turn *The Wars* runs counter to the usual expectations about what a war novel is or should be. Most are Big Books, volumes of ponderous heft and authority. Tolstoy's *War and Peace*, Mailer's *The Naked and the Dead*, Jones's *From Here to Eternity*, even Hemingway's relatively slender *A Farewell to Arms* and *For Whom the Bell Tolls* leave *The Wars* looking like a mere pamphlet. Perhaps only Remarque's *All Quiet on the Western Front* manages so efficiently to compress and distill the horrors of combat in so few pages. But unlike Remarque, Findley achieves his impressive economy by piecing together a collage of arresting images and brief, telling scenes that not only cohere in a compelling narrative, but whose form mimics the fractured lives of soldiers and civilians shattered by war. Like the narrator who painstakingly assembles Robert Ross's story from interviews, photographs, and archival materials, or like the inhabitants of the "Stained Glass Dugout," Findley builds a magnificent construction from carefully selected scraps. The picture he presents is never whole and complete, yet it is all the more evocative, all the more transfixing because we are constantly made aware of its brokenness.

But the word *picture* may be misleading, suggesting something static and fixed rather than the flow of images that animates *The Wars*. This is an intensely cinematic novel. Jump-cuts leap back and forth in time, dart from location to location. The opening tableau might have been lifted from a film by Akira Kurosawa. Riveting in its initial stillness, pregnant with possibility, it is the departure point for a train of swiftly accelerating scenes that inexorably gather momentum and power. Imagine the camera holding on a horse frozen in a hieratic pose, head bowed, right front hoof raised. A dog lies beside her. In the background, a warehouse burns. The camera moves to Robert Ross, motionless as the horse, his uniform in disarray, his nose broken. The camera pans the field, registering icons of destruction. Robert Ross moves, action commences.

Pairs of horses and dogs appear like solitary markers throughout the novel, statuary modelled in slightly varying attitudes. When Clifford Purchas and Robert Ross chance on Eugene Taffler on the prairie, Taffler's mount is seen grazing nearby, the dog sitting with its ears erect. Outside the whorehouse in Lousetown they are encountered once more, the horse standing head lowered. As Ross passes through Regina, his train is watched by a group of Indigenous people. One is mounted and the horse's head is bowed. The image resurfaces again and again like a recurring dream until, as the climax of the novel approaches, Findley repeats verbatim the two pages that begin *The Wars*, every gesture coalescing with the force of a premonition ripened into a reality.

Although I stress how visual a book *The Wars* is, it needs to be said that Findley manages words every bit as craftily and subtly as he composes pictures. "She was standing in the middle of the railroad tracks," the first sentence announces; this is followed by "her head was bowed and her right front hoof was raised as if she rested." "Right front hoof" delivers a mild surprise, corrects assumptions. Oh, we say, it is not a woman he describes but a *horse.* The deployment of pronouns carries as much weight in the novel as the images that represent them. Midpoint in *The Wars*, Rodwell refers to the toad he harbours in the dugout as "he," and Levitt immediately attempts to put him right. "I thought it was improper, sir, to refer to animals as *he* and *she*," he says. Rodwell replies, "Well—I suppose in the strictest sense—perhaps. It depends on how well you know them." For Findley, even something as apparently trivial as pronoun choice is a judgment on perspective, a declaration of how characters inhabit and regard the world. Rodwell and Ross acknowledge the universality of suffering, whether animal or human, and that empathy destroys them both. Faced with the likelihood of his own death, Ross notes, "Anyone in hiding was an imitation animal." Sheltered in the barn with the horses he hopes to rescue, Ross dooms himself by calling out to the troops that have encircled them, "We shall not be taken." For Mickle, the officer in command, "we" can mean only one thing, that Ross has human accomplices, and so the fateful step to fire the barn is made. A devastating outcome hinges on a single word, a word that is also a moral emblem.

Like Mickle, who could not grasp the meaning of Ross's *we*, I have never been able to decipher Findley's eccentric use of the plural in his title, *The Wars*. By now, I'm sure hundreds of undergraduate essays have been written and graded, earnest attempts to measure its meaning. It may suggest that war is an endless continuum, the natural state of humankind, and that peace is the real anomaly. It may refer to the domestic and sexual violence that dwells in the novel, even perhaps to the conflicting impulses that lurk in Robert Ross's heart and that tear him apart. Et cetera, et cetera. But in the end, an index doesn't satisfy. That Findley set great store by the phrase is obvious because he employs the plural again and again: "Just like a savage painted for the wars," "the Civil Wars." It even appears highlighted in italics. As Robert Ross departs Montreal bound for England, and his mother, drunk and unable to say goodbye, watches the leave-taking between her husband and son, Findley writes, "*Come on back to the raf*', *Huck honey.*' And this is what they called *the wars.*" But these two sentences defy logic. Who are *they*? And what is the relationship of this poignant appeal quoted from *The Adventures of Huckleberry Finn* to the assertion that follows?

The connection cannot be construed, only felt, and felt for what it is, a moment so emotionally charged, so apposite to circumstances, as to take your breath away. Like the frieze of horse and dog, or the occasional glimpse of Harris's blue scarf, *the wars* hovers in the reader's consciousness, heard as the faintest of dire whispers. It is as impossible to boil simple meaning from these two words as it is to impute clear and unambiguous motives for Ross's actions, or to determine how many angels can dance on the head of a pin.

Just as I *sense* the appositeness of Findley's title, I *feel* I understand Robert Ross in some deep, gut-wrenching way despite the fact that Findley supplies only limited access to the consciousness of his hero, whose interior world is largely shielded from prying eyes. Certainly, he offers little of what could be described as Ross's thoughts—no tortured musings, no probing or dissecting of his precarious psychological state. Only Marian Turner and Lady Juliet d'Orsey, the latter a "Boswell in bows," speculate or draw inferences about what lies at the root of Ross's conduct. Perhaps Findley's apprenticeship as an actor led him to adopt the inspired approach of letting Ross reveal himself only by his actions. After all, as Findley maintains in *The Wars*, "People can only be found in what they do." This is where I find Robert Ross.

If Ross is dramatically located in what he does, the anonymous narrator of *The Wars* is a spectral presence. Who is he? Or she? What relation exists between this narrator and Ross, which is strong enough to compel her or him to pursue his story so relentlessly? Knowing that Findley relied on family photographs, as well as the wartime correspondence of his uncle, Thomas Irving Findley, to help him write *The Wars* might prompt one to identify the author with his ghostly narrator. Yet that would be to fall into the mistake of the biographical fallacy, and also to fail to recognize that this unnamed figure is, above all, a cunning narrative strategy.

I am convinced *The Wars* is as much a novel about the writing of history as it is about war, which makes it a distant cousin to Tolstoy's *War and Peace*, and it is the narrative voice that leads me to make this supposition. A lesser novelist would have adopted a more obvious route, neatly tying up what appear to be loose ends by establishing the narrator in the foreground of the novel and providing answers about her or his identity and motivation. Instead, Findley exploits this disembodied voice in as ingenious and fluid a way as he does the imagery of the book. Sometimes this voice provides tiny historical essays to place events in the novel in a larger context; sometimes it slyly confesses to restricted knowledge and transparently speculates about what may or may not have actually happened; sometimes it simply offers a record of the interviews; and at other times it assumes a godlike authority, supplying specific details or emotions that any human narrator, no matter how diligent, could not be privy to and would have had to imagine. This unique and flexible way of telling the story also provides a running commentary on the problems encountered by any attempt to comprehend the past, mingling as it does evidence resurrected by research with rational interpretation while still managing to shrewdly draw our attention to the subjectivity of all observations and assumptions.

The Wars is the finest historical novel ever written by a Canadian and, like all serious historical novels, is as much about the present as the past that they claim to spread before our eyes. The people historical novels portray are often us, disguised in our grandfathers' and grandmothers' clothes. In this novel, Findley states that "distance [is] safety." From the safety of thirty years' distance, I see now that my first, visceral response to *The Wars* was not just to a work of art, but also to an important cultural and historical document. *The Wars* was published in 1977, and the seventies were a decade that saw a marked renewal of nationalism in English Canada. A residue of the euphoria brought on by the Centennial celebrations of 1967 and the success of the Montreal Expo still lingered, and along with it, a certain pride in and sense of national possibility. This was countered by a growing anxiety about American economic, cultural, and political influence in the country, particularly among Canadian artists and intellectuals, many of whom had been roused to action by George Grant's warnings in *Lament for a Nation* that a distinct Canadian identity was being eroded by the implacable force of America's homogenizing tendencies. In broad strokes, this was the mood of the times. In *The Wars*, Findley reminds us of the need "to clarify who you are through your response to when you lived. If you can't do that, then you haven't made your contribution to the future." Findley's contribution to the future of Canadian literature was to write *The Wars*.

By this I don't mean to say that he sat down and wrote a political tract disguised as a novel. Nothing could be further from the truth. What Findley did do was to dare to write a novel that radically shifted historical perspective. He moved Canadians from the periphery of a seminal event in world history and set them firmly down in its centre. He didn't do this in a jingoistic or tub-thumping fashion, but rather as discreetly as he used *he* or *she* or *we* when referring to animals—so that the realignment of viewpoint seems *matter of fact*. The second section of the novel contains this observation: "At the centre of the world is Ypres." Here the novel moves abruptly from past tense to present, as if the Canadian soldiers' experience of the Great War as their "centre of the world" endures, remains fully alive, can never be extinguished. And it does something more: it once again asserts that perspective depends on experience. All roads lead to Rome, but perhaps only if one is Roman.

During the seventies on a visit to London, I met a young Australian woman who was stunned that her employers expected her to show up for work the next day. "How could that be?" she wondered aloud. "Tomorrow is Anzac Day." It was inexplicable to her that an Australian national holiday consecrated to the memory of the Australians and New Zealanders who had perished on the beaches of Gallipoli could possibly be ignored in Britain. As naïve as her bewilderment was, it merely drives home Findley's point about historical perspective.

Using his own unerring historical instincts, Findley situates his novel in Ypres, the killing field where Canadian troops doggedly held the line against German gas attacks and where, in one day, the Canadian Division lost half its infantry in captured, dead, and wounded. The battle of Vimy Ridge is most often celebrated as a clear-cut Canadian victory, but those who survived Ypres proudly dubbed themselves the Old Originals in honour of the unique identity, as Canadians, that they believed they had forged there. If others failed to see them as distinct, they knew who they were. A Belgian peasant whom Robert Ross encounters refuses to see him as anything but English, but Ross asserts, "*Je suis canadien!*"

I was twenty-six or twenty-seven when I first encountered *The Wars*, and I saw my country in it. The novel did not prompt any bogus, hyperventilating patriotism, simply a thrill of recognition. A prairie boy, I even took a small satisfaction in the mention of Regis from Regina. Perhaps this is laughable, but I had been required to make scrupulously exact drawings of the Union Jack in the first grade, and from twelve years of public schooling I had managed to acquire the notion that, in the grand scheme of things, Canadian was a synonym for second-rate.

As a young man who wanted to write fiction and to write it about Canada, I was unknowingly in search of a model, some reassurance that it could be done, and done well. Reading *The Wars*, I found that reassurance. More than anything else, this is what I wanted to thank Timothy Findley for the night I accosted him after his reading.

The Wars is a great book, rich in its images, its language, its construction, and, ultimately, its conception. Its richness cannot be exhausted; although every reading yields something new, *The Wars* remains an elusive work that jealously guards its mysteries. Perhaps this has something to do with the ultimate irreducibility of meaning that is the hallmark of great literature. Interpretations of *The Wars* multiply and expand; it is both familiar and strange each time I engage with it. This, too, I wished I could have said to Timothy Findley that night long ago—to have given him some sense of how I appreciated his gift, to have let him know that *The Wars* has always been and, shall remain for me, the loveliest, the most moving of novels.

Introduction to *The Wars*, by Timothy Findley (Penguin, 2005)

Literature and the
Teaching of History

IT IS NOT UNCOMMON for our sense of a particular historical period or historical figure to be conditioned by a purely literary experience. For a good many English-speakers, what knowledge they have of ancient Rome, of Julius Caesar, of Mark Antony, of Brutus or Octavius has its source in Shakespeare's *Julius Caesar*. Efforts at rehabilitating the reputation of Richard III are confounded because the same playwright's portrait of a treacherous, tyrannical, and malignant prince is not easily expunged from the public mind. Examples multiply. The French Revolution is Dickens's *A Tale of Two Cities*, while Margaret Mitchell's *Gone with the Wind* is the final word for many on the American Civil War. In fact, it could be argued that it has been imaginative writers and not historians who have taught most of us our history.

To teachers of history this may simply be seen as something to be regretted and lamented. What they ought not to do is shrug their shoulders and despair. Obviously, literature is a potent force in the shaping of historical understanding, so potent that it often prevails over the versions expounded in high school history texts. It is tempting then to regard literature as the antagonist of history, a seductive spinner of dazzling lies while virtuous Clio clings to the truth and nothing but the truth. That would be a misreading of the situation. The success of literature simply lies in this: fiction and poetry often do well those things that historians frequently neglect to do or do badly. Literature, in an immediate and sensual way, provides some notion of the texture of life in the past. A novel can convey graphically to a student how women and men of a previous time worshipped, fought, dined, traded, married, died. This makes literature a marvellous supplement to the typical textbook. It puts flesh on the historical skeleton, supplies missing pieces to the bewildering historical puzzle.

Textbook history has difficulty in providing students with an appreciation of the realities of the past. By and large, its goals are to reduce and abstract. Confronted with the task of encompassing vast stretches of time and explaining complex and tangled events, textbook writers must condense and generalize. They do this job well, but it is difficult to deny that in the process something is lost. By necessity, condensation and compression diminish detail and particularity, those things which help to distinguish one epoch or people from another. Unless led to see otherwise, students can readily assume that aside from certain minor oddities (powdered wigs and cocked hats) or technological backwardness (no television, no airplanes), the people of long ago were very much like ourselves in the way they envisioned the world. When this occurs, students become trapped in a type of provincialism; they cannot conceive of any point of view but their own, and this point of view achieves the status of something universal and constant. If the facts belie these suppositions, all history is apt to appear absurd and inexplicable. Even historical analogy is rendered impossible. A secular age cannot begin to fathom the religious wars of the seventeenth century because most of our contemporaries in the western world don't see religion as something worth fighting over. This makes it difficult for us to understand that for many people of the sixteenth century religion was so important that they were prepared to persecute their fellows over questions of doctrine or go to war against princes who promulgated heresy. Deep in their bones, people of the seventeenth century believed that religion was of the utmost importance. If we lack the imagination to grasp that, how can we detect the similarities between those religious wars and the great ideological wars of our own century?

Literature can be a springboard that assists us to make this imaginative leap through the centuries. By dramatizing thought and belief and emotion, by making them stir fictional women and men to action, by placing these people in the grand or homely circumstances appropriate to their station in life, we can experience a fleeting flavour of the past.

Consider attempting to explain to today's students how the prospect of sudden death from disease might have influenced the behaviour of people in an earlier time. It is unlikely they have lost loved ones to communicable disease or faced such death themselves. It is true they live in an age of great anxiety, but anxiety of a different kind. What can they know of this particular dread? A teacher or a textbook can *tell* them what the consequences of the ever-present fear of contagion are likely to be, but the impression made is likely to be faint.

But what if they could be conducted back into history and have as their guide a master realist such as Daniel Defoe, a man desperately concerned in his own time with the prevention and control of epidemics? Defoe's *A Journal of the Plague Year* was written at a time when England faced the prospect of a recurrence of the plague of 1665 which had decimated London, a plague which still lived in memory. Defoe's book touches on phenomena that an outbreak of contagion would have had an influence upon: medical practice, the weakening of social and moral codes, the rise of superstition and sorcery, the growth of antagonism between the rich and the poor. In his selection of a single, telling anecdote, Defoe enables us to see and understand what pages of exposition could not. In a simple paragraph that eschews all exaggeration and melodrama he shows us how the fear of human contact that accompanies the spread of plague permeates life. Defoe writes:

> It is true, people used all possible precaution. When any one bought a joint of meat in the market, they would not take it of the butcher's hand, but took it off the hooks themselves. On the other hand, the butcher would not touch the money, but have it put into a pot full of vinegar, which he kept for that purpose. The buyer carried always small money to make up any odd sum, that they might take no change. They carried bottles of scents and perfumes in their hands, and all the means that could be used were used, but then the poor could not do even these things, and they went at all hazards.

That pot of vinegar fixes itself in the mind and speaks volumes.

Of course, this is not an argument in favour of supplanting the high school history text with novels, plays, and poems. It is an argument for the judicious use of these things (or even short passages from them) to give students a fuller, more complete appreciation of history. It is also an acknowledgement that the good text accomplishes what the novel, play, or poem cannot accomplish. Literature is likely to concern itself with the intimate and personal response to the motions of history; textbooks seek to convey the sweep of time, the march of events, the consequences of cause and effect. Each offers a unique vantage point from which to regard the past.

If using literature in a history class is a valuable exercise, decisions about what books to use are never easy. First of all, the choices must be appropriate, capable of being understood, and there is no sure guide to that. The more distant the time being studied, the more likely its literature is to erect barriers to comprehension in the form of archaic language and outdated literary

conventions. For many students, such barriers may be insurmountable. Sometimes the historical novel offers a workable compromise. While a medieval romance is likely to prove impenetrable to
the vast majority of students, one of Alfred Duggan's novels of
life in the Middle Ages, presented in lucid prose, may be able to
engage, delight, and inform them.

However, as a general rule, I think it better to allow the past
to speak for itself in its own accents whenever possible. For a sense
of the impact of nineteenth-century industrialization, Dickens is
likely to be a better and truer source than a historical novelist
writing with hindsight and the condescension that hindsight so
often occasions. The value of Dickens lies in two things. First,
he weaves a rich tapestry of the textures of Victorian daily life,
the sort of detail that Defoe provides. Second, Dickens himself
and his attitudes provide insight into the convictions and preju-
dices of a liberal middle-class gentleman of his day. In his novel
Hard Times, Dickens clearly condemns the deplorable conditions
of working men and women, but it is also clear that he despises
and distrusts unionism. The novel has a lot to teach us about the
cast of the Victorian reformer's mind when it came to the sanctity
of property and the aversion to granting any real power to the
lower orders. Novels written in the midst of dispute and ferment
are likely to capture the spirit of such times more authentically
than the common run of historical novel because, oddly enough,
many practitioners of this genre appear to be deficient of real
historical sense. Bad historical novelists ignore the psychological
realities of the period they attempt to depict, believing their job is
done when they have scrupulously researched the externals: dress,
cuisine, weapons, and so on. That done, the novelist transports
contemporary people into the past, costumed in armour or togas
as if they were got up for a fancy-dress ball, and leaves it at that.
Perhaps this reluctance to truly imaginatively inhabit the past is
a result of the writer understanding all too well how difficult it

is for many readers to care about characters whose opinions may be opposed to those now widely held. So readers' sensibilities are often soothed by some hero or heroine advocating ideas that we currently regard as self-evident but would have been dismissed as lunatic in an earlier epoch. Unfortunately, all but the very best of what goes by the name of historical fiction is often profoundly unhistorical.

On the other hand, the literature representative of a particular period often gives access into the minds of those who lived it. From the vantage point of the 1980s, how can we grasp the feelings of liberation and joy with which young men all over Europe and the British Empire greeted the outbreak of the First World War? Maybe a few lines from Rupert Brooke's "Peace," written at the beginning of hostilities, sum it up best.

> Now, God be thanked Who has matched us with His
>   hour,
> And caught our youth, and wakened us from sleeping,
> With hand made sure, clear eye, and sharpened power,
> To turn, as swimmers into cleanness leaping,
> Glad from a world grown old and cold and weary,
> Leave the sick hearts that honour could not move,
> And half-men, and their dirty songs and dreary.
> And all the little emptiness of love!

And what clearer or more moving statement of the disillusioning road such young men travelled than Wilfrid Owen's ironically entitled "Dulce et Decorum Est," written after his horrific experience of trench warfare. The "swimmers into cleanness leaping" are now

> Bent double, like old beggars under sacks,

Knock-kneed, coughing like hags, we cursed through
    sludge,
Till on the haunting flares we turned our backs,
And towards our distant rest began to trudge.
Men marched asleep. Many had lost their boots,
But limped on, blood-shod. All went lame; all blind;
Drunk with fatigue; deaf even to the hoots
Of gas-shells dropping softly behind.

A similar record of disenchantment with war from the German side is to be found in Erich Maria Remarque's harrowing *All Quiet on the Western Front*, which also reflects, like Owen's work, the alteration in the European spirit produced by the First World War. Both writers illustrate the rewards of using literary works in the teaching of history, giving students the opportunity to note change other than technological change, allowing them to see how great events can alter consciousness. The change may not be measurable, but it can easily be remarked and felt imaginatively. By putting a face to our forebears, literature provides students with an opportunity to see the human in historical processes, to let them see the vinegar pot in the shop. Most importantly, literature provides the student with something that approaches unmediated contact with the past. Most of the time, something or somebody stands between the student and the past itself, either a teacher or a textbook. In the pages of Homer's *Odyssey*, or Robert Penn Warren's *All the King's Men*, students are addressed directly by voices from another age. If they listen closely and with respect to these voices, they may travel a long way towards gaining a truer historical understanding.

The History and Social Science Teacher, Spring 1987

Apprehending the Past: History Versus the Historical Novel

I WOULD LIKE to express my deep appreciation to St. Thomas More College for inviting me to give this year's Keenan Lecture and to thank the Keenan family for their generosity in funding this lecture series in memory of the first dean of STM, Dr. Michael Keenan. In the past, many distinguished scholars, men and women of great learning, have delivered these addresses. I fear that this evening the college breaks with tradition since I can make no claim to scholarship. In fact, it has been a long, long time since I was required to dangle a footnote in a text.

Most of my adult life has been spent writing fiction and teaching creative writing—occupations not acclaimed for their theoretical or analytical rigour. Although my topic tonight touches on the disciplines of history and literature, I am a specialist in neither. Much of what I have to say is informed by my experiences as a working writer who has devoted the past twenty years of his life to attempting to apprehend the past in historical fiction, and I use the word "apprehend" in its several senses: to take into custody, to understand, and to approach with anxiety. In my case, an anxiety heightened by the fact that I once contemplated a career as an academic historian but abandoned that plan when I realized I was an unfit candidate for the profession, like a myopic aspiring to be a fighter pilot. Nevertheless, that said, most writers of historical fiction, whether they studied history or not, exhibit uneasiness in the presence of the senior sibling, history proper, which is likely, at best, to give them a patronizing pat on the head and consign them to the children's table.

And yet historians themselves display a certain uneasiness of their own, appear not to be all that serene about the state of historical studies, are prone both to worry about its declining influence and to fear that trespassers are invading their territory. One concern is the enormous popularity of works produced by amateur historians, much of which the celebrated historian Margaret MacMillan judges to be shoddy, inferior goods. She states in *The Uses and Abuses of History*:

> Bad history tells only part of complex stories. It claims
> knowledge which it could not possibly have, as when, for
> example, it purports to give the unspoken thoughts of its
> characters. It makes sweeping generalizations for which
> there is not adequate evidence and ignores awkward facts
> which do not fit. It demands too much of its protagonists,
> as when it expects them to have had insights or made
> decisions they could not possibly have done. The lessons
> such history teaches are too simple or simply wrong.

J. L. Granatstein, in his polemic *Who Killed Canadian History*, offers another perspective, ascribing a good deal of the blame for the perceived failing health of the discipline to professional historians themselves. Granatstein, a man who shows a preference for the meat cleaver over the scalpel when it comes to carving up his colleagues, caustically asserts that

> the vast majority of scholarly books are destined to
> remain unread on university library shelves.... The
> point is not that scholarly publishing is unnecessary. It is

vitally necessary that research into our past and present be undertaken in the universities. However, one may legitimately question the use of public funds to publish books whose only true value is to secure tenure or promotion in the universities for the authors. The unreadable sludge could be circulated to the three interested readers in *samizdat* form or made available on the internet.

Both MacMillan's and Granatstein's dismissals are based on the *quality* of the historical production, examples of Gresham's Law at work: bad currency pushing out good coin of the realm. On the one hand, the counterfeiters are clumsy amateurs, on the other, ivory-tower careerists. Yet as pointed as these criticisms may be, perhaps the most searching critique of historical practice is to be found in the work of Hayden White, an academic historian himself, a man of whom Robert Doran says, "... one would have to return to the nineteenth century to find a thinker who has had a greater impact on the way we think about historical representation, the discipline of history, and on how historiography intersects with other domains of inquiry, particularly literary studies."

What White dared to do was to question and dissect the often-repeated assertion that history is both a science and an art. The aspiration of history to be "scientific" was first enunciated by Leopold von Ranke who, in the nineteenth century, famously insisted that only a thorough study of primary sources, of original documents, could provide the foundation for historical truth. Ranke assumed that diligent research could supply historians with raw material to which they could turn an "innocent eye," an eye objective and essentially scientific, fully capable of uncovering the truth about former times. The claim that history was a science was reasserted by Marx and, later in the twentieth century, by the

Annales school in France, which emphasized the role of analysis in revealing abstract historical laws. The *Annales* school was critical of political and narrative histories because they fell into the trap of false "dramatic" and "novelistic" representations of the past, which they scorned for aping the conventions of fiction.

The Anglo-American tradition, where the narrative mode of history has largely predominated, has been inclined to be more accepting of the science and art description, although given the immense prestige accruing to science and scientists, the emphasis chiefly came to be placed on the science aspect of the formulation. For most historians, the "art" side of the equation has been taken to be synonymous with the "style" or "ornamentation" of the historical narrative, the flavourful gravy spooned onto the beef.

White took issue with these assumptions. In an influential essay, "The Burden of History," he claimed that historians' notions of what constituted science were laughably outdated and naïve, writing, "Many historians continue to treat their 'facts' as though they were 'given' and refuse to recognize, unlike most scientists, that they are not so much found as constructed by the kinds of questions which the investigator asks of the phenomena before him."

This kick to the historical hornet's nest produced a buzz of outrage. White was accused of undercutting the prestige of a discipline that based much of its credibility on its respect for "facts." But White went even further by suggesting that history had stronger resemblances to fiction than many had been willing to credit. I have neither the time here nor the acumen to attempt any explication of White's assertion that "emplotment," and master tropes such as metaphor, metonymy, synecdoche exist at a deep structural level in a historical text, governing not only the formal structure of a history but investing it with meanings beyond those of simple cause-effect explanations. It is sufficient to point out that it is White's conviction that history *cannot be written* without recourse to "story-types that form the cultural patrimony of every civilization and community."

But while emphasizing the "art" element in history, White most certainly did not depart from the Rankean notion that recourse to the archives is the bedrock of historical writing, noting that

> in the research phase of their work, historians are concerned to discover the truth about the past and to recover information either forgotten, suppressed, or obscured, and, of course, to make of it whatever sense they can. But between this research phase, which is really quite indistinguishable from that of a journalist or a detective, and the completion of a written history, a number of important transformative operations must be performed in which the figurative aspect of the historian's thought is intensified rather than diminished. In the passage from a study of an archive to the composition of a discourse to its translation into a written form, historians must employ the same strategies of linguistic figuration used by imaginative writers.... The kind of interpretation typically produced by the historical discourse is that which endows what would otherwise remain only a chronologically ordered series of events with the formal coherency of the kind of plot structures met with in narrative fiction.

In *The Content of the Form*, White argued further that aesthetic form has a content or meaning that cannot be disentangled from the message it is designed to deliver, advancing a radical claim that history is merely another kind of story, asserting,

Stories are not lived; there is no such thing as a real story. Stories are told or written, not found. And as for the notion of a true story, this is virtually a contradiction in terms. All stories are fictions. Which means, of course, that they can be true only in a metaphorical sense and in the sense in which a figure of speech can be true. Is this true enough?

For conservative historians "all stories are fictions" was a red flag to the bull. In their eyes, it introduced a dangerous relativism to the writing of history. True, historians had always conceded a subjective element in their work—their own differing takes on the same events made that difficult to deny. It was the *degree* of subjectivity that White seemed to be suggesting was inherent in the discipline that raised the alarm. Was White saying that the past could be represented in any way a historian chose? What then was to separate history from propaganda, and was he not giving carte blanche to wild-eyed conspiracy theorists and Holocaust deniers? But this attack on White overlooked his wholehearted acceptance of the legitimacy of documentary evidence. And it ignores the distinction that he drew between writing about "real events" as opposed to writing about "imagined events" and the constraints that the former inevitably imposes on the historian, and how these constraints necessarily influence and shape the creation of a text. White does not suggest that a novel is *exactly* the same thing as a history, only that both tell stories using similar techniques. He maintains that historians are not simple recorders of fact, but interpreters of it, and interpretations can never be literal or absolute. The only legitimate question that can be asked of them is, Is this true enough? Such a standard does not imply that historical interpretations are exempt from judgments about their evidentiary, ethical, or epistemological coherence, simply that they are not incontestable.

Like evidence offered in a court of law, the facts presented by historians may be incomplete, flawed, or distorted. Differing conclusions may be drawn from them. But they ought to be subject to inquiry, debate, and scrutiny about the evidence they offer in the way novels seldom are or should be. To grant an element of subjectivity does not mean that *no* grounds exist for evaluating the "truthfulness" of a work of history. However flawed and provisional those tools of evaluation may be, they are essential and necessary. *Mein Kampf*, too, might be considered as a "subjective interpretation," but does that mean it is impossible to offer a judgment on the coherence and validity of its claims?

Responses to White within the community of academic historians about what constitutes the nature of history play out in the misunderstandings that exist between historians and historical novelists. If academic historians accuse amateur historians of being purveyors of inferior goods, they are likely to condemn historical novelists for being peddlers of far shoddier wares. In the eyes of many historians, writers of historical fiction are nothing but magpies who pick up all the shiny, entertaining bits from the past, tart them up even more, and pass off their gaudy, cheap trinkets on an ignorant, unsuspecting public. In prickly self-defence, historical novelists are likely to retort that the autopsies academic historians perform on the past drain all the blood from it; little wonder that the public recoils from the grey, grinning, lifeless corpse they lay out to be admired in the morgue.

Admittedly, these are caricatures, but like editorial cartoons often do, they capture a little truth. What they don't reveal is that the writing of history and the writing of historical fiction are essentially *different ways of attempting to apprehend the past*. In my view, two things distinguish historical novelists from historians: the intellectual temperament that characterizes the gaze they turn upon the past, and the points of view they habitually employ to express that gaze in words.

I turn to Isaiah Berlin's famous essay on Tolstoy, "The Hedgehog and the Fox," to give some sense of what I mean by "intellectual temperament." Berlin uses the Greek poet Archilochus's observation that "The fox knows many things, but the hedgehog knows one big thing" as a way of classifying different sorts of writers and thinkers. The hedgehogs incline to "one system less or more coherent or articulate ... [while foxes] pursue many ends, often unrelated and contradictory, connected, if at all, only in some *de facto* way...."

Although Berlin applies his formulation to writers of fiction, I would like to alter it somewhat by emphasizing that writers of fiction are temperamentally more fox-like than historians, more likely to be leery of coherent and articulate systems, more comfortable with *de facto* connections and less at ease with the analysis, synthesis, and interpretation that exemplify history proper. What initially drew me to the study of history was the wide-ranging and capacious nature of the discipline, how it touches on so many varieties of human experience. Initially, history looked to be the ideal match for someone like me who has the temperament of a fox, or perhaps, more truthfully, that of a dilettante. History intrigued me because it traversed such a vast, far-flung territory. But what I failed to recognize in my student days was that while the *reading* of history is fox-like, the *writing* of history is essentially the province of the hedgehog.

The second feature that might be said to distinguish historical novels from histories is their narrative tone and how that tone influences their reception by the reader. By tone I mean how a piece of writing *sounds* in the reader's ear, and that is chiefly a product of the point of view adopted, of how the story is told. Most nineteenth-century novelists wrote predominantly, if not exclusively, in the third-person omniscient, a point of view that is all-knowing, its tone detached, distant, and godlike. A tone that conveys *authority*. Twentieth- and twenty-first-century novelists, on the other hand, have not much employed this narrative strategy, opting for other means of storytelling which are more subjective, which strive to create the illusion in the reader of having a more intimate, unmediated access to the thoughts and emotions of the characters in a novel. Experiments in stream of consciousness, a predilection for first-person narration, or some version of a third-person limited (subjective in tone) are common features of contemporary fiction.

As a teacher of creative writing, I bore my students to tears by harping on how the choice of a narrative stance profoundly influences or changes the story told. The content may be the same, but how the reader experiences it is influenced by the manner of telling it.

For instance, fairy tales are typically told in the third-person omniscient. "Once upon a time, a princess lived in a lonely castle high atop a hill, and she was the fairest lady in the land and her hand was sought by countless worthy knights."

Switching the perspective to first-person narration is likely to change the story, even though the information conveyed is much the same. "Like, I knew this princess once who lived in a big old castle on a big old hill, and, like, all the knights thought she would be very *significant* arm candy." The second example is facetious, but the tone has significantly changed the story, even though the "facts" of it are much the same.

Historians favour a narrative stance imbued with an omniscient, godlike tone. This is how it happened; these are the reasons why it happened. Speculation on many points may be tentative but it is couched in measured, judicious tones. The overall impression it leaves is of the *authority* of the narrator. One might say that the subjectivity of the narrator, the historian, is disguised by an essentially omniscient point of view.

As I have suggested, fictional texts generally have a more intimate, subjective tone to them. The American novelist Wallace

Stegner observed, in speaking of his mentor, Bernard DeVoto, a man who wrote both fiction and history:

> A novelist these days is seldom judgmental or omniscient
> in the historical sense. Benny was much better at the
> historical judgment, holding a lot of facts in his head,
> seeing the whole picture, making these pieces fit the pic-
> ture, and being a kind of god manipulating the machine,
> than he was at being a ventriloquist and speaking out
> of a single mouth, or, as he would have to if he were
> a real fictionist, speaking serially out of many mouths.
> Faulkner could speak out of any mouth and be absolutely
> right. That's a major difference between a Benny DeVoto
> and a Faulkner.

Which is only to say that the tools of production—the nar-rative strategy—inevitably result in different products. My first stab at writing historical fiction was defeated because I could not grasp this rather simple and obvious distinction. In 1982, I began a novel that would eventually appear under the title *The Englishman's Boy*, a book that only saw the light of day fourteen years later, an elephantine gestation period. My problem writ-ing it was twofold. One difficulty was that the lingering resi-due of historical training I had received as a graduate student was continually at war with my fox-like novelistic impulses. I was constantly interrogating my divided self: What are you up to? What should you be up to? Which master do you serve? History or the novel? It took me a long time to realize that in the case of the historical novel, the noun was of greater importance than the adjective. The book was dead as a novel because it *sounded* like a history; the narrative voice was stately, judicious, even-handed, measured. It was only when I adopted a first-person narration for the section of the novel dealing with Hollywood in the 1920s and a third-person point of view that frequently veered into a subjective third-person for events taking place in the 1870s that some of this trouble was alleviated.

The historical novel, I would argue, eschews the attempt to *be* history in favour of being a reflection *on* and *about* history. So much so that, in some instances, history achieves the status of a shadowy character, as it did in Leo Tolstoy's *War and Peace*. As the Marxist literary historian Georg Lukács observed:

> At the heart of Tolstoy is the contradiction between the protagonists of history and the living forces of popular life. He shows that those who, despite the great events in the forefront of history, go on living their normal, private and egoistic lives are really furthering the true (unconscious, unknown development) while the consciously acting "heroes" of history are ludicrous and harmful puppets.

One can see the same particular, sometimes eccentric historical thinking underpinning the work of many historical novelists. The works of Stendhal, Pushkin, Gogol, Balzac, and Fenimore Cooper all demonstrate highly personal conceptions of what history is and what its meaning is for the present. In the case of Gore Vidal, one of the most prolific American practitioners of the historical novel, his conviction that the United States had turned its back on republican virtue for the blandishments of imperial glory was a frequently, almost obsessively reiterated theme, a cry of despair for, if not paradise lost, then paradise as missed opportunity.

If historians must juggle and negotiate the demands of science and art, historical novelists are faced with the even thornier problem of mingling "real events" with "imaginary events." The nineteenth-century Italian writer Alessandro Manzoni wrestled with just this quandary. Manzoni is best remembered for his historical novel *The Betrothed*, which first appeared in Italy in 1827 to great acclaim, the publication of which occasioned Goethe to remark that Manzoni's novel suffered from his fastidious attachment to the historical record, a criticism that prompted Manzoni to spend the next two decades composing *On the Historical Novel*, a treatise that he hoped would demonstrate how history and the novel could be reconciled—a compelling instance of what tender orchids novelists are, how defensive they can be, and how easily they wilt when touched with critical frost.

To his credit, Manzoni's tizzy did not blind his incisive and unflinching mind from recognizing that historically minded readers would wish to know what was "real" and what was invention, while readers of a literary bent would complain that the aesthetic unity of a work was damaged if any such revelation was attempted.

In the end, Manzoni found the problem philosophically insoluble. The historical novel is undoubtedly an awkward, ungainly species of literature, centaur-like because it is composed of "real" and "imaginary" events. Historians are apt to look at it and declare it isn't history. This is undoubtedly true, but it raises the question, If it is not history, why would historians presume that the same standards of judgment apply to it? And the reverse applies to the criticism of histories levelled by historical novelists. Why complain that they do not exhibit the qualities associated with novels when we know they aren't? But as I say to my creative writing students, If you wish to argue or prove a point, write an essay. If you wish the reader to experience and inhabit an issue, *dramatize* it.

Literary scholars have long harboured their own reservations about the hybrid nature of the historical novel and been reluctant to give it a pass because of its perceived aesthetic failures. A. S. Byatt has written:

During my working life as a writer, the historical novel has been frowned on, and disapproved of, both by academic critics and by reviewers. In the 1950s the word "escapism" was enough to dismiss it, and the idea conjured up cloaks, daggers, crinolined ladies, ripped bodices, sailing ships in bloody battles. It can also be dismissed as "pastoral." My sister, Margaret Drabble, in an address to the American Academy of Arts and Letters, spoke out against the "nostalgia/heritage/fancy dress/costume drama industry." She believes passionately that it is the novelist's duty to write about the present, to confront an age which is "ugly, incomprehensible, and subject to rapid mutations."

This raises the perplexing question, Why have so many Canadian novelists chosen to adopt a form likely to encounter criticism and disapproval from two fronts, to have their flanks nipped by both historians and literary critics? Certainly, their attraction to the historical novel is relatively new. Herb Wyile in his book *Speculative Fictions* writes,

> Speaking of the lack of historical fiction during the flourishing of Canadian literature in the 1960s, Margaret Atwood recently observed that the writers of that generation "were instead taken up by the momentous discovery that we ourselves existed, in what was then the here and now, and we were busily exploring the implications of that."

Yet the last three decades have seen a remarkable upsurge of historical fiction, Atwood herself entering the fray. Stephen Henighan in *When Words Deny the World: The Reshaping of*

Canadian Writing believes this change in literary direction is attributable to a precise moment in Canadian political history.

> In a political sense, the collective idea of Canada was demolished on November 21, 1988, when Canadians voted to subordinate our national project to the requirements of continental free trade. Though we were constantly assured that culture was "off the table," it is obvious that in the absence of some shared national ethos endogenous literature—perhaps all endogenous culture—becomes unsustainable in a medium-sized country speaking two world languages.

And he goes on to say that

> in retrospect, history seems likely to view the early 1990s as a time of wrenching cultural change, even of collective trauma.
> How have our novelists responded to the annihilation of our intimate selves?
> Primarily with averted eyes.... Our most prominent novelists have collaborated in rewriting history as a stately foreign pageant...

Among the reasons he gives for this betrayal is that economic globalization increased the cultural power of Toronto, lent even more heft to the influence wielded by its media and its publishing houses, which gave rise to something he describes as "TorLit," which supplanted the older regional configuration that produced CanLit. In Henighan's estimation, Toronto publishers became the gatekeepers to success in the new global literary market, and access to that market was predicated on a number of things. Novelists of contemporary life had to suppress any overt engagement with Canadian social or political issues, which would bewilder foreign readers, and they had to ensure that their depictions of Canadian life were not too "Canadian." Faced with these demands, he suggests that many retreated, seeking refuge in more commercially viable historical fiction.

Here I must confess that Henighan uses my own work as illustrating "an exceptionally graphic chronicle of how one significant Canadian writer began to write more commercial 'literary blockbuster fiction' for the international market," noting that the kind of stories I had published in a book called *Things As They Are?* "had become deeply unfashionable. TorLit critics slammed the book for being everything they no longer wished Canadian writing to be: white, male, rural," and dismissed it for being "troublingly out of tune with globalized literary taste..."

Now in challenging what Henighan has to say, I run the risk of appearing whiny, petulant, and self-serving, perhaps a congenital condition that afflicts writers, who have a reputation for being notoriously thin-skinned. Nevertheless, I do grant Henighan his insights. With reservations, I agree that the cultural power wielded by Toronto does lead to an undervaluation of regional, rural literature, which in some circles is viewed as an atavism, embarrassingly out of touch with Canada's increasingly urban and multicultural society. And I do believe that for those Canadian writers who experienced the heady cultural nationalism of the sixties and seventies, the North American Free Trade Agreement (NAFTA) was a disturbing and ominous sea-change, which seemed to mark a profound alteration in the mood of the country, a step back from the cultural and political nationalism that shaped my generation of writers who had teethed on George Grant's *Lament for a Nation*.

Whatever NAFTA's merits or demerits as public policy, many writers of my generation were likely to feel it was a renunciation of the desire to frame an English-speaking Canadian identity. For those who saw themselves as contributors to that enterprise it gave them pause and, in that pause, I contend, some came to see history as playing as large a role in the formation of a Canadian identity as discovering ourselves in the here and now.

The historical novel has always been concerned with the probing of national identity. Walter Scott's resurrection of Scottish culture and history, Manzoni's radical introduction of Italian peasantry as a subject in *The Betrothed*, Gogol's celebration of Cossack life in *Taras Bulba*, or James Fenimore Cooper's search for an essential Americanism in *The Leatherstocking Tales* all point to this. For English-speaking Canadians, the definition of identity is *the* perpetual question and anxiety, and the recent rise of the historical novel may be just another revisiting of that perennial, nagging subject. The Canadian past may even have begun to look more distinctly Canadian than the Canada of the 1980s, which was embracing the globalization enterprise, and seeming to fold itself more completely into the warm and welcoming arms of our neighbour to the south.

Of course, it is impossible to identify any *one* reason for Canadian writers embracing historical fiction; there are likely to be many. What I am talking about is a mood, nothing programmatic. This is a hunch on my part, a suspicion. I have not canvassed novelists as to their motives for resorting to historical fiction; any such questions would likely be greeted with unrestrained hilarity.

In my own case—if I may be permitted to descend into the abyss of personal anecdote—I certainly did not wake up one morning and say, NAFTA is now a fact, how will I respond? Aha, it seems the time has come to take out that historical novel that has been gathering dust in a drawer since 1982 and get back to work on *The Englishman's Boy!* What will be my conception for it? Well, it is essential that the book deal with the birth of the Hollywood dream factory and its globalizing cultural influence, and one of the characters, who is a Canadian working in Beverly Hills in the 1920s, should make statements questioning Canadians' fragile grip on their own identity so as to draw a parallel with contemporary politics. Perhaps I will have him say things like

> Canada isn't a country at all, it's simply geography.
> There's no emotion there, not the kind that Chance
> is talking about. There are no Whitmans, no Twains,
> no Cranes. Half the English Canadians wish they
> were *really* English, and the other half wish they were
> Americans. If you're going to be anything, you have
> to choose.

I also did not decide from the moment I first put pen to paper—yes, it was a long time ago—that the novel must concern itself with an obscure massacre of First Nations people, which helped prompt the Macdonald government to form the North-West Mounted Police and to march them west to lay claim to that region, nor did I conceive of that as an act of imperial possession having inescapable consequences for the configuration of the country and for Indigenous peoples, consequences with which we are still living. The book was not framed as an illustration of ideas; the ideas emerged in the writing of it. I assuredly did not say, I must write a historical novel; it is the duty of the moment. That is not the way writers of fiction work. But their convictions and beliefs do surface in their work, and the Canadian historical novel presently provides plenty of evidence that, if nothing else, an awareness exists among writers of fiction that Canadian history is an essential component of any formulation of Canadian identity, a radically different tactic from the approach of novelists who in the sixties, seventies, and eighties principally focused on contemporary Canadian life, the "here and now" of those decades.

In the first half of the twentieth century, it was Canadian historians who did the most to define a hesitant and hazardous

Canadian identity; the influence of fiction writers in that period was minimal, even negligible. In giving weight to historical knowledge in creating a sense of ourselves, I am not invoking the dead hand of the past or succumbing to a nostalgic yearning for some *better time*. If nothing else, history is a reminder of change, fluidity, mutability. None of us, as much as we would like to, can own history, neither historians nor historical novelists. Nor can we fix a Canadian identity in time, immure it like a fly in amber. It is as changeable as quicksilver, utterly mercurial.

Still, earlier traces of the past are detectable in the present, and that is why knowledge of the past is so important to contemporary life. Every aspect of the work of historians takes on value if viewed in this light: the specialized studies that reveal bypassed incidents or failed aspirations that still glimmer faintly in the present; the overarching interpretations that touch on common experiences shared by Canadians of all kinds and that argue, maybe, just maybe, amidst the welter of our divisions there is a centre, and that centre may hold. We are frequently a divided and fractious country, but not an *entirely* fractious country.

So what role can the Canadian historical novel play in depicting Canadian identity? It can do little of what the historian is capable of. Fiction writers have neither the command of facts nor the ambition necessary to attempt grand interpretations. However, centuries ago, the Italian philosopher of history Giambattista Vico posited an idea earth-shaking for his time: a claim that history derived from humble human origins, not divine providence. Now of course, there may be a divine plan, but arrogant claims to discern it and act on it frequently produce disastrous outcomes. Historical fiction, I believe, reinforces the sense that our responsibilities as actors in history are rooted in our humble human origins. While the analytic, authoritative, omniscient voice of the historian may leave the impression that historical forces have the omnipotence of divine providence, Wallace

Stegner's serial voices of fiction remind us that history is never as clear or simple for those who lived it as we might imagine. The lesson of the historical novel may be that the past was every bit as problematic as the present we are floundering about in. The clamour of voices in the historical novel, each speaking its own brand of truth, may prompt in us the realization that our understanding of past and present is won by our own efforts, that these are subjects to be pondered as citizens and individuals. *The Englishman's Boy* contained a warning: Beware of anyone who hands you the past too neatly packaged in a history, in a historical movie, or, of course, in a historical novel. Test them all.

In an age in which mammoth bureaucracies, faceless corporations, unfettered financial institutions, and vague concepts such as globalization assume the robes of divine providence and increasingly suggest that human beings are powerless to influence their own destinies or to assert their own identities, history and historical fiction may help provide a sober second voice that reminds us that we live with the consequences of our own choices, that we are responsible for and deserve the world and the country we get. In an age when political discourse has become increasingly Manichaean, increasingly simplified and reductionist in outlook, to insist on the complexity of the past is to insist on the complexity of the present, a reminder that true cosmopolitanism not only recognizes and applauds difference in the present, it acknowledges it in the past.

Both the writing of history and literature are creative acts, by different means that lead to different results. Novelists speak a different language, more confiding and visceral than that of historians. Alessandro Manzoni wrote that history gives us

> events, which, so to speak, are known only from the
> outside; what men have performed: but not what they
> have thought, the feelings which have accompanied

their deliberations and their plans, their successes and their misfortunes: the conversations by which they have impressed or tried to impress their wills, by which they have expressed their anger, poured forth their grief, by which in a word, they have *revealed their individuality*: all this history passes by almost in silence; and all this is the domain of poetry.

I do not claim one voice is better or more valuable than the other. Like the parable of the six blind men each touching a part of the elephant and drawing conclusions about what the elephant is from whatever they lay hands on, neither history nor the historical novel alone can do justice to the elephant that is the past. We need many and complementary stories. As Canadians, we not only locate ourselves in stories, we discover ourselves in them. No one can apprehend the past in the sense of taking custody of it; it is a common heritage, this country of ghosts. These ghosts walk among us. It is my conviction that the more ghost stories we tell ourselves, of every kind and variety, the better we may come to understand who we are, and the less strange we Canadians may come to appear in one another's eyes.

Lecture given at St. Thomas More College, University of Saskatchewan, Saskatoon, October 24, 2013

From Hero to Villain
and Villain to Hero

IN HER ACKNOWLEDGEMENTS to her novel *Wolf Hall*, Hilary
Mantel thanks Dr. Mary Robinson, who the novelist says is
an academic whose business "has been the facts" of Thomas
Cromwell's life but who, Mantel notes, "encouraged me and lent
me her expertise through the production of this fiction, put up
with my fumbling speculations and been kind enough to recognize the portrait I have produced."

Given my own experience writing historical fiction, Mantel's
phrase "fumbling speculations" is one that I find an apt description for the blind grappling with the demands of the historical
novel that I have indulged in. Typically, only with hindsight can
I perceive hints of the motivations, both conscious and subcon-
scious, which might have played a role in making a book. It is this
experience that informs tonight's talk in which I will make some
guesses—perhaps thoroughly wild speculations—about how two
writers, Robert Bolt and Hilary Mantel, arrived at depictions of
Thomas Cromwell and Thomas More that stand in such stark
contrast to one another.

How "correct" these portraits are to the historical record is
not the topic of my talk, although the history of the Tudor period cannot be entirely dismissed from it. What I wish to discuss
is More and Cromwell as fictional characters and what they may

indicate about the preoccupations of both the authors and the societies in which they were created and received. Of course, the "real" More and Cromwell were men who occupied positions of power in sixteenth-century England, eminent lawyers and scholars who each served King Henry VIII as lord high chancellor and who wielded power only exceeded by that of the monarch in a time far different from Bolt's and Mantel's.

Historians, of course, quite properly avoid speculating about the undocumented inner lives of history's movers and shakers, which is the province of novelists and dramatists, and a job that Bolt and Mantel undertake in rich detail, Bolt in his play *A Man for All Seasons*, and Mantel in her novel *Wolf Hall*. And it strikes me that those explorations are inextricably linked not only to the personal preoccupations of the writers but also to the preoccupations of the contemporary worlds in which they wrote. Bolt's stage play premiered in London in 1960 and Hilary Mantel's novel in 2009, a separation of close to fifty years, a half-century that marked great change in British attitudes and society.

Bolt's play was largely responsible for introducing More to a non-Catholic British public and was instrumental in forming its notion of him. It might be said that Bolt was to More what Shakespeare was to Richard III. The playwright was clearly obsessed with More's story, reworking a 1954 radio drama into a television play that was followed up by a longer stage version, which later became a celebrated movie that won eight Oscars in 1967. Until I saw that film, I had no inkling who Thomas More was. At the age of sixteen, I wasn't much interested in the ins and outs, the rights and wrongs of Henry VIII's domestic troubles, but the life-and-death moral decisions More faced in dealing with his monarch's marital woes were unexpectedly thrilling, even for a naïve high school student.

Any attempt to succinctly and fairly sum up the issues that led to the English church's break with Rome and the disastrous consequences it brought down on More's head is a dicey proposition. In the broadest strokes, Henry VIII's marriage to Catherine of Aragon had failed to produce a son. England had bitter memories of the decades-long civil war known as the War of the Roses that was a result of a contested kingship. The court feared that if Henry VIII did not produce a male heir, another bloody dynastic struggle was inevitable. The only solution they could see to the problem was for Henry to find a young and ostensibly fertile woman, remarry, and give the country a Prince of Wales. But for that to happen his union to Catherine of Aragon had to be annulled. A young lady at court, Anne Boleyn, had caught Henry's eye and was conveniently lurking in the wings.

Still, the king needed to find a seemingly plausible justification for setting aside his wife and delegitimizing his daughter, Mary. He and his advisers decided that grounds for an annulment existed because Pope Julius II had wrongly granted a dispensation that permitted Henry to marry Catherine, his dead brother Arthur's wife. Since this dispensation was a contravention of canon law, which forbade marrying the widow of a brother, Henry requested one of Julius's successors, Pope Clement VII, to put Henry right with God by dissolving his bond with Catherine. According to the king's compliant advisers, Pope Julius had flouted divine law, which had prompted a vengeful deity to punish Henry by denying him a male heir.

But Catherine refused to yield her place to Anne Boleyn and appealed for assistance to her nephew, the Holy Roman Emperor Charles V. The emperor had ample military power to bring to bear on Pope Clement if he made the wrong decision and invalidated the marriage of Henry and Catherine. The sack of Rome in 1527 by Charles V's troops had given savage proof that the pope would not necessarily be spared if he earned the displeasure of the emperor.

The question of the annulment of the king's marriage was a Gordian knot, a knot in which the religious, political, and personal strands were so tightly bound together that it grew impossible to separate one from another. As the decision whether the pope would release the king from his marriage vows dragged on interminably, the increasingly impatient Henry came to see his domestic difficulties as a naked contest between the authority of the English Crown and the authority of the church, a dispute that involved ever growing numbers of lawyers and churchmen, who in turn produced ever more dizzyingly intricate and arcane arguments concerning the case.

Thomas Cromwell and Thomas More were at the centre of this imbroglio. Put in the simplest, perhaps simple-minded terms, Cromwell was in favour of raising the power of the monarchy above the power of the church, while More was not. This conflict is at the root of Bolt's drama, which sets More, the generous, wise, principled protagonist, against Cromwell, the venal, ruthless, unprincipled antagonist.

Mantel, however, takes a far different view of the matter, exchanging the roles of protagonist and antagonist in her novel. In *Wolf Hall*, More is cast as a cold-hearted, heretic-hunting religious fanatic and Cromwell as a warm-hearted statesman of sturdy, commonsensical tolerance, someone who is willing (more or less) to live and let live. Fifty years after audiences had embraced Bolt's More and detested his Cromwell, Mantel's readers were led to feel the opposite.

What might account for these radically different portraits? Certainly, the temperament and personal experiences of the writers surely have something to do with their responses to these long-dead historical figures. But beyond that, the mood of the times also must have played a role in how Bolt's More and Mantel's Cromwell were received by their respective publics.

Let me turn first to Bolt's drama, *A Man for All Seasons*. In his preface to the play, Bolt writes, "I am not a Catholic nor even in the meaningful sense of the word a Christian. So by what right do I appropriate a Christian Saint to my purposes?"

The question is germane, but Bolt's answer to it provides more confusion than clarity. The hinge of the play is More's unwillingness to swear an oath affirming the Act of Succession, which stated that any children of Henry VIII and Anne Boleyn would be the rightful heirs to the throne. The Act also named the king head of the English church, divesting the pope of all authority over it. Historically speaking, there is little doubt that More did everything he could to avoid swearing to the Act of Succession because he could not countenance the idea that anybody *but* the pope had a right to head God's church in England. Yet in the play, when More explains to his daughter why he will not falsely swear to this Act, More says, "When a man takes an oath, Meg, he's holding his own self in his own hands. Like water. *(He cups his hands)* And if he opens his fingers then—he needn't hope to find himself again." For Bolt, the question of the oath has little to do with whether or not it is a pledge made under the eyes of God. Rather, he views it as an act that affirms or denies one's selfhood; in essence it is an existential act.

Bolt knows he is imposing existential ideas fashionable in intellectual circles in the 1950s and 1960s on More and that these ideas would likely be incomprehensible to a sixteenth-century believer. For a devout Catholic of the time, steeped in the literature of martyrdom, swearing to an oath that broke God's law would be a renunciation of faith, a renunciation that would have put More's soul in jeopardy of eternal damnation. But whether one was saved or damned was an archaic question for most mid-twentieth-century artists and thinkers. The pressing question for many of them was how to live without faith, how to live "authentically," how to own up to your self-defining choices and construct meaning in your life. The explanation for his actions that

More offers his daughter is obviously more a nod to Camus and Sartre than it is to Aquinas or Augustine.

Yet Bolt willingly admits how hard it was for him and his contemporaries to arrive at More's adamantine sense of self. He writes, a "clear sense of the self can *only* crystallize round something transcendental in which case, our prospects look poor, for we are rightly committed to the rational." This is a strange assertion, since commitment to the rational dispenses with any appeal to the transcendence that Bolt claims to be a precondition to sustaining a firm sense of the self. However, wanting to have his cake and eat it too, the dramatist swiftly dances over this thin ice, boldly declaring,

> I think the paramount gift our thinkers, artists, and for
> all I know, our men of science, should labour to get for
> us is a sense of selfhood without resort to magic. Albert
> Camus is a writer I admire in this connection.
> Anyway, the above must serve as my explanation and
> apology for treating Thomas More, a Christian Saint, as
> a hero of selfhood.

It's possible to accept the apology, but the apology doesn't settle the contradiction. More did what he did because he *had* a conception of transcendence. And Bolt grudgingly acknowledges that without that conception a clear sense of self is nearly impossible to acquire. Nevertheless, his solution to that philosophical contradiction is to create a protagonist who apparently *does* arrive at selfhood without recourse to transcendental support. More is refashioned into a very contemporary figure, a Camus-like character who shares many of the qualities exhibited by Dr. Rieux and Jean Tarrou in *La Peste*. Now to my mind, there's certainly nothing wrong in remodelling the past to illuminate the present, if you are skilful enough to get away with it. But what is curious about

Bolt is that he exposes his writer's sleight of hand in the preface of the published play, revealing the magician's tricks which might have gone undetected if he hadn't chosen to point them out.

The twentieth century was a time of relentless inquiry into the political opinions of artists and intellectuals. Bolt stages More's existential defiance in a courtroom, the arena in which many of these people found themselves when they ran afoul of their governments, courts in which they were forced to decide whether standing firm in regard to previously publicly professed principles was worth the loss of livelihoods, their families, and in the most extreme cases, their lives. Understandably, few measured up to the standard of conduct More set and were willing to pay for their principles with their lives. More was an anomaly; he exemplified the lonely individual who pits himself against the implacable power of the state, is cynically and brutally crushed by it, yet manages to confirm his moral integrity by his death.

For many left-leaning writers like Bolt, the immediate postwar period was a difficult time. The United States was gripped by a Red Scare that put Communists and Communist sympathizers in professional jeopardy, especially if they happened to come to the attention of the House Committee on Un-American Activities or the red-hunting Senator Joe McCarthy, attention that often made them unemployable in universities, government services, or most famously, Hollywood, where the glare of publicity was particularly fierce. In such an atmosphere, many in the motion picture industry hurriedly flocked to declare their anti-Communism and their wholesome "Americanism." Director Elia Kazan, writer Ayn Rand, actors Gary Cooper and Ronald Reagan, and studio heads Jack L. Warner, Louis B. Mayer, and Walt Disney were just a few of those who fully cooperated with HUAC by naming names and stridently condemning Communist influence in Hollywood.

Of course, on the other side of the ideological divide, there were those who suffered for their past and present convictions.

The group known as the Hollywood Ten became heroes for left-leaning progressives by refusing to testify before the committee and snitch on colleagues. Eventually, they were charged with contempt of Congress and handed one-year prison terms. The Ten did not stand entirely alone. In September of 1947, an action group called the Committee for the First Amendment was formed to lend them moral support. It included some of the biggest names in Hollywood, stars such as Humphrey Bogart, Lauren Bacall, Gene Kelly, Burt Lancaster, Frank Sinatra, Henry Fonda, Bette Davis, Judy Garland, etc.

But with the anti-Communist hysteria showing no signs of abating, a number of prominent entertainers, among them Ira Gershwin, Humphrey Bogart, John Garfield, and Edward G. Robinson, began making statements or writing articles retracting their support for the Ten. Although their reasons for doing this can never be absolutely ascertained, their critics believed that these men feared their careers would be destroyed if they didn't quickly and publicly backtrack. Even among the staunchly intransigent Hollywood Ten, a rift opened in the ranks. The director Edward Dmytryk did a complete about-face by volunteering to appear before HUAC, where he contritely admitted to having been a member of the Communist party and then helpfully provided HUAC with more names of supposed Hollywood Communists (twenty-six) than any other "friendly witness."

A Communist witch hunt was not the only problem bedevilling party members and "fellow travellers" during this period. Uncomfortably for them, a growing body of evidence detailing a long history of Soviet terror, atrocities, and political double-dealing had put them in an awkward position regarding their earlier political allegiances. Some, of course, reflexively labelled uncomfortable facts as anti-Communist provocations and lies. Bolt was not one of them. He had joined the Communist party in 1942, but disenchantment with it led him to resign his membership sometime in 1947.

Still, even for those who left the party as early as Bolt did, it was difficult to reconcile how the retreat from Communism had been such a slow, reluctant withdrawal for many writers and artists. In 1938, when George Orwell published *Homage to Catalonia*, his memoir of the Spanish Civil War, the majority of British left-wing intellectuals condemned as an outright lie his account of Soviet agents actively working behind the scenes to undermine their political allies in the Republican coalition government. The more well-informed, while privately acknowledging that there might be some truth in what Orwell was saying, still took the position that he had no business airing the party's dirty linen because that might bring the reputation of the Soviet Union and Stalin into disrepute.

The next left-wing writer to break ranks was Arthur Koestler, whose novel *Darkness at Noon*, published in 1940, incisively dissected the psychology of those Communists who had confessed in Soviet courts to committing fictional crimes in order to prevent undermining the very Communist leadership that was prosecuting them on trumped-up charges. But this trickle of criticism of the USSR in left-wing artistic circles virtually ceased when Hitler attacked Russia in 1941, an event that brought the Soviet Union into the war on the side of Great Britain. Only with the defeat of Nazism and the emergence of the Cold War did books like Orwell's *Animal Farm* and *1984*, which offered trenchant critiques of totalitarianism, win favour with anti-Communist Western governments and a wide reading public.

The book, however, that really marked a significant turning away from Communism by European thinkers and artists was *The God That Failed*, a 1949 collection of essays written by prominent literary figures such as Koestler, André Gide, Richard Wright, Stephen Spender, and Ignazio Silone, all of whom repudiated their former association with the party and condemned Communism for having degenerated into a slavish personality cult devoted to the worship of Joseph Stalin.

This slow shifting of political perspective among those in the literary community who had been supporters of Communism had an echo within the USSR. In 1956, the unimaginable happened. Premier Khrushchev denounced his old boss, Stalin, for orchestrating vicious and baseless purges of party stalwarts, for subjecting innocent Soviet leaders to torture, and for having them tried and summarily executed on the basis of false confessions and bogus evidence. Khrushchev was revisiting the Moscow show trials between 1936 and 1938 in which Old Bolsheviks such as Zinoviev, Kamenev, and Bukharin had been wiped out for their suspected opposition to Stalin's leadership. Forced to make humiliating confessions to imaginary crimes, they were swiftly dispatched by Stalin's secret police after their "sins" were paraded before a gullible public. But just as they had been condemned in the blink of an eye, the criminals of 1936, 1937, and 1938 were exonerated in 1956 every bit as quickly by the party that previously had condemned them.

Against this background, it's difficult not to read *A Man for All Seasons* as a meditation on the precarious position writers, scholars, and intellectuals find themselves in when they attract the ire of the state. Although the trial in the play might be seen as bearing some resemblance to the workings of the House Committee on Un-American Activities, it's the Moscow show trials that most clearly mirror the situation More found himself in. And there is little doubt that *A Man for All Seasons* was intended to speak to people much like Bolt himself, an educated public familiar with the political atmosphere of the thirties, forties, and fifties who could poignantly recall the idealism surrounding the Spanish Civil War and the anti-Fascist struggle that recruited significant numbers of Oxford and Cambridge undergraduates into Communist party ranks.

Bolt borrowed Robert Whittington's description of Thomas More ("a man for all seasons") as the title of his play, but the postwar period was to prove to be very much the season for More. Bolt

provided a public which had witnessed a long procession of intellectuals who had compromised their principles under state duress
with a tonic symbol of political virtue and integrity. Thomas More
appeared to be the antidote for Joseph Stalin and Joe McCarthy.

Of course, Bolt's secular canonization of More was not
greeted with universal approbation. Those who still retained
Marxist leanings of one sort or other were inclined to dismiss the
play as irredeemably, tritely bourgeois. Bolt's fellow playwright
David Mercer, who claimed to have passed sixteen years educating
himself in the Marxist-Leninist view of history, commented that
Bolt's "talent is so encapsulated in a kind of bourgeois mind that I
doubt it'll ever come free." The theatre critic Kenneth Tynan, who
in 1966 sweetly described his politics for the *New York Times* by
declaring himself "a believer in noncoercive Socialism; above all,
[I believe] that we must have a sexual revolution with a political
revolution," found the play deficient in seriousness. He wrote in
The Observer that for Bolt it mattered "little whether More's beliefs
were right or wrong: all that matters is that he held them, and
refused to disclose them under questioning." Tynan speculated
that unlike the Communist Brecht, whose play about Galileo
celebrated the struggle of science against religious obscurant-
ism, Bolt presented truth as subjective, the implication seeming
to be that Bolt lacked a Marxist's "objective" grasp of history. "I
have no idea whether Mr. Bolt himself is a religious man," Tynan
mused, "but I am perfectly sure that if someone presented him
with irrefutable evidence that every tenet of Catholicism was a
palpable falsehood, his admiration for More would not be dimin-
ished ... nor would he feel tempted to alter a word of the text....
If, upon completing *Galileo*, Brecht had suddenly learned that
his protagonist's hypotheses were totally untrue, he would either
have torn up the manuscript or revised it from start to finish."

It must be admitted that Tynan has put his finger on something. He is correct in assuming that Bolt wasn't very much

interested in More's Catholicism, but that doesn't mean Bolt admired More simply because he refused to yield to the imperious Henry. What Bolt's More puts his faith in is one of the fundamental tenets of that most bourgeois of political doctrines, liberal democracy. The thing that More most eloquently professes belief in during the course of the play is England's laws. He is confident these laws will provide him with a safe harbour if and when the royal tempest begins to blow in his direction. Of course, what More is banking on, the rule of law and respect for due process, are anathema to all totalitarian and authoritarian governments and were not notions given much credence in sixteenth-century England.

And since More is a "man of Bolt's time" in disguise, his faith in the law is his downfall; just as twentieth-century liberal democrats were swept aside by those on both the right and left who argued that individual rights ought to count for nothing when weighed against the will of the masses or the will of the master race, More is fated to share the fate of those future political innocents.

There is something touching about More's reverence for the law. When his mercurial son-in-law, Roper, decides the law gives shelter to God's enemies and announces that he'd cut down every law in England to get to the devil, More answers, "And when the last law was down, and the Devil turned round on you where would you hide, Roper, the laws all being flat? ... This country's planted thick with laws from coast to coast—man's laws, not God's—and if you cut them down—and you're just the man to do it—d'you really think you could stand upright in the winds that would blow then? ... Yes, I'd give the Devil benefit of law, for my own safety's sake."

Roper angrily retorts, "I have long suspected this; this is the golden calf; the law's your god." More replies, *"(wearily)* Oh, Roper, you're a fool, God's my god ... *(Rather bitter)* But I find him rather too *(Very bitter)* subtle ... I don't know where he is nor what he wants." This is scarcely a ringing endorsement of the deity. In fact, this sounds more like the despondent cry of an anguished mid-century existentialist adrift in an indifferent universe than it does the declaration of faith of a true believer willing to stake his life and soul on what he is sure is God's eternal plan.

And yet perhaps it is the unresolved tension in Bolt's More between Christian belief and existential despair that made him such a seductive example of the "hero of selfhood" for so many experiencing political and religious disappointments in the postwar world. In an interview with Richard Duprey in 1962, Bolt leaves the impression that the figure of More brought him face to face with his own philosophical and moral quandaries. Bolt found the meaningless and absurd universe that existentialists proposed as likely to be too pitiless a vision for human beings to bear. But orthodox Christianity hardly seemed a viable proposition, given what recent history and science had revealed about human depravity and a universe of inconceivable and impersonal vastness. Was the only solution, then, a return to the values which might be loosely called the Christian tradition? Bolt rejected that as a possibility because he felt that Christian ethics stripped of Christian dogma was pure and simple hypocrisy. For Bolt, there were only two respectable intellectual positions. The first was an admission that Christian ethics depended on a belief that Christ was God "or the incarnation of God or the son of God ... that he was crucified, died and rose from the dead. This ... is, at least to my mind, what really makes a Christian distinct from somebody who is mushily going along with something he vaguely thinks of as Christian." The other alternative was to recognize and admit the absurdity of human existence, to resign oneself to the fact that transcendence was a lie, and to try to construct meaning for oneself, even if a human being amounted to nothing more than a mere speck in a daunting cosmos.

But having laid out the unpalatable choices, Bolt then makes a disarmingly honest confession to his interviewer. He confides, "I'm halfway between either of the respectable positions and the position I am in is not respectable, but I believe that it is the position that 99.9% of the people are in today, and I think the only thing that can endow you with any kind of respectability is the effort that you put into sustaining it and trying to resolve it."

Bolt's More is a compromise, a man who, by turns, acts as if human beings are responsible for creating their own "selfhood," their own meaning in life, but who then trustingly puts his life in God's hands because to do otherwise would be to deny God. In describing Bolt's More as an uneasy compromise, I don't mean to diminish him as a character or to disparage Bolt's skill as a dramatist. It is hard to deny that in some essential way *A Man for All Seasons* is a success and that that success owes something to the contradictions that More contains, and that these contradictions are felt as the nuances and vagaries that complicate human existence rather than as clumsy attempts to fudge philosophical issues that Bolt cannot satisfactorily resolve even in his own mind. When all is said and done, despite its shaky philosophical underpinnings, *A Man for All Seasons* emerges as a compelling drama of conscience and More a compelling example of grace under pressure.

If Bolt's More is a divided soul, a man hung between two impulses, secular and religious, the same might be said of many of the theatre- and moviegoers who flocked to see *A Man for All Seasons*. For many who had been raised as Christians, their former faith now seemed a dead article, worn away to nothing by the wholesale atrocities of the twentieth century, which suggested that if a loving God wasn't dead, he was definitely asleep on the job. And for many Communists and Communist sympathizers, even some Democratic Socialists, the idealistic belief in the power of political action to make the world a virtual paradise now appeared to be a chimera.

What's more, as the Cold War proceeded and nuclear holocaust threatened, governments, whether capitalist or communist, came to make greater and greater demands on the loyalty of their citizens, insisting on ever greater conformity to the state's interpretation of the world, and if citizens demurred to fall into line with that interpretation, the state made sure they paid a price for their dissent, a price that was certainly higher in Communist countries than Western democracies, but even in some democracies could be onerous enough to give pause to anyone thinking about bucking the prevailing orthodoxy.

More's case is an example of the state's insatiable need to enforce political conformity. At first, and for as long as he could manage it, More was a silent dissenter to Henry's claim to be supreme head of the English church. He did not choose to be a boat-rocker. Just as those who disagreed with Stalin did not set themselves *actively* against the head of state, More offered no challenge to Henry. Nevertheless, the former lord high chancellor's refusal to swear an oath proclaiming the monarch the head of the English church displeased the king because More's reputation as a lawyer and a scholar stood very high in both England and Europe and his silence promoted speculation as to what his position on the matter really was.

More doggedly clung to the assumption that he could not be condemned for what *he did not say*. Just like some who appeared before HUAC took the Fifth in an attempt to save themselves, More made use of the sixteenth-century English common law version of protection against self-incrimination. In a standoff with Thomas Cromwell, the two men argued what More's silence meant. More said that since he had not voiced an opinion on the legitimacy of the Act, no one could say he had denied that Henry was head of the church. Thomas Cromwell retorted that More's silence was "not silence at all, but most eloquent denial."

In rebutting Cromwell, More, the consummate lawyer, cites a long-established principle of English common law, reminding his interrogator that "the maxim of the law is 'Silence gives consent.' If therefore you wish to construe what my silence betokened, you must construe that I consented, not that I denied."

And Cromwell rejoins, "Is that in fact what the world construes from it? Do you pretend that is what you wish the world to construe from it?"

More answers, "The world must construe according to its wits; this court must construe according to the law."

But Henry's great fear is *what* the world might construe. Just as Stalin needed show trials that would demonstrate he was surrounded by would-be assassins and traitors, trials that would provide justification for the purges that sent thousands upon thousands of his countrymen to their deaths in the gulags, King Henry needs More to declare in open court that the monarch is head of the church or to categorically deny that he is. If More swears that Henry is the rightful head of the English church, so much the better. If he says Henry isn't, then More is guilty of treason, a capital crime, and his execution will remove a focus and rallying point for dissent.

Of course, the law is an inconvenient sticking point for even the king. And so he relies on Thomas Cromwell, the dirty hands of power, a character who might have been patterned on Nikolai Yezhov or Lavrentiy Beria, the sinister heads of Stalin's secret police, men who unquestioningly and unflinchingly carried out the autocrat's wishes. Cromwell's approach to his duties is cynically straightforward. "When the king wants something done, I do it." And in explaining his duties to his underling, Richard Rich, he says that if the king "wants to change his woman he will … And our job as administrators is to make it as convenient as we can."

Bolt's Cromwell is hardly what E. M. Forster would have called a well-rounded character. He is a flat abstraction, little more than the cold, bureaucratic manifestation of evil, although never a stupid manifestation of evil. Cromwell is not only the willing servant of unrestrained power, he understands the psychology of it. He muses, "If the King destroys a man, that's proof to the King that it must have been a bad man, the kind of man a man of conscience ought to destroy…"

This is an acute insight into the perverse mind of the totalitarian. Absolute power knows it can make no mistakes; what it desires is the definition of right. And because Cromwell understands what and who he serves, he is unrelenting in his attempts to get Henry what Henry wants from More. The king wants the approval of a good and honest man, which More stubbornly withholds because to give his approval would be to turn his back on everything that gives meaning to his life.

More does not *seek* martyrdom; he would be a less attractive character if he did. Bolt's More is not a religious mystic or ascetic but a man immersed in the world, a devoted husband and father who loves his illiterate, blustering wife as much as he does his adored and scholarly daughter, Margaret, who under her father's fond instruction has become a sixteenth-century oddity, a young woman of considerable learning. The More who graces Bolt's stage is invariably temperate and wise, a dependable dispenser of good advice to those who need it most: the ambitious office-seeker, Richard Rich, and Margaret's suitor, William Roper, a young man who veers erratically between fervent Protestantism and equally fervent Catholicism. More is also the model statesman, an honest, diligent, and loyal servant of the king—that is, until the king asks for what he cannot give.

More wraps himself in the comforting blanket of the law, but Cromwell suborns Richard Rich into perjuring himself. Rich swears that he has heard More say that Henry is not head of the church of England, something the wary More would never do. The realization that Rich's lie has doomed him gives More the freedom to make clear what he thinks of Henry's claim to be the rightful head of the church of England. This he does eloquently and forcefully. He does what the men Stalin condemned to death did not have the opportunity to do or did not take the opportunity to do. He goes on the record with his opposition.

More understands it is his *unvoiced* thoughts that have sealed his fate. That someone has reserved a corner of their mind for their own thoughts is regarded as criminal by totalitarians, who require from their subjects not only outward compliance to their dictates but inward compliance as well. As More says to Cromwell, "What you have hunted me for is not my actions, but the thoughts of my heart. It is a long road you have opened. For first men will disclaim their hearts and presently they will have no hearts. God help the people whose Statesmen walk your road." And this prophecy is borne out by much of the history of the twentieth century.

A few years after the initial success of *A Man for All Seasons*, Bolt would fail a much less onerous test of principle than the one that More so courageously passed. A member of the militant Committee of 100, a group that advocated a ban on all nuclear weapons, Bolt was arrested in an anti-Bomb demonstration. Signing a declaration that he would not participate in such actions again would have freed him from custody, something Bolt refused to do, a refusal that earned him a one-month jail term. But after he had spent two weeks in jail, Sam Spiegel, the producer of *Lawrence of Arabia*, for which Bolt had been engaged to write the screenplay, paid him a visit and talked him into finally signing the declaration, which brought about his release from prison. It was a step Bolt retrospectively regretted all his life and one that he never forgave Spiegel for persuading him to take.

That Bolt, an admirer of the unswerving More, had wavered in his principles merely underlines the uncomfortable position intellectuals have always occupied in highly political ages. Those who accept the role of public intellectual are subject to scrutiny and criticism from governments, employers, fellow intellectuals, and sometimes even the average citizen. How to weather these pressures is what concerns Bolt in *A Man for All Seasons*. Unfortunately, artists and intellectuals often talk and write as if their principles are inviolate; and unfortunately, their record indicates they frequently fail to adhere to their code of ethics at about the same rate as any other segment of humanity. But unlike most people, given their access to forums in which to parade their virtue, their failure is often played out in public. I feel free to make that observation because I don't make it from any position of moral superiority. I know all too well which camp I would be likely to fall into if subjected to pressure from a Henry VIII or even a Sam Spiegel. I am confident I would not be able to number myself among the indomitable "heroes of selfhood."

For a generation that had seen so many flinch under coercion, Bolt's More was an inspirational, aspirational example of an individual capable of defying the iron imperatives of the state and preserving his "self." More does not fail his ideals but, sadly, his ideals fail him. Perhaps the greatest villainy Bolt's villainous Cromwell perpetrates is to demonstrate to More just how tenuous the rule of law is, how easily it is abrogated and manipulated by those who can lay their hands on the levers of power. In his preface to *A Man for All Seasons*, Bolt writes, "Cromwell's contemptuous shattering of the forms of law by an unconcealed act of perjury showed how fragile for any individual is that shelter. Legal or illegal had no further meaning..." This was the lesson of Nazi Germany and Soviet Russia, which subjugated their populations not only by the exercise of extralegal terror but also by seeing to it that the legal system itself was answerable to no one but the monsters in charge. To a lesser degree, American politicians bent the judicial system to punish dissent they deemed un-American. Little wonder that in *A Man for All Seasons* the state is portrayed as a pitiless piece of machinery and Thomas Cromwell one of its cogs prepared to grind to bits whoever or whatever is perceived to be a source of opposition. In Bolt's words, Cromwell is a creature characterized by a "self-conceit that can cradle gross crimes in the name of effective action"; utility is his motive and goal.

For close to a half-century, *A Man for All Seasons* was the dominant imaginative narrative focusing on the lives of Cromwell and More, a narrative in which Cromwell was the king's conscienceless jackal and Thomas More was his unrecognized, unappreciated servant, a peerless example of ethical conduct in government. Then, in 2009, Hilary Mantel's Booker Prize–winning novel *Wolf Hall* offered a counternarrative to Bolt's play, one in which Thomas Cromwell was elevated from a position as the agent of "gross crimes in the name of effective action" into a talented, farsighted statesman who, while hardly a saint, laboured by pragmatic and effective action to further the common good of the common people. And in a surprising twist, More was reduced to a small-minded, vindictive, self-righteous, and cold-hearted Pharisee.

When *Wolf Hall* appeared, Mantel's depiction of More excited considerable controversy. Some were quick to jump to the conclusion that Mantel was exacting revenge on the faith in which she had been raised but no longer professed by denigrating a saint beloved by English Catholics. As so often happens, the controversy found vociferous life in online forums where a war was conducted between those who regarded More as irreproachable and those who saw him as a cruel fanatic intent on consigning every Protestant he could lay his hands on to a fiery death at the stake.

Reputable scholars were, of course, more circumspect in weighing More's reputed fanaticism. They, too, were divided, but their arguments tended to centre on whether or not he displayed a greater or lesser degree of religious intolerance than was common in a time in which, by present standards, religious intolerance was the norm.

Largely overlooked in these heated debates was the realization that the picture of More readers received was moderated by the fictional Cromwell's consciousness. Mantel chose to embed readers of *Wolf Hall* deeply in Cromwell's mind, make them privy to his observations and rumination. The point of view of the novel is principally third-person limited, which focuses on the protagonist's perspective and thus filters everything we learn through Cromwell's mind. Occasionally, Mantel makes a barely perceptible shift into a first-person narrative offered in Cromwell's voice, which diminishes even further the distance between reader and character because of its confidential, confessional air, a tone that promotes a sense of intimacy and trust that turns the reader into the privileged confidant of the narrator. At other times, when Mantel needs to provide information difficult to deliver in a third-person limited or first-person point of view, she adopts a curiously *personal* third-person omniscience that bears little relation to the magisterial, godlike tone favoured by most nineteenth-century novelists, but which still manages to achieve a compelling authority, sketching background as indisputable *fact*. I offer the following as an example of Mantel's subtle third-person omniscient voice.

It is said [Cromwell] knows by heart the entire New Testament in Latin, and so as a servant [of Cardinal Wolsey, Chancellor of England] is apt—ready with a text if abbots flounder. His speech is low and rapid, his manner assured; he is at home in courtroom or waterfront, bishop's palace or inn yard. He can draft a contract, train a falcon, draw a map, stop a street fight, furnish a house

and fix a jury. He will quote you a nice point in the
old authors, from Plato to Plautus and back again. He
knows new poetry, and can say it in Italian. He works all
hours, first up and last to bed. He makes money and he
spends it. He will take a bet on anything.

It's Cromwell's voice we hear whenever More is discussed,
and antagonists are likely to get short shrift when protagonists pass judgment on an adversary. In the world of the novel,
not every character receives even-handed, fair dealing. Here is
Cromwell commenting on the attitude of Cardinal Wolsey, his
former employer, to those who stray from orthodoxy.

Sometimes one of his people—Stephen Gardiner, let's
say—will come to him denouncing some nest of heretics
in the city. [Wolsey] will say earnestly, poor benighted
souls. You pray for them, Stephen, and I'll pray for them,
and we'll see if between us we can't bring them to a better state of mind. And tell them, mend their manners, or
Thomas More will get hold of them and shut them in his
cellar. And all we will hear is the sound of screaming.

While Bolt renders More's last meeting with his wife Alice in
loving and tender terms, an exchange that ends with Alice saying,
"I understand you're the best man that I ever met or am likely
to…," a statement that leaves More's face "shining," Cromwell
shows us a very different More, one given to belittling and ridi-
culing his wife in the presence of company. As she sits mute and
browbeaten before guests, More sarcastically remarks,

"That expression of painful surprise is not native to her
… It is produced by scraping back her hair and driving
in great ivory pins, to the peril of her skull. She believes

her forehead is too low. It is, of course. "Alice, Alice," he
says, "remind me why I married you."

"To keep house, Father," Meg says in a low voice.

"Yes, yes," More says. "A glance at Alice frees me
from stain of concupiscence."

Needless to say, Bolt's angelic husband has been supplanted
by the husband from hell.

While Mantel's treatment of More shocked many, what
intrigues me is the novelist's success in promoting Cromwell, at
least in the public's mind, from villain (or failing that, obscure
footnote in English history) into a skilful, dynamic, preternatur-
ally effective player in the great game of nation-building. In fact,
Mantel's creation penetrated the consciousness of the chattering
classes and purveyors of opinion so deeply that in an opinion piece
in the May 27, 2019, edition of *The Guardian*, Alex Clark wondered where England could find its "contemporary Cromwell, the
man who Mantel portrays as finding Machiavelli's work a little
too trite for his tastes?" He answers himself, saying, "Certainly
not, on recent evidence, in the corridors of Westminster. Today's
crop of fixers, plotters and negotiators resemble the characters in
a Feydeau farce far more strongly than they do skilled practitioners of realpolitik."

Writers' tastes may differ concerning everything imaginable,
including styles of leadership. Bolt lived and wrote in an age in
which democratic politicians professed to be directed by principle. Whether or not they were is another question, but voters
thought it necessary that their leaders pretend they were creatures
of principle. Bolt votes for More; he casts his ballot for a qualified,
measured idealism. However, by the dawning of the twenty-first
century even a qualified idealism seemed a quaint notion. Labour
Party leader Clement Attlee's 1945 plans to build a "New Jerusalem"
in Britain, Kennedy's promise of a "New Frontier" for Americans,

and Johnson's confident proclamation that a "Great Society" would come to fruition in the U.S.A. were hopes that appeared to have ignobly expired on the drawing board. The twenty-first century was a harder-headed time that appeared to ask for a different sort of hero, a competent can-do guy, a qualified pragmatist. And Mantel's version of Cromwell fit that bill perfectly.

That is not to suggest that the success of a historical novel or play can be attributed solely or even principally to being in step with the zeitgeist of its era. Necessarily, its level of accomplishment as a work of art is decisive for any lasting success. But the readiness to accept the premises of that work of art must also have something to do with how it speaks to the prevailing social and political climate. Granted all that, what needs to be emphasized is that Mantel's technical virtuosity as a novelist and her imaginative empathy are fundamental to how readers respond to her novel. I have already alluded to how her skilful manipulation of point of view in *Wolf Hall* draws readers into Cromwell's mind, allows them to share his motives, reasoning, and emotions. All of this subtly evokes the humanity of the protagonist. And in Mantel's rendering, Cromwell becomes an enormously sympathetic individual.

However, what also needs to be admitted is that for some time Cromwell's character had been undergoing renovation at the hands of historians. In her 2014 biography, *Thomas Cromwell*, Tracy Borman writes:

> The records provide a glimpse of a loving husband and
> father, a devoted friend and a tireless helper of the poor,
> widows and others in distress who appealed for his
> assistance. He was also intensely loyal to those whom
> he served, from his first master in Italy, Francesco
> Frescobaldi, to the man who launched his political career,
> Cardinal Wolsey, and—above all—his royal master.

These are the characteristics Cromwell displays in Mantel's novel, and it is worth noting that *Wolf Hall* precedes the Borman biography by five years. Interestingly, both biographer and novelist dwell on a little-known calamity in Cromwell's life in their work. Borman draws attention to a will made by Cromwell that divided his estate between his son, Gregory, and his daughters, Anne and Grace. The daughters were left very substantial amounts of money, something highly unusual in an age when men like Cromwell assumed that their female children would marry well and be provided for by their husbands. Borman points out that this will is the only documentary evidence of the existence of the girls and thinks it likely that Anne and Grace died during outbreaks of the "sweating sickness" that swept London during their childhoods, an inference Borman makes because she notes their names were struck from the will at a later date.

Mantel draws much the same conclusion about the fate of Cromwell's daughters. But Mantel stresses the importance of these deaths to Cromwell to a much greater degree. Making imaginative forays into his life that are denied historians, she immerses readers in Cromwell's sorrow at the loss of his dear daughters, so tenderly cared for and loved by their father. Wrenching visions of his dead children dressed in the angel wings they wore one Christmas haunt him throughout the novel, his grief evoking a sympathy for him that Bolt's depiction of a heartless bureaucrat is incapable of awakening.

But unlike Bolt's More, Mantel's Cromwell is hardly a faultless man. In his youth, he is fond of brawls and shady deals, behaviour that the reader is not likely to judge too harshly since Cromwell is a young man desperately trying to pull himself up by his bootstraps in an unforgiving and vicious world. Through stupendous efforts, he does just that, leaving behind his lowly origins (his father was a blacksmith and brewer, in constant trouble with the law) to become a Tudor Horatio Alger success story, a Renaissance man who knows Greek and Latin, is proficient in several other languages, is an accomplished entrepreneur well versed in the arcane details of banking and the Flemish cloth trade. In his final incarnation, Cromwell emerges as a highly respected lawyer renowned for the sharpness of his mind, a mind that proves its worth to Cardinal Wolsey, lord high chancellor of England, and eventually earns Cromwell a position as one of Henry VIII's most trusted advisers and then, finally, as his lord high chancellor.

But rising to these heights has its costs, as Cromwell readily acknowledges in *Wolf Hall*: "This is what the world and the cardinal conspire to teach him. Christ, he thinks, by my age I ought to know. You don't get on by being original. You don't get on by being bright. You don't get on by being strong. You get on by being a subtle crook…"

Cromwell is a Machiavellian, but a measured and restrained Machiavellian. A practitioner of realpolitik, when it is necessary to do so he manipulates people, but in the service of what he sees as some larger, often humane, purpose. The man who had sold himself as a mercenary in Europe's wars and who killed men who had intrigued to kill him, Cromwell has learned that it is better to compromise than to fight and that diplomacy is a better alternative to disputes than recourse to the battlefield. Nevertheless, his hard past has marked him, and sometimes he is brought up short when he learns that others think he has the face of a murderer, a judgment that disturbs him and which he mulls over ceaselessly.

In many ways, Mantel's picture of Cromwell is more nuanced than Bolt's of More, who is presented as a uniformly virtuous man, a paragon of morality. But just as Bolt's Cromwell strikes one note, evil incarnate, Mantel's More is, at best, agonizingly bad company, a sanctimonious rule-enforcer, reputed to practise self-flagellation and wear a penitential hair shirt. In Mantel's novel More comes across as being an irritating hair shirt for anyone unfortunate enough to have dealings with him.

But beyond the portrait of Cromwell as a man of great gifts, how and why did this fictional character capture the fascination of England in the first decade of the twenty-first century? Here is one of those wild speculations I promised at the beginning of this talk. Perhaps it is because *Wolf Hall* is an attempt to locate the beginnings of modern England in the Tudor past, and because the novel poses fundamental questions about what concessions politicians must make to provide effective government for the nation. Perhaps it is also because *Wolf Hall* asks how nations reform and renew themselves. G. R. Elton noted in his study of the Tudor commonwealth, *Reform and Renewal*, that it was a period of English history which inaugurated a "concept of a responsible state committed to social, political and religious reform," much of which, he pointed out, was ably guided by the hand of Cromwell.

If Bolt's More provides an illustration of the individual fallen prey to the whims of a vengeful ruler, Mantel's depiction of Cromwell shows us a statesman bent on making the apparatus of government work for the benefit of the country, a leader who anticipates change and skilfully manages it. Cromwell is sensitive to the threats and opportunities that present themselves; he senses the little shifts of power that are transforming England in ways the king, the nobility, and the church hierarchy cannot grasp. Cromwell wants to teach Henry VIII how to navigate this new world. Thinking of the king, he asks himself,

> How can [Cromwell] explain to him? The world is
> not run from where he thinks. Not from his border
> fortresses, not even from Whitehall. The world is run
> from Antwerp, from Florence, from places he has never
> imagined.... Not from castle walls, but from counting
> houses, not by the call of the bugle but by the click of
> the abacus, not by the grate and click of the mechanism
> of the gun but by the scrape of the pen on the page of

the promissory note that pays for the gun and the gun-smith and the powder and shot.

For Mantel, More is the defender of the old, the decrepit, the defunct. Cromwell is the torchbearer for the new, the energetic, the forward-looking. She writes,

> But when More, a scholar revered through Europe, wakes up in Chelsea to the prospect of morning prayers in Latin, [Cromwell] wakes up to a creator who speaks the swift patois of the markets; when More is settling in for a session of self-scourging, he and Rafe are sprinting to Lombard Street to get the day's exchange rates.

Cromwell may be rather lukewarm when it comes to religion, but if he sides with anyone, it is with the reformers, those who he refers to as the Bible men. Unlike More, he believes it would be a good thing if the common people could read the word of God in their own tongue. When Cromwell bumps up against some church doctrine that he considers preposterous, his constant refrain is, "Show me where it says in the Bible ..."—a predictably Protestant response.

It is noteworthy that Cromwell stands for reinvention of the state, a preoccupation that has dominated Britain ever since the Second World War drove home to an exhausted, virtually bankrupt nation that it was now a second-rate power, that the British Empire was dissolving before its very eyes, and that all its former assumptions about what it meant to be British (or English) were gone. At the conclusion of the Second World War, the U.K. set about redefining itself. Churchill, Britain's indefatigable leader in the fight against the Nazis, was ousted from power by Clement Attlee's landslide electoral victory. The new Labour government immediately embarked on a program of unprecedented social reform that saw the establishment of the welfare state, steps toward taking control of key sectors of the economy by the government, the gradual divestiture of colonies, and investments in education intended to weaken class and income difference.

But this was only the first of the "quiet revolutions" that sought to reconfigure Britain and adjust its perspective on the world. Attlee's domestic and foreign policy were largely reversed three decades later by the Thatcherite revolution, which adopted a neoliberal agenda intent on breaking the power of the unions, privatizing many government services, and returning to an unapologetically jingoist stance that saw Britain fight a war with Argentina over possession of the Falkland Islands and another as the enthusiastic ally of the United States in the Gulf War of 1990.

The election of Tony Blair and a less ideologically stringent Labour Party seemed to offer a synthesis of Attlee and Thatcher policies in what came to be known as the Third Way, a doctrine that accepted features of both capitalism and traditional Socialism. In foreign policy, Britain continued to make much of the so-called "special relationship" that supposedly linked the interests of the United Kingdom with its former colony, the U.S.A. As Thatcher had, Blair entered into a war against Saddam Hussein in support of American foreign policy aims.

Yet percolating underneath the surface of all this domestic chopping and changing was a question that Britain had largely avoided addressing since the conclusion of the Second World War and that was, What should its relationship to Europe be? This is also the question that simmers in Cromwell's mind as he tries to manoeuvre the English ship of state.

Ever since the Hundred Years War effectively ended the dynastic claims of English kings to the throne of France, there has been a wide difference of opinion in Britain about just how involved in the affairs of Europe it should be. Many of its citizens have seen themselves as absolutely distinct from Europe and have regarded the English Channel as a moat girdling their little island, holding at bay incursions from Continental powers. But there have always been others who have argued that not to fully engage with Europe would deny their country a more prosperous, secure future and condemn it to benighted provincialism.

The truth is that until the Brexit vote, the British hadn't decisively answered that question. After their entry into the European Community in 1973 there had been referendums on membership and fluctuating levels of support for British participation in what later became the European Union, all of this accompanied by attempts to renegotiate the terms of the United Kingdom's membership in the organization. After all this hedging of bets and second thoughts, in the June 2016 referendum a bare majority of Britons (51.9 per cent) voted to exit the European Union. Wales and England (with the exception of London) voted for Brexit while Scotland and Northern Ireland voted to remain within the EU. The leaders of both the country's major parties were opposed to severing the connection to Europe. Most commentators attribute the vote to leave the European Union to several factors, among them anxiety that the French and Germans harboured ambitions for an even more comprehensive political and economic union that would diminish British sovereignty. This, along with fears about losing control of the entry of immigrants and refugees that fuelled a sometimes ugly, racist, populist nationalism in England, likely led to the success of the Eurosceptics.

Just as Bolt's More seems to contain tendencies associated both with a Christian belief in transcendence and twentieth-century existentialist psychology, the attitudes of Mantel's Cromwell swing between an intense British patriotism and a fondness for the offerings of European culture. Many of the tensions that factored in the Brexit vote contend in Cromwell's mind. He is drawn to Europe but remains jealously protective of British sovereignty. Cromwell is a multilingual sophisticate who has lived abroad and knows the people of Europe and their ways; he is culturally accomplished in the fashion admired by the English elites who made sure that their sons made the Grand Tour of the continent to finish their education. His experience of Europe has taught Cromwell a lot. Mantel writes, "Florence and Milan had given him ideas more flexible than those of people who'd stayed at home." And distance from England has allowed him to see things about his own country that stay-at-homes cannot discern. Cromwell recognizes the inherent conservatism that so many foreign observers have noted as a salient feature of the English. "There cannot be new things in England," Cromwell says. "There can be old things freshly presented, or new things that pretend to be old." This insight into the national character enters into many of his political calculations, which include the recognition of how suspicious the English are of outsiders. Cromwell remembers well Evil May Day, when Londoners rioted against the presence of foreigners, particularly Flemish workers and Italian bankers on Lombard Street, the same street to which he hurries each morning to check the exchange rates. Cromwell has measured the depth of English nationalism, or patriotism if you prefer a softer word, and he knows how strongly it plays in his country's affairs. The English may

> mislike or fail to understand recent measures in the Parliament. But instinct tells [Cromwell] this; they will knit together against foreign interference…. They are the same people who rioted against foreigners, on Evil May Day; the same people, narrow-hearted, stubborn, attached to their patch of ground. Only overwhelming force—a coalition, say, of Francis and the Emperor— will budge them.

Readying himself to rework England in the image of the king to whom he gives his wholehearted, unstinting support, Cromwell muses,

> For hundreds of years the monks have held the pen, and
> what they have written is what we take to be our history,
> but I do not really believe it is. I believe they have sup-
> pressed the history they don't like, and written one that
> is favourable to Rome.

In the spring of 1532, Mantel's Cromwell declares to himself,

> It is time to say what England is, her scope and bound-
> aries: not to count and measure her harbour defences and
> border walls, but to estimate her capacity for self-rule. It
> is time to say what a king is, and what trust and guard-
> ianship he owes his people: what protection from foreign
> incursions moral or physical, what freedom from the pre-
> tensions of those who would like to tell an Englishman
> how to speak to his God.

This is Cromwell's project, to define what it means to be English in a rapidly changing world. This messy struggle of definition is not very different from the messy struggle that has engaged every British government since the end of the Second World War, and this may be why Mantel's portrait of Cromwell has spoken so strongly to the British public: simply because it reminds it of its divided soul. *Wolf Hall* recalls for the British and us, too, that the process of change is never-ending. How do we negotiate the growing gap between wealthy and poor, the influence of social media, the rise of populism, the threat of climate change, the host of problems that assail us? Our bewilderment and desperation mount as did the bewilderment and desperation of the people of Tudor England as the Middle Ages gave way to a new, unimaginable order.

Mantel holds up to our eyes a picture of a farsighted, common-sensical, pragmatic, yet compassionate statesman, the sort of leader that most of us yearn for in an age in which politics has descended into empty gestures, tweets, and thirty-second soundbites, an age in which blowhards bloviate and patriotism is, indeed, the last refuge of the scoundrel.

Just as Bolt's More touched upon the anxieties and the preoccupations of the age in which he was created, so too is Mantel's Cromwell a reflection of current concerns and worries. What I choose to label the "fictional" More and Cromwell are products of editing and emphasis: certain aspects of their personality and talents are thrown into high relief to make them comprehensible for the audiences and the times the writers address. Other traits and habits that these men might have possessed are discreetly consigned to the shade for the sake of contemporary sensibilities. For instance, it didn't serve Bolt's purposes to have More scourge himself; the practice is too medieval for the playwright's purposes. On the other hand, Mantel's More wields the whip on himself simply because the practice *is* medieval. At the behest of one author a character will exhibit more virtues than sins; at the behest of another the same character will display more sins than virtues.

Mantel knows that historians and historical novelists edit our pasts, but she also knows that every human being indulges in that editing. Mantel writes, "It's the living that turn and chase the dead. The long bones and skulls are tumbled from their shrouds, and words like stones thrust into their rattling mouths: we edit their writings, we rewrite their lives."

The reputations of historical figures rise and fall, sometimes with amazing speed. The celebrated and acclaimed are swiftly toppled from their pedestals. Although Canada's first prime minister,

John A. Macdonald, was once widely admired, now his policies towards Indigenous people have led to his name being removed from a prize given by the Canadian Historical Association for scholarly writing. All across Canada calls have come for statues of him to be removed from view. The hero becomes villain. And the formerly humiliated and maltreated are seen in a new light. A portrait of Viola Desmond, a black woman once summarily ejected from a Nova Scotia movie house for occupying a seat implicitly reserved for whites, is now featured on Canadian ten-dollar bills.

As England did in Cromwell's time, nations reinvent themselves and, in doing so, reinvent their histories. We take from the past what we feel we need and make our uses of it. What we need to be a little more aware of is what that process entails and why we are doing it. It might be wise to remember that the past we so confidently rewrite as *the* truth will, not so very far down the road, be rewritten in the interests of others. It might also be of some benefit to entertain the thought that what we feel we need isn't necessarily what we *ought* to have.

To recognize that the historical novel—even history itself—is more about the present than it is the past is a humbling thought. Or at least it ought to be.

This article is based on a talk slated to be given at St. Thomas More College, University of Saskatchewan, in March 2020 but which was never delivered because of the Covid pandemic. I have extended it beyond the forty-five-minute limit of the originally planned talk because I wanted to explore the works in question in a little more depth.

Permissions and Acknowledgements

As indicated, some of these pieces were first published in the following periodical publications: *Canadian Geographic, The Canadian Forum, Canadian Literature, The Globe and Mail, The History and Social Science Teacher, Montage, Music and Literature, The National Post, Time, The Washington Post, The Walrus,* and *Western Living.*

In addition, the following pieces were first published in book form: "Troubled Wit and Moralist" as the afterword to *St. Urbain's Horseman* by Mordecai Richler (McClelland & Stewart, New Canadian Library, 1989); "A Walk around the Leacock Monument" as "Leacock and Understanding Canada" in *Stephen Leacock: A Reappraisal,* ed. David Staines (University of Ottawa Press, 1986); "Strangerhood" as the afterword to *The Tomorrow-Tamer* by Margaret Laurence (McClelland & Stewart, New Canadian Library, 1993); "Finding Home in Heule" in *Writing Home: A PEN Canada Anthology,* ed. Constance Rooke (McClelland & Stewart, 1997); "Brand Name vs. No-name: The Western Canadian City in Fiction" in *The Urban Prairie* (Saskatoon: Mendel Art Gallery & Fifth House Publishers, 1993); "The University and the River" in *Many Lives Mark This Place: Canadian Writers in Portrait, Landscape, and Prose* (Vancouver: Figure 1 Publishing, 2019, reprinted by permission of Figure 1); and *"The Wars"* as the introduction to *The Wars* by Timothy Findley (Toronto: Penguin Books, 2005; this piece, and those published by McClelland & Stewart as indicated above, reprinted with permission of Penguin Random House Canada). I wish to thank all the editors and publishers involved in these publications.

I also want to gratefully acknowledge a grant I received from SK Arts that assisted in the preparation of this book for publication.

Many thanks to my editor Melanie Little for her astute eye and gentle guidance in helping this book arrive at its present form.

And, as always, my heartfelt appreciation to Sylvia for her unstinting encouragement and her presence in my life.

GUY VANDERHAEGHE is a three-time winner of the Governor's-General Award for English language fiction for his collections of short stories, *Man Descending* and *Daddy Lenin*, and for his novel, *The Englishman's Boy*, which was also shortlisted for the Giller Prize and The International Dublin Literary Award. His novel, *The Last Crossing*, was a winner of the CBC's Canada Reads Competition. *August into Winter*, his most recent novel, won the Saskatchewan Book Award for Fiction and the Glengarry Book Award and was shortlisted for the Writers' Trust Atwood Gibson Fiction Prize. He has also received the Timothy Findley Prize, the Harbourfront Literary Prize, and the Cheryl and Henry Kloppenburg Prize, all given for a body of work.